What the Buddha Thought

Oxford Centre for Buddhist Studies Monographs
Series Editor: Richard Gombrich

The Oxford Centre for Buddhist Studies promotes teaching and research into all Buddhist traditions, as found in texts and in societies, and is equally open to the study of Buddhism by methods associated with the humanities (philology, philosophy, history) and the social sciences (anthropology, sociology, politics). It insists only on using sources in their original languages and on aiming at the highest scholarly standards.

Previously published by Routledge

Richard F. Gombrich, *How Buddhism Began: The Conditioned Genesis of the Early Teachings,* 2nd edition

Soon-il Hwang, *Metaphor and Literalism in Buddhism: The Doctrinal History of Nirvana*

Tse-fu Kuan, *Mindfulness in Early Buddhism: New Approaches through Psychology and Textual Analysis, of Pali, Chinese and Sanskrit Sources*

Karma Phuntsho, *Mipham's Dialectics and the Debates on Emptiness: To Be, Not To Be, or Neither*

Peter Alan Roberts, *The Biographies of Rechungpa: The Evolution of a Tibetan Hagiography*

Noa Ronkin, *Early Buddhist Metaphysics: The Making of a Philosophical Tradition*

Sarah Shaw, *Buddhist Meditation: An Anthology of Texts from the Pali Canon*

Will Tuladhar-Douglas, *Remaking Buddhism from Medieval Nepal: The Fifteenth-century Reformation of Newar Buddhism*

Alexander Wynne, *The Origin of Buddhist Meditation*

Published by Equinox

Venerable Seongcheol, *Sermon of One Hundred Days: Part One*

What the Buddha Thought

Richard Gombrich

equinox

LONDON OAKVILLE

First published in 2009 by

UK: 1 Chelsea Manor Studios, Flood Street, London SW3 5SR
USA: DBBC, 28 Main Street, Oakville, CT 06779

www.equinoxpub.com

British Library Cataloguing-in-Publication Data
A catalogue record for this book is available from the British Library.
ISBN 978 1 84553 612 1 (hardback)
978 1 84553 614 5 (paperback)

Library of Congress Cataloging-in-Publication Data
Gombrich, Richard F. (Richard Francis), 1937–
What the Buddha thought / Richard Gombrich.
p. cm.—(Oxford Centre for Buddhist Studies monographs)
Includes bibliographical references and index.
ISBN 978-1-84553-612-1 (hb)—ISBN 978-1-84553-614-5 (pb)
1. Gautama Buddha—Teachings. I. Title.
BQ915.G66 2009
294.3'63—dc22
2008049777

Typeset by S.J.I. Services, New Delhi
Printed and bound in Great Britain by Lightning Source UK Ltd, Milton Keynes

CONTENTS

For Geoff Bamford and Sarah Norman,
fellow enthusiasts

PREFACE

This book argues that the Buddha was one of the most brilliant and original thinkers of all time.

While the book is intended to serve as an introduction to the Buddha's thought, and hence even to Buddhism itself, it also has larger aims: it argues that we can know far more about the Buddha than it is fashionable among scholars to admit, and that his thought has a greater coherence than is usually recognized. Interpreters both ancient and modern have taken little account of the historical context of the Buddha's teachings, but relating them to early brahminical texts, and also to ancient Jainism, gives a much richer picture of his meaning, especially when his satire and irony are appreciated. Incidentally, since many of the Buddha's allusions can only be traced in the Pali versions of surviving texts, the book establishes the importance of the Pali Canon as evidence.

Though the Buddha used metaphor extensively, he did not found his arguments upon it like earlier thinkers: his capacity for abstraction was an intellectual breakthrough. His ethicizing older ideas of rebirth and human action (karma) was also a breakthrough for civilization. His theory of karma is logically central to his thought. Karma is a process, not a thing; moreover, it is neither random nor wholly determined. These ideas about karma he generalized to every component of conscious experience – except nirvana, the liberation from that chain of experience. Morally, karma both provided a principle of individuation and asserted the individual's responsibility for his or her own destiny.

The book is based on the Numata Lectures which I gave by invitation at the School of Oriental and African Studies, London University, in autumn 2006. I gave ten lectures under the general title 'The Origin and Greatness of the Buddha's Ideas'. I am extremely grateful to the Numata Foundation, Bukkyo Dendo Kyokai, for financing those lectures; they are by far the greatest patrons of the study of Buddhism in the world. I thank Dr Tadeusz Skorupski and Dr Kate Crosby for inviting me. The lectures were open to the public, and I am particularly grateful to members of the audience who came long distances and asked excellent questions, some of which have, I hope, enabled me to improve my material.

Like the lectures, the book is ambitious in being intended for two audiences. It contains much that is new, so that I dare to hope it will interest, perhaps even excite, experts in the field. It is, however, also intended to reach a wider public – in fact, anyone remotely interested in Buddhism – even though it does not fully cater for those who have no idea whatsoever about the Buddha's teachings. I have not used up space by providing the rudimentary knowledge which can be picked up from any work of reference – or better, perhaps, from such books as *What the Buddha Taught* by the Ven. Walpola Rahula or *The Buddha's Way* by the Ven H. Saddhatissa. On the other hand, I have included, for easy reference, the text of a handout which was distributed at the lectures, entitled 'Background Information'.

As I explain more fully below, I have tried to make the book accessible by not using foreign words in the body of the text when it is not absolutely necessary, but there are also places where I cannot convey my message without discussing Pali words in detail. I do hope that those discussions will not deter non-linguists; they should not. I have used initial capitals for some English words to indicate that they are standard translations of Pali fixed terms.

The title of this book is a gesture of homage to the late Ven. Dr Walpola Rahula, who taught me much of what I understand of early Buddhism. I trust it will not be taken amiss if I admit that at the same time I not only wish to supplement his book by approaching the subject more from a historical angle, but even on one topic, nirvana, venture to clarify what I fear is a somewhat muddled presentation.

This book is intended to be read through, rather than dipped into, since it contains some quite complex arguments and builds up the case for the Buddha's coherence and brilliance as a thinker cumulatively. Nevertheless, readers may find a brief guide to its contents useful.

After introductory remarks, the first two chapters are mainly occupied with karma. Chapters 3 and 4 then deal respectively with the brahminical and the Jain backgrounds to the Buddha's ideas.

Chapter 5 shows how some of the Buddha's main concepts relate to concepts in the Upaniṣads and thus how they relate to each other.

Chapter 6 is a case study of a very important topic, the Buddha's view of love and compassion; it aspires to show by example how my approach, as a historian of ideas, can cast fresh light on the Buddha's thought. Chapter 7 then discusses the method I have exemplified in Chapter 6, and gives my view of the evidence for what I am saying. I realize that it is unusual not to explain my method until halfway through the book, but I hope it keeps people reading.

The next three chapters, 8 to 10, present what I take to be the main ideas underlying the Buddha's teaching; one might even call them his 'philosophy'. I would have liked to make my text as accessible as *What the Buddha Taught,* but here at least I have surely failed, because I have to deal with some sophisticated and unfamiliar ideas. Should any readers feel so discouraged that they lay the book down, I hope that they will nevertheless persevere with the remaining chapters, because those are not only more colourful but also (particularly Chapter 11) important for getting to know the Buddha's extraordinary mind and personality. The centrality of the theme of karma in the Buddha's thought is summarily reviewed in the final chapter.

❧

In arriving at my own ideas, I owe enormous intellectual debts, above all to Joanna Jurewicz and to Sue Hamilton. I am conscious that my text does not adequately convey how much I owe to Sue Hamilton's insights; in particular, had I felt it appropriate to devote more space to cognition in Chapter 10, I would have cited her at length. Her demonstration that the Buddha is always talking about experience chimes beautifully with Joanna Jurewicz's early work on the Ṛg Vedic 'Hymn of Creation', in which she shows how from the recorded beginnings of Indian thought, existence and consciousness are intertwined. Though the Buddha disentangled them, this philosophy of experience, as one might call it, influenced him profoundly. Joanna Jurewicz's other discoveries are no less momentous. Not only has she deciphered the original meaning of the chain of dependent origination. Her discovery of belief in rebirth in the Ṛg Veda also makes the entire early history of Indian religion far more plausible and coherent. I wonder whether any other single scholar in the last hundred years has made so important a contribution to the field.

I must also make special mention of my comparatively recent students Noa Gal Ronkin and Alexander Wynne. Teachers can have no greater reward than to find their pupils reaching higher by standing on their shoulders. This is central to the process of conjecture and refutation which I regard as the only way forward.

BACKGROUND INFORMATION

You are advised to read this through quickly, and then use it for reference.

LANGUAGES

Sanskrit (S) is native to India. It is an Indo-European language, and therefore is related to English. The oldest texts in Sanskrit go back to the second millennium BC, but through an oral tradition (therefore very hard to date); writing was first used in India in the third century BC. The oldest texts are called the Vedas (see below) and were preserved as sacred by the males of a hereditary priestly group, the brahmins.

Prakrit is the Indian term for languages directly derived from Sanskrit. The oldest extensive Indian inscriptions, put up by the emperor Asoka in the mid-third century BC, are in Prakrit. Some words in Prakrit are the same as in Sanskrit.

Pali (P) is a Prakrit language. It is not exactly what the Buddha spoke, but fairly close to it. The sacred texts of the Theravada tradition, also known as Southern Buddhism, constitute the Pali Canon. Though not immune to change over time, some of these texts must be our oldest evidence for Buddhism.

For more on Pali, see my introduction, entitled "What is Pali?", to Wilhelm Geiger's *Pali Grammar* (1994).

BASIC DATA ON BUDDHISM

The Three Jewels

Buddhism consists of the 'Three Jewels': the Buddha, the Dhamma and the Saṅgha. They are also known as the 'Three Refuges', meaning that Buddhists rely on them, place trust in them. Though many dislike calling Buddhism a 'faith', it is not unfair to say that Buddhists have faith in the Three Jewels.

Buddha (S/P) is, strictly speaking, a title. Literally it means 'Awoken' but we tend to use 'Enlightened'. His family name was Gotama (P).

Non-Buddhists simply regard the Buddha as the founder of Buddhism. For Buddhists he re-founded it in the area and period of the universe in which we are living; there are other similar Buddhas who do the same when and/or where Buddhism is extinct.

Dhamma (P) or **Dharma** (S) is what the Buddha taught (according to Buddhists: what all Buddhas teach). The term has many applications and many translations, according to context. It is both descriptive and normative, the law of the universe.

Dhamma translates 'Buddhism' if by the latter is meant the system of ideas. For Buddhism as a historical, empirical phenomenon, Buddhists use a different word, *sāsana* (P) or *śāsana* (S) (accent on first syllable). This word also means 'teaching', but 'dispensation' captures the purport better. So a Buddha founds a *sāsana,* but the *dhamma* is a set of truths, eternal but sometimes forgotten.

Saṅgha (S/P) means 'community'. This term too has several applications but they are not hard to distinguish. The Buddha may originally have used it to refer to all his followers who had reached the first stage of spiritual progress. But by far its commonest use is to refer to the ordained: monks, nuns and novices of both sexes. (However, in orthodox Theravada the female Saṅgha is extinct.) The term may refer to the monastic community as a whole or to a particular local community.

The Saṅgha is governed by rules, collectively known as the ***Vinaya*** (S/P) 'discipline'. This term may refer to the rules or to the texts containing those rules.

Fundamental texts

The **Pali Canon** is in Pali called the ***Tipiṭaka***, 'Three baskets'. They are (the order matters):

1. ***Vinaya Piṭaka***, the rules for the Saṅgha, both for individual members and for the whole community. The two codes of disciplinary rules for individuals (one for monks, one for nuns) are called the *pātimokkha* (P)/*prātimokṣa* (S). Though much of the *Vinaya Piṭaka* is a commentary on these rules, so that they are embedded in it, strictly speaking they stand outside the Canon; they have a kind of supreme status, because one cannot receive full ordination (at least in theory) without knowing the *pātimokkha* by heart.

2. ***Sutta Piṭaka***. *Sutta* is P, *sūtra* is S. A *sutta* is a text, prose or verse or both, containing teachings. Many are in a narrative setting. The main collection of the Buddha's sermons is in the four ***Nikāya***, collections arranged mainly on formal criteria.

3. ***Abhidhamma Piṭaka***, 'higher teachings', the teachings analytically rearranged into a systematic and wholly literal presentation. While the early schools have the main texts of the first two *piṭaka* in common, they differ in *abhidhamma* (S: *abhidharma*).

When one says something like 'the early canonical texts', one is usually referring to most of the *Vinaya Piṭaka*, the four *Nikāya*, and a few other verse texts from the *Sutta Piṭaka*.

HISTORICAL AND CULTURAL BACKGROUND

Time

Since the Buddha lived well before writing was used in India, it is not surprising that the various Buddhist traditions differ widely about his date. The canonical account of his death says that he passed away aged eighty. For a while modern scholarship dated this to 483 BC or thereabouts and this dating is still found in many reference works. But it is too early. He must have died round 405 BC.

For more detail, including an explanation of the limits of possible precision, see my 'Dating the Buddha: a red herring revealed', in

The Dating of the Historical Buddha/Die Datierung des historischen Buddha, Part 2 (Symposien zur Buddhismusforschung, IV, 2), Heinz Bechert, editor (Göttingen: Vandenhoeck and Ruprecht, 1992), pp. 237–59. For a less technical account, see my 'Discovering the Buddha's date', in Lakshman S. Perera (ed.), *Buddhism for the New Millennium,* London: World Buddhist Foundation, 2000, pp. 9–25.

The emperor Asoka, who was largely responsible for the spread of Buddhism, ruled from *c.*269 to *c.*231 BC.

Space

The Buddha was born close to the modern border between India and Nepal, which did not then exist, into a tribe called the Shakyas. He spent his life in the part of north-east India now known as Bihar (the name is derived from the Buddhist word for 'monastery') and the eastern UP. Modern Benares (Varanasi in Indian languages) already existed; Patna (ancient name: Pataliputra), which was to be Asoka's capital, was founded soon after his lifetime.

Social environment

The Buddha lived when the first cities were coming up in India. (We ignore the prehistoric Indus Valley civilization.) With this arose larger and better organized states, mostly monarchies, and a great increase in trade, which led to contact with the world beyond India.

A complex religious and cultural system had already been articulated by the brahmins. Their leadership was, however, contested by the new political and mercantile classes, who tended to support heterodox teachers. ('Heterodox' means not accepting the authority of the Vedas and hence of their brahmin interpreters.) The Buddha's contemporary Mahāvīra was one of them; he taught, though he did not found, Jainism, a religion still alive today.

See my *Theravada Buddhism: A Social History*, 2nd edition. London: Routledge, 2006, Chapters 2 and 3.

Brahmin religion and society

Brahmin ideology posited a hierarchic social structure which we call 'the caste system'. According to this, society had four strata, which they called 'colours' (S: *varṇa*). The brahmins (S: *brāhmaṇa*) were at the top, then came the nobility (S: *kṣatriya* or *rājanya*), then the *vaiśya*, originally stock-rearers and farmers but by the Buddha's day primarily traders, and then the *śūdra*, artisans and labourers. Even below these came the outcastes, who in theory were associated with unclean work dealing with corpses and/or excreta. This brahmin theory is first mentioned in the tenth book of the *Ṛg Veda.* Kings were supposed by the theory to enforce its rules. In fact, however, enforcement has always been extremely variable.

Early brahmin religious literature is vast. It all carries the name *Veda*, meaning 'knowledge', and is all in an ancient (but not uniform) kind of Sanskrit. It is internally stratified by genre and to some extent the genres also constitute a chronological sequence. The oldest genre is sometimes known in the West as the Vedas, which is confusing. The *Ṛg Veda*, a collection of 1,028 hymns, is the oldest text in this genre. The latest genre/stratum is that of the *Upaniṣads.* These were composed over several centuries; the oldest and longest is the *Bṛhad-āraṇyaka Upaniṣad*, which was certainly known to the Buddha, though not necessarily in exactly its present form, so it must antedate 500 BC.

Kinds of Buddhism

There are two main Buddhist traditions in the world today: Theravada and Mahayana. Theravada is a Pali word (*Theravāda*) meaning 'Doctrine of the Elders'. Mahayana is a Sanskrit word (*Mahāyāna*) and means either 'Great Path' or 'Great Vehicle' – it is ambiguous. The Theravada regards only the Pali Canon as authoritative, the Mahayana arose around the beginning of the Christian era and venerates many other texts. Theravada is dominant in most (not all) of South and Southeast Asia, Mahayana in East and Central Asia. Further details are not relevant to this book.

ABBREVIATIONS

AN	*Aṅguttara Nikāya*
BĀU	*Bṛhad-Āraṇyaka Upaniṣad*
Ch.Up.	*Chāndogya Upaniṣad*
Dhp.	*Dhammapada*
Dhs.	*Dhammasaṅgaṇī*
DN	*Dīgha Nikāya*
J	*Jātaka*
MLD	*Middle Length Discourses*
MN	*Majjhima Nikāya*
PED	*Pali-English Dictionary*
RV	*Ṛg Veda*
Ś.Br.	*Śatapatha Brāhmaṇa*
SN	*Saṃyutta Nikāya*
Snip.	*Suttanipāta*
Thg.	*Therīgāthā*
Ud.	*Udāna*
Vin.	*Vinaya Piṭaka*
Vism.	*Visuddhimagga*

Chapter 1

INTRODUCTION

I have been motivated to write this book mainly by two feelings: admiration and exasperation.

My admiration is for the Buddha, whom I consider to be one of the greatest thinkers – and greatest personalities – of whom we have record in human history. Ranking people in an order of merit is a pursuit fit only for parlour games, but I maintain that the Buddha belongs in the same class as Plato and Aristotle, the giants who created the tradition of western philosophy. I think that his ideas should form part of the education of every child, the world over, and that this would help to make the world a more civilized place, both gentler and more intelligent.

This does not mean that I consider that all the Buddha's ideas were correct. Given the distance between the Buddha and me in time and space, it would be extraordinary if I did. I disagree with some of his theories and do not subscribe to all his values. I therefore do not call myself a Buddhist. However, I believe that my understanding of his ideas makes me at least as sincere an admirer of the Buddha as the millions who identify as Buddhists. Moreover, my admiration extends to a great deal of what those born into the Buddhist tradition think and do. And that admirable part of the Buddhist tradition, or traditions if you will, goes back, in my view, to the Buddha himself.

Those Buddhist traditions, which have lasted for over two and a half millennia and extended over a vast geographical area, are so diverse that some scholars scoff at the very notion that one can talk about 'Buddhism', and insist on using the word in scare quotes, if it has to be used at all. I disagree. Granted, Buddhism itself, as a human phenomenon, is subject to the Buddha's dictum that 'All compounded things are impermanent'.[1] It would be astonishing if over such a long time, as it moved to different regions and cultures, it had not undergone vast changes; the same has happened to every human tradition. But the historian should be able to trace every branch of the tradition back to another branch, until we arrive at the trunk and root, the Buddha himself. To change the metaphor from trees to rivers: on their way, the various streams of the Buddhist tradition have been joined and adulterated by streams from other cultures, whose influence must likewise be analysed. Yet I think that in most traditions – or at least in the scriptural traditions, which have done most to shape human history – it is what owes its origin to ancient Buddhism that preponderates.

Many will remain sceptical. They may grant that the Buddhist Order of monks and nuns, the Saṅgha, is the oldest institution in the world, and easily recognizable as the same institution from age to age and country to country; but they may protest that Buddhist beliefs today are hopelessly diverse, and ask why. I believe I have an answer. The Buddha was startlingly original. Many of his ideas were formulated to refute other ideas current in his day, but to put them across, he had inevitably to use the language of his opponents, for there was no other. As I shall explain at many points in this book, he infused old terms with new meanings. This inevitably led to misunderstandings, especially among those who knew his teachings only partially or superficially.

Let me give a salient example. Again and again I find propagated in modern Indian university teaching and publications the view that the Buddha taught virtually the same as the *Upaniṣads*, texts sacred to the brahmins, and significantly differed from them only in attacking the caste system. This arises from the fact that the Buddha's main ideological opponents were brahmins of Upaniṣadic views, so he used their own terms to attack them. Moreover, those attacks were conducted mainly by using metaphor and irony, registers imperceptible to the literal-minded. To illustrate this will be one of the main themes of this book.

But more needs to be said. In many cases, the Buddha was not asking the same questions as his opponents, or indeed as the successors of his opponents in India down the centuries. He did not always follow the unspoken rules of what philosophy, or systematic thought, was supposed to be about. Naturally, this led to misunderstandings after his death, even well before Buddhism became implanted in countries beyond India. Another salient example may clarify this. The orthodox tradition, Vedic thought, was much concerned with ontological questions: what exists? The

Buddha said that this is a wrong question. But this was too much for his followers. One major school, the *abhidharma*, gave his teachings a realist interpretation; another, the *Vijñānavāda*, an idealist interpretation; it is possible to derive both these interpretations from the early Canon, particularly if one highlights certain texts and ignores others. There are indeed also texts which, if taken in isolation, seem to be ambiguous on this matter.

Before many centuries had elapsed, things went even further than this. When Buddhism reached China, the great difficulties of translating Indian texts into Chinese, difficulties both of a practical character and inherent in the vast difference between the cultures of the two countries, soon led to mysticism: mysticism in the sense that the Buddha's teaching was held to transcend rationality and to be inexpressible in language. Though not the only view, this view has been dominant in Far Eastern Buddhism, particularly in the school known in the West by its Japanese name, Zen. While I shall show in this book that I agree that the Buddha held the goal of the religious life to be an experience which language has no power to express, I strongly disagree with interpretations of his teachings, which are of course expressed in language, as being mystical in the vulgar sense of defying normal logic.

I therefore hold that a successful interpretation of the Buddha will make clear not only the ideas he expressed but also how those ideas lent themselves to the various interpretations which are in fact historically attested. The Buddha will thus stand as the source for a successful history of Buddha ideas – even though to compose such a history, even in outline, may be beyond the powers of any single scholar. Moreover, that must be beyond the scope of this book.

MISUNDERSTANDING AND PSEUDO-PROFUNDITY

The above paragraphs may give the reader a first hint of why one of the motives that drives me to write is exasperation. However, I can put the matter even more plainly from another angle. I find the Buddha's ideas extraordinarily powerful and intelligent, a work of genius. I do not think those powerful ideas, properly understood, are very complex or difficult to grasp. Yet Buddhists and non-Buddhists alike persist in regarding the Buddha's thought as immensely 'deep' in the sense of complex and therefore difficult to understand. I do not share this view.

Just as traditional exegesis of the Four Gospels has not taken much account of Jesus' Jewish background, traditional exegesis of the Buddha operated in almost total ignorance of his historical context. After all, if he preached eternal truths, historical context did not appear to have any relevance! That may excuse the blinkered approach of the early commentators, but it will not serve for modern scholars. Statements, obviously, derive their meaning largely from context. Therefore to understand what anyone is saying, particularly if it transcends the banal, one needs to try to reconstruct its historical context.

I have taken first steps in this direction in the early chapters of my book *Theravada Buddhism: A Social History*, and gone further in my next book, *How Buddhism Began*. I shall follow the same path in this book; this will lead to my repeating myself a little, but I hope not too much. My method is therefore historical.

Most books written by academics – and I confess that I am one of those – feel that they must begin with a chapter on what they call methodology, i.e., 'How do I set about writing this book?' For historians this usually means how they find what they consider relevant evidence and how they treat it. For me, the proof of the pudding is in the eating, and I find it boring and unhelpful to read about how something can or could be done in theory, before one has witnessed the practice. For this reason I discuss my method, i.e., my use of evidence, only halfway through the book, once the reader has had a chance to see how my method works.

Why do I think that the Buddha's thought has been so undervalued? I would not go so far as to say that the undervaluation is in proportion to the veneration; but there is something in that nevertheless. While I consider that Buddhism has been by and large a great force for good in human history, a civilizing influence, I think that regarding the Buddha purely as a religious teacher can be unhelpful. It is of course a fact that he founded what we call a religion; in his terms, indeed, he saw himself as teaching a path to salvation. But to stress that can be a hindrance in the educational systems of today. Naturally, I am not disputing that as the founder of a religion the Buddha can be classed with Moses, Jesus or Mohammed. But let us not thereby exclude him from the category of thinkers like Plato, Aristotle and Hume.

TERMINOLOGY AND CLARITY

One of my teachers, the Ven. Dr Walpola Rahula, was given to saying that one could teach Buddhism to a non-Buddhist audience in their own language without using any foreign words at all. I agree. And yet at the same time I have always held that if one wants fully to grasp the meaning of a Buddhist text, one needs to read it in the original language. What do I mean?

The key terms in Buddhism – and probably in any system of ideas – do not refer to external objects, such as nose, tree, cup. They are abstractions. Linguists understand that there are very few words which have *precise* equivalents in another language, except sometimes in a closely related language: the word 'cup' will not have a precise equivalent in Chinese, because the Chinese traditionally have a different range of utensils from English-speakers, and the closest Chinese word may, for instance, cover a broader or a narrower range than 'cup'. Nevertheless, once the word 'cup' is used in a context, it is often no problem to convey what it refers to with enough precision to serve the needs of communication.

The translation of abstractions is much more problematic. This is not just because the terms do not have precise equivalents in foreign languages, though in the case of abstractions the ambiguities and semantic range of a term may well baffle translators and those dependent on their translations. Let me give two simple examples. Italian *coscienza* can be either 'conscience' or 'consciousness'. German *Geist* can be 'soul', 'spirit', 'ghost', 'mind' or 'wit'. The problem becomes far worse when the ideas one is trying to understand are expressed in the original by relating one to the other or even explaining one in terms of the other.[2]

The oldest extensive evidence for the Buddha's ideas, I hold, is found in large parts of a huge collection of texts known in English as the Pali Canon.[3] Pali is a language derived from pre-classical Sanskrit and closely related to it – even more closely than Italian is related to Latin. It is also closely related to the language (likewise derived from Sanskrit) that the Buddha himself must have spoken. Of that language we have no direct record, because writing was not used in India, so far as we can tell, in the Buddha's lifetime (unless it be that there was a system of writing numerals). For most purposes one can expound Indian Buddhism equally well whether one uses the Sanskrit terms or their Pali equivalents; there are a few exceptions to this, but they are mostly irrelevant to the contents of this book. On the other hand, Sanskrit has a very long history and many different genres of texts, and to gain insight into the meanings of Pali words one needs to compare them not to Sanskrit in general but to the Sanskrit of the Buddha's day – what is generally referred to as late Vedic Sanskrit.

From this point on, the discussion will use only Sanskrit (S) and Pali (P) terms; on the other hand, it is not useful in this context to stick to either S or P consistently.

THE BUDDHA'S USE OF METAPHOR

The preaching recorded in the *sutta*s, the texts containing the Buddha's sermons and discourses, is mainly delivered with what Pali calls *pariyāya*.[4] Literally, this word means 'way round' and so 'indirect route', but it refers to a 'way of putting things'. The translation 'circumlocution' will not quite do, because that wrongly suggests long-windedness or evasiveness. *Pariyāya* refers to metaphor, allegory, parable, any use of speech which is not to be taken literally. A text delivered 'with *pariyāya*' is contrasted with one delivered without, in other words, with a text which is to be taken literally. In the early canons, it is the *abhidharma* texts which are 'without *pariyāya*' and thus claim to give us the Buddha's meaning literally.[5]

What does this mean for us? It is the primary task of a modern expositor like myself to present in our language what the Buddha meant, literally. Removing the figurative use of language which fills and enlivens his discourses is likely to make them less vivid and interesting; besides, it is always debatable to what extent that which is expressed by a metaphor can be conveyed by its literal equivalent, particularly when the subject matter is religious. I can, of course, try introducing metaphors of my own, but unless I am very careful to make clear what I am doing, this runs the risk of distorting the message, particularly because our own world is so far removed from that of ancient India. I had better stick to the task of decoding what the Buddha said by recognizing when he is speaking figuratively, and preferably also understanding why. But simply to ignore the metaphors is to lose an essential part of the meaning.

SKILL IN MEANS

The Buddha's use of metaphor is linked to what became known as his Skill in Means. In the Mahayana, Skill in Means (S: *upāya-kauśalya*) acquired the status of a technical term. That term is not found in the early Pali texts, but what it stands for is found all over them.[6] The term refers to the Buddha's skill as a communicator. This, in turn, is manifested by the Buddha's ability to adapt what he says to his audience, to their prejudices, expectations and capacities. When he encounters non-Buddhists, the Buddha hardly ever initiates a discussion or begins by putting forward his own views. As T. W. Rhys Davids pointed out a century ago,[7] this reminds us of Socrates, who always got discussions going by asking the other party to state their views. When the Buddha's interlocutor has spoken, the Buddha's normal technique is to agree – and then to carry on. He says, 'Yes ... and ...'

This is a wonderful bargaining or diplomatic tactic, from which anyone can learn. The Buddha avoids an adversarial stance. What he does after his initial agreement is to take what has apparently been agreed on and turn it upside down. One of his main ways of doing that is to make the words used by his opponent mean something quite different.

The way in which the Buddha infuses new meaning into accepted terms is so bold that in some instances one might almost call it outrageous. The word 'karma' itself[8] offers a perfect example. It is a noun derived from one of the commonest of all Sanskrit roots, *kṛ*, meaning 'to do' or 'to make'. Sanskrit *karman* and Pali *kamma* thus mean 'act, action, deed'. Regardless of what kinds of action the word is used to refer to, an action is something which takes place in the physical world. So when the Buddha said, 'It is intention that I call karma,'[9] he was doing something logically analogous to saying that he chose to call black 'white', or to call left 'right'. This example is so extreme that perhaps it does not describe it adequately to say that what his opponents meant literally he took metaphorically. There are, however, many examples of the latter procedure. When he took a word for sacrifice which the brahmins meant literally, and turned that into a metaphor, we are on more familiar territory.

Already in ancient times, this matter became explicit in the Buddhists' view of their own tradition. Though every Buddha was thought to have attained moral perfection in a whole set of virtues, two were of paramount importance: compassion and wisdom. Odd as it may sound to our ears, the prime instance of his compassion was his preaching. There was no necessity for him to preach, but he was kind enough to do so, and thus show to all living creatures the path to liberation from rebirth. Consonant with the idea of individual responsibility, the Buddha's compassion consisted above all in helping others to help themselves. And it was his wisdom that provided the Skill in Means which made his preaching so effective.

DECODING AN IDEOLOGICAL STRUCTURE

The meaning of Buddhist texts is never going to be clear to us if we stick to reading word-for-word translations, or exegesis which clings closely to such translations. Here is a typical statement of one of the Buddha's basic teachings: 'The Buddha taught that living beings have no self, but what we think of as the self in fact consists of five aggregates.' Many people are so used to sentences like this, which are so obscure as to be meaningless, that they read (or listen) on without a murmur of complaint. Some even fancy that if they cannot understand such profundities, it must be their fault!

Of course, the teacher making such a statement may well have explained that 'self' here corresponds to S: *ātman* (P: *attā*), which besides 'self' can be translated 'soul', and that 'aggregates' translates S: *skandhāḥ* (P: *khandhā*). True. But as an explanation of what the Buddha was teaching, this is still totally inadequate.

The only way fully to explain matters to an English-speaker is to use clear, normal English. This will not be possible through just translating terms or sentences containing those terms. However, a large part of the explanation will consist of dealing with those terms, exploring their semantic range and discussing their uses, both literal and metaphorical.

Let me begin with the 'self', briefly postponing the 'aggregates'. Throughout ancient times, in the cultures where it was known, the salient doctrine of Buddhism, its most distinctive feature, was held to be the doctrine of No Self or No Soul. Both these two-word English phrases translate S: *anātman* and P: *anatta/anattā*. When Buddhism was discovered by the West (mainly in the nineteenth century), it was being expounded by and to Christians, who were no less struck by Buddhism's denial of a supreme creator god; but for modern scholars too, the denial of a self or soul has been the most striking characteristic of Buddhism and of the teaching ascribed to the Buddha.

It will be easiest to grasp my argument if I come straight to the main point, and say baldly that all the fuss and misunderstanding can be avoided if one inserts the word 'unchanging', so that the two-word English phrases become 'no unchanging self' and 'no unchanging soul'. I shall explore the matter in detail later in the book, but here it suffices to say that for the Buddha's audience *by definition* the word *ātman/attā* referred to something unchanging; in that linguistic environment, to add a word meaning 'unchanging' would have been redundant. Thus, there are several ways of expressing this doctrine clearly and accurately in English. One can say, for example, 'There is nothing in living beings that never changes,' or 'There is no unchanging essence in living beings.' (Since the main concern is with people, it may be helpful to substitute 'people' or 'human beings' for 'living beings'.)

So far, so good. If Buddhism is just a way to gain salvation, it seems enough to know that this applies to us humans. In fact, however, the doctrine is far wider. It applies to everything within our normal experience. In this broader context, the word 'soul' becomes inappropriate and one wants a word like 'essence'. So the cardinal teaching becomes: 'Nothing in the world has an unchanging essence,' or 'There is nothing in our normal experience that never changes.'

On the one hand, these are simple, intelligible statements. On the other hand, 'in the world' has been equated with 'in our normal experience'. Thus each statement of the doctrine leads us on to another. In other words – and this is my most fundamental point – we are dealing with a system which is not merely coherent but interlocking. It is perfectly understandable, but to understand it correctly you have to know how the entire set of key terms is being used. Thus, for the Buddha 'the world' is the same as 'that which we can normally experience'.

Yes, we should now go on to explain what is meant by 'normally'. But if we were thorough about following from link to link, the introduction would become the whole book. So for the moment it must suffice to point out that the Buddha is not primarily concerned with what exists – in fact, he thinks that is a red herring – but with what we can experience, what can be present to consciousness. For his purposes, what exists and the contents of experience are the same. At this level, if we want a label, his doctrine looks like pragmatic empiricism.

To go a step further: this accords with what is known as the First Noble Truth. Traditionally, this is expressed in a single Pali word, *dukkha* (S: *duḥkha*). This 'truth' is expressed as a single word, not a sentence, and thus looks more like an exclamation than a proposition. Again, there has been a lot of argument over how to translate the word *dukkha*; and again, the choice of translation must depend heavily on the context. But what is being expressed is that life as we normally experience it is unsatisfactory.

Thus we arrive at what is known in Pali dogmatics as the *ti-lakkhaṇa*, 'the three hallmarks'. The hallmarks of what? Of life as we can normally know it. The hallmarks are that it is *anicca, dukkha, anatta*: 'impermanent (i.e., ever-changing[10]), unsatisfactory, not/without self/essence'. We have already seen that since by definition self is unchanging, the first and third hallmarks are virtually tautologous. In Chapter 5 we shall show that the same applies to *dukkha*: that in the terms in which the Buddha was thinking and preaching, nothing impermanent could be fully satisfactory. This may not be obvious to us, and indeed it sets the bar for satisfaction far higher than many of us would want to, but for the Buddha, we shall see, this is a fundamental postulate.

Another point which we must for the moment be content to gloss over is the ambiguity between not *being* a self or essence and not *having* a self or essence. For the purposes of this summary exposition, the ambiguity hardly matters, and we shall return to it in Chapter 5.

The most basic point of the Buddha's teaching that we have so far displayed is that everything in our lives changes: that most of us have no experience of anything unchanging. Moreover, in this view of the world, to 'exist' is not to change: existence and becoming are defined as opposites. But is change random? Surely not. Even if we and everything around us change all the time, life could not go on if we did not recognize continuities at every step. The change, in other words, is not random. The Buddha axiomatized this in the proposition that nothing exists without a cause.

Another, simpler way of saying that all phenomena exhibit non-random change is to say that *everything is process*. That is indeed, in my view, the Buddha's position. But now the question must surely be: if the Buddha was saying something so simple and straightforward – which is not to say that all the implications are straightforward –

why is this not what we read in every book about Buddhism? I am going to suggest that this may well be because Pali and Sanskrit lacked a word which closely corresponds to the idea of 'process', and had to express it figuratively. I also believe that the word *saṃkhārā*, which is translated in an astonishing variety of ways, often comes closer to 'process' than has hitherto been recognized.

KARMA AS PERSONAL CONTINUITY

It is time to return to where I began this summary exposition: to the human being, the suffering individual, doomed to continual change, while for both him and his loved ones the great change of life to death is forever looming. It is time, indeed, to say more about karma. Karma is my favourite point of entry to the Buddha's world-view. Rather than begin with a demolition job, as I did when I showed that the common understanding of No Soul is severely deficient, I can introduce karma as a positive doctrine. I believe that it is not only fundamental to the Buddha's whole view of life, but also a kind of lynchpin which holds the rest of the basic tenets together by providing the perfect example of what they mean.

If the doctrine of No Soul means that there is no personal continuity, this suggests the alarming consequence that there is no moral responsibility. But the slightest acquaintance with Buddhism, in virtually any of its forms, shows that this cannot be the correct interpretation, because Buddhism teaches that when people (or other beings) die, they are reborn according to their moral deserts. For those who consider the soul to be the locus of good and evil in the individual, this makes Buddhism bafflingly incoherent. How did such an illogical religion ever survive, let alone appeal to millions?

The answer, of course, is that the idea that Buddhism denies personal continuity could not be further from the truth. In fact, Buddhism probably has the strongest idea of personal continuity found anywhere. Christians, for example, believe in personal continuity through just the one life that we live here on earth, and perhaps in a second life in a place or state of reward or punishment, a heaven or a hell – although, since that is often considered to be 'outside time', it is not clear how the term 'continuity' can there apply. Buddhists, by contrast, believe in personal continuity over an infinite series of lives.

Infinite? Well, the series can have no beginning, because the Buddha established that nothing can come into being without a cause. So, like the world, life cannot have a beginning. (The Buddha advised against spending time on racking one's brains about this.) All of us have already lived infinitely many lives. The series can, however, have an end: that is achieved by the attainment of nirvana. One who has attained nirvana, according to the Buddha, will not be reborn.

We are thus heirs of our own deeds over an infinite number of lives. The best-documented series of lives in Buddhism is that of the person whose last life was as the Buddha, Gotama Buddha. This person resolved to attain Buddhahood a vast number of years ago. (The Buddhist term for someone who takes such a resolution is *bodhisattva.*) Stories of more than five hundred of his previous lives (called *Jātaka*) are retold in scriptures[11] and sermons, painted on temple walls and dramatically recited or re-enacted; they form an integral part of Buddhist culture.

Karma is not the only element of continuity in our lives. Those lives have five sets of components, and each of these five sets is denoted by the term which above was translated by the English word 'aggregate'. In fact, the word should not be detached from a word that precedes it in a Pali compound, *upādāna-khandha,* and that compound is complicated, because it is a pun of which one meaning is a metaphor: 'a mass of burning fuel'. In this latter sense it is part of the same metaphorical structure as nirvana (P: *nibbāna*), which means the going out of a flame. I shall explain this metaphor in Chapter 8. For the moment, we need only note that these five masses of burning fuel are, metaphorically, the five sets of processes which constitute our lives. In the traditional order, these five are: interactions with the physical world through the five senses, feelings (as of pleasure and pain), apperceptions (perceptions which serve to identify objects), *saṃkhārā* and consciousness.

I have left the fourth untranslated. Common translations are 'mental formations' and 'volitions'. *Saṃkhārā* in this context refers to those mental processes not covered by the second, third and fifth categories, and they are indeed emotions and volitions. Far the most important of these processes is intention. While it is admitted that some intentions are morally neutral, the focus is on intentions which are morally good or bad.

The Buddha taught that all thoughts, words and deeds derive their moral value, positive or negative, from the intention behind them. This does not make the effect of actions irrelevant: Buddhism is no less familiar than is modern law with the idea of negligence. But the basic criterion for morality is intention. Morality and immorality are mental properties of individuals. Metaphorically they were often referred to as purity and impurity. Each good deed makes a person purer and thus makes it slightly easier to repeat such a deed. For instance, I may find it a wrench to give money away the first time, but each time I do so the generosity will come more easily. The same applies to bad qualities, such as cruelty. An intention, carried out, becomes a propensity. A proverb cited by Damien Keown in his little book *Buddhism: A Very Short Introduction*[12] puts it admirably: 'Sow an act, reap a habit; sow a habit, reap a character; sow a character, reap a destiny.'

Though karma, ethical volition, is thus only one of the elements of continuity in an individual's life (and beyond), from the religious point of view it is the most important. This volition, moreover, is presented as a process. It is far from random, and is partially conditioned by preceding volitions; but it is not wholly determined. If it were, the volition could not be the responsibility of its agent, and for that agent to suffer consequences would be completely unjust, and indeed make nonsense of the very idea of volition as a separate category of thought or mental event. While I shall have more to say about karma and determinism below, it suffices here to say that the entire Buddhist ideology depends on the proposition that karma is on the one hand conditioned but on the other not strictly determined.

INDIVIDUAL AUTONOMY AND RESPONSIBILITY

Since ethical value lies in intention, the individual is autonomous and the final authority is what we would call his conscience. There is no external agent, such as a God, who can take the blame for our decisions. We have free will and are wholly responsible for ourselves. Further, this responsibility extends far beyond this present life. So we are entirely responsible for our moral condition and what we make of it.

As a general rule, a monk could not be disciplined for an offence to which he did not admit. Similarly, the moral rules laid down for the laity (which also apply, *a fortiori,* to the Saṅgha) are formulated as personal undertakings: the Buddhist layman declares, 'I undertake to abstain from taking life' and so forth, and thus articulates personal conscience. At least in theory, even the recitation of the words is useless and pointless unless one is consciously subscribing to their meaning.

The point of ritual lies in doing, not in intending. Thus ritual is ethically neutral for the Buddhist. It has no moral and hence no soteriological value. It is not normally forbidden, unless it involves an immoral act such as killing, but it is certainly not commended. The Buddha, following his custom of putting new meanings to old words, often asked his followers to substitute moral for ritual practices. One of the Three Fetters which tie men to continued existence in this world was declared to be infatuation with ritualistic observances,[13] clinging to the letter rather than the spirit of actions.

The Buddha took the brahmin word for 'ritual' and used it to denote ethical intention. This single move overturns brahminical, caste-bound ethics. For the intention of a brahmin cannot plausibly be claimed to be ethically of quite a different kind from the intention of an outcaste. Intention can only be virtuous or wicked. The very term *sva-dharma,* the Sanskrit word meaning one's own particularistic duty, is absent from the Buddhist Canon. It is 'purifying action' (*puñña kamma*) which brings the good Buddhist rewards in this and future lives. But since acting is really mental, doing a good act is actually purifying one's state of mind. In meditation, such purification is undertaken directly, without any accompanying action. Thus there is a logical continuum between the moral actions of a man in the world and the meditations of a recluse. This shows why the Buddhists claim morality to be a prerequisite for meditation. The system is all of a piece.[14]

A great deal of modern education and psychotherapy consists of making people aware that they are responsible for themselves. In fact, we consider that it constitutes a large part of what we mean by becoming a mature person. It is amazing that someone should have promulgated this idea in the fifth century BC, and hardly less remarkable that he found followers. In Chapter 2 I shall suggest what socio-economic conditions made this possible – though certainly not inevitable.

Introductions to Buddhism written for westerners tend to begin by quoting the Buddha's advice to a group of people called the

Kālāmas.[15] They had complained to him that various teachers came and preached different doctrines to them, and they were confused about which to follow. The Buddha replied that everyone has to make up their own mind on such matters. One should not take any teaching on trust or external authority, but test it on the touchstone of one's own experience. Naturally, the implication is that people would then find out for themselves that it was the Buddha whose teaching their experience showed to be correct. It is natural and appropriate for modern authors to highlight this teaching: its implications for tolerance and egalitarianism, at least on the intellectual level, resonate with post-Enlightenment thought. The attitude was not unique in the ancient world: one can imagine the same advice coming from Socrates – though not from Plato. But it is astonishing to find it in the generally hierarchic society of India.

The Buddha's views on politics are fascinating, but since I have virtually nothing to add to what I have written about them elsewhere,[16] I shall leave them out of this book. So let me at this point draw attention to his egalitarianism: that the only true criterion for ranking people is moral, and that morality is closely linked to intellectual ability. The first of these propositions may remind us of Christianity, but the second less so.

If people are responsible for their own decisions, and in particular for deciding which teaching to follow, this sets a high premium on intelligence. The usual term that the Buddha seems to have used for a morally good act was a word, *kusala*, which in Sanskrit[17] can mean either 'healthy, wholesome' or 'skilful'. Scholars have debated which of these translations is more appropriate in Buddhism. Perhaps one need not really decide between them, for the ambiguity could have been intentional and words may be selected not only for their literal meanings but also for their overtones. Nevertheless, let me concede that it may make sense to ask which metaphor was uppermost in the Buddha's mind. My answer is that for him *kusala* primarily means 'skilled', because a good moral choice is an intelligent and informed choice. I have little doubt that 'skilful' fits the bill.[18]

If you have intellectual autonomy, you had better have the brains to make good use of it. In every traditional society, including that into which the Buddha was born, education consists largely in parroting what the teacher says. If later some Buddhists parroted, 'The teacher says I must think for myself,' we cannot blame the Buddha for that. The Buddha even made a monastic ruling that one of the duties of a pupil towards his teacher is to correct him when he is wrong on doctrine or in danger of saying something unsuitable.[19] That, I think, has few parallels in world history.

Though the Buddha's advice to the Kālāmas may not follow logically from his doctrine of karma, I see the two as closely connected: everyone is ultimately responsible for themselves and has to use their intelligence to make their own choices.

WHY HAVE I STARTED HERE?

In this Introduction I have tried to summarize, briefly but I hope clearly, what I consider to be the most important of the Buddha's ideas. I have shown that to take the key concepts in isolation is almost bound to lead to misunderstanding. Thus, the concept of 'no soul', commonly held to refer to the most characteristic Buddhist teaching, has at least to be taken in conjunction with the doctrine of karma.

It turns out, I would argue, that if one wants to expound the Buddha's core teaching, quite a lot hangs on where one begins. I have used No Soul and karma (moral causality) as my points of entry. The Buddhist tradition is unanimous that the Buddha began by preaching the Four Noble Truths, which deal with *dukkha* (let's call it 'suffering'). I have mentioned the First Noble Truth, that all living beings experience suffering, but neither did I make it my point of entry, nor have I yet explained the other three Noble Truths. Why?

Because the Buddha was preaching to an audience who already had a set of preconceptions, most of them very different from our own. They took rebirth for granted; they believed in some enduring entity at the centre of each human being, an entity which transmigrated from life to life; probably most of them believed that the cycle of rebirth could be brought to an end, but that that central entity would somehow survive eternally. Some of them believed that the form in which one was reborn was affected by how one behaved previously, but whether and how this happened was a hotly contested issue. So I have had to make these preconceptions explicit from the very outset; and indeed, after I have explained the Buddha's view of karma in more detail in the next chapter, the following two chapters will deal with the views of karma and rebirth which led up to the Buddha's own.

Virtually everything I have so far written requires further elaboration, and I have not even touched on such important matters as nirvana, the Buddha's view of language, and – perhaps most important of all – ethical values. Other important features of the Buddha's teaching and practice, such as meditation and the monastic Order, must remain almost entirely outside the scope of this book. I hope, however, that I have done enough to show that the ideas here presented are not only powerful but also form a coherent system.

SUMMARY: DID ONE PERSON REALLY THINK OF ALL THIS?

I have mentioned above that some scholars do not like to talk of Buddhism in the singular at all, unless it be in scare quotes. Probably even more common, at least in the United States, is the view that if such a historical figure as the Buddha existed, we can know nothing about him. Academics who are prey to this fashion for 'deconstruction' are reluctant to consider anything in a Buddhist text to be older than that text itself. Since it is most unlikely that any text was written down before the reign of the Emperor Asoka in the middle of the third century BC, some 150 years after the Buddha's death, and indeed hardly any texts that we have were written down even that early,[20] the same sceptics claim that we can know nothing about Buddhism before it had already split into schools and sects. That means, of course, knowing nothing about the Buddha or his ideas. On this view, Buddhism emerges into the light of history from impenetrable darkness.

Surely this defies common sense. Firstly, it makes no sense to assume that Buddhism could have arisen without a historical person who founded it, and provided it with ideas and institutions. (About the ideology of the institution I shall have something to say in Chapter 11.) It is equally implausible, in my view, to claim that these ideas could just have accumulated among Buddhists as time went on, and that their coherence is a matter of historical accident. One remarkable brain must have been responsible for the basic ideology. The owner of that brain happens to be known, appropriately, as the Buddha, the 'Awakened'.

Moreover, as I began to show in *How Buddhism Began* and will further demonstrate below, that brain was strongly influenced by ideas current at a certain place and time. The ideas were original and brilliant, but fully to understand them requires also an understanding of what preceded them. It is because exegetes have had too little such understanding that the ideas have often been misinterpreted.

Chapter 2

MORE ABOUT KARMA, AND ITS SOCIAL CONTEXT

For the Buddha, the idea of karma is inextricably connected with the idea of rebirth. He saw karma, intentional action, as a matter of cause and effect. Good karma would bring good effects for the doer, bad karma bad effects. It would not be right to call these rewards and punishments,[1] because there is no rewarder or punisher. The effects are produced, rather, by a law of nature, analogous for us to a law of physics. For the Buddha and others in ancient India, however, the model was agriculture. One sows a seed, there is a time lag during which some mysterious invisible process takes place, and then the plant pops up and can be harvested. The result of an intentional act is in fact normally referred to as its 'fruit'.[2] The time between the act and its fruit is unpredictable.

All the world religions face the problem known in theology as theodicy, literally 'god's justice'. This is also known as the problem of suffering, though its main concern is with apparently unjust suffering. It seems that sometimes wicked people die without having got their comeuppance, and that often babies who cannot yet have done wrong suffer and die too. This evidence from our common experience would seem to refute the doctrine of karma – if people had only one life. Karma works as a theodicy by claiming that the explanation for both triumphant rogues and suffering babies lies in what they have done in former lives.

For karma to work as an ethical doctrine, it must steer between the extremes of determinism and randomness. If we have no free will, if our actions are rigidly determined, we are not ethical agents and the rest of the Buddha's teaching makes no sense at all. So it is not surprising to find in the Pali Canon his condemnation of the determinist doctrines of the Ājīvaka teacher Makkhali Gosāla[3] and others. On the other hand, the teaching is equally flawed unless actions have consequences.

For the middle way between determinism and randomness, there is an important *sutta* in the *Saṃyutta Nikāya*.[4] A non-Buddhist renunciate called Moliya Sīvaka asks the Buddha what he thinks of the view that everything one experiences, whether pleasure, pain or neutral, is the result of what one has done. The Buddha replies that this view is wrong and goes beyond both what one can know for oneself and what is commonly accepted to be true. One can know for oneself, and it is commonly accepted, that feelings arise from eight causes. He lists them. The first five are perfectly clear and refer to the medical knowledge of those days. First there are the three humours: bile, phlegm and wind. The fourth is a combination of these three. The fifth is a change in season. (We, with our more variable climate, would call it a change in the weather.) The sixth the *PED* translates as 'being attacked by adversities';[5] but I think the reference is still medical and it means inappropriate or inadequate care or treatment.[6] The seventh seems to mean 'caused by an act of violence'.[7] Only the eighth cause, says the Buddha, is the result of karma. In other words, he seems to be saying that ascribing good or bad experiences to karma is only suitable when no medical or common-sense explanation is available. But is this logical?

The Buddha's teaching of karma was a moral exhortation. So it is intended to be seen from the front, to be taken as an answer to the question 'How should I behave?' Since people are lazy, and tend to be more interested in saying, 'How did I get into this mess – surely it was not my fault?', the tendency has always been, probably from the Buddha's day until now, to see the same doctrine from the other end, backwards. Thus, it is easy for belief in karma to become a kind of fatalism, the very reverse of what the Buddha meant. In this perverse form of the doctrine, people say, 'This is my karma', when what they mean, to use the original terminology, is 'This is the result of my karma.'

Still, one can ask, 'Granted that we create our own futures, to what extent are things that happen to us the result of our own acts in this or a former life?' The Buddha's answer to Moliya Sīvaka, just quoted, says that medical conditions are to be explained by medical causes without having recourse to karma. But does this always apply? When we pose the problem of theodicy, often the first example of unjust suffering that comes to mind is the child born with AIDS.

Does the fact that this is a condition of which we understand the medical causes mean that it is not a case of karmic causation? If so, what use is karma as a theodicy?

It seems that karma operates on a grand scale, for example, in determining where one is born and when one dies. At first sight the example of the child with AIDS may appear to contradict this. But no. One must realize that karma must operate through some specific cause; it is, as it were, the cause behind causes. In that sense the Buddha's answer to Moliya Sīvaka is misleading, for karma and the other causes cited are not on the same level.

The account that I wrote in my first book, based on fieldwork in a Sinhalese Buddhist village, will serve to give us a picture of how the Buddhist view of the results of karma probably has always operated:

> Bad karma means that one is due for misfortune ... Specific misfortunes are caused by other beings – gods, men or devils – who operate as freewill agents, or they may result from natural causes such as eating the wrong food. These causes interlock and cannot be rigidly schematised. A man who falls ill will probably first try western medicine at the local hospital, and if that fails try Ayurvedic medicine administered by a village specialist. If that fails his next resort will be determined by his sub-culture and individual temperament. He may ascribe it to human agency (black magic) and employ suitable counter-measures (white magic). He may ascribe it to demons of disease or to malign planetary influences ... and banish or appease them by more or less elaborate exorcistic ceremonies. He may ascribe it to the actions of a god, or rather the failure of that god's protection, and make the god a vow, promising him some present or service if he recovers. If the remedy does not work this may be due to a wrong diagnosis, or, much more likely, it may be because the man's karma is too bad, and he is due to suffer longer. The theories and remedies listed are not mutually exclusive.[8]

In practice, people tend to apply the theory backwards: when one has an illness and no treatment seems to do any good, one starts saying that this must be an effect of bad karma. The Buddha himself listed the effects of karma as one of the four things which are not to be thought about, because thinking about them will drive you crazy.[9] Presumably this warning is directed to unenlightened people, because the second of the three knowledges which are said to come with Enlightenment is the ability to see how beings are reborn in accordance with the moral quality of their deeds (*yathā-kammūpaga*).[10] So he witnessed the workings of karma, but we cannot. And what he saw convinced him that nothing could be as urgent as putting a stop to the whole process.

Very rarely in human history have people accepted that they are wholly responsible for themselves. Most people have lived under such conditions that this teaching has no plausibility. It has no plausibility for those whose food supply depends on the vagaries of the weather. A high rate of morbidity must also be demoralizing. Equally important, in societies where power is very unequally distributed, and those with little or none of it depend on the goodwill of their overlords, it is natural to believe that the world is run by a god or gods. What, then, were the exceptional circumstances which allowed the Buddha's teaching of individual responsibility to take root in a large segment of society, at least for a few generations?

My claim is not that the Buddha's conceiving these ideas was determined by the society and the economy in which he lived, for I think that remarkable individuals are capable of generating ideas under almost any circumstances. But we would never have heard of the Buddha and there would be no Buddhism had not a lot of people accepted his ideas, and it is their acceptance which I think can be attributed to their material conditions.

All historians agree that Buddhism arose early in India's second period of urbanization. (The first was the Indus Valley civilization, irrelevant to our story.) This urbanization must have come about through the production of an agricultural surplus. Radical changes in society and the economy ensued. The larger towns (still very small by modern standards) developed into city states, with courts, nobility and an administrative class. The surplus agricultural production led to trade on an ever increasing scale, and this in turn led to contact with more distant societies and a broadening of cultural horizons. Traders kept accounts; kings enforced laws. I have described all this in Chapter 2 of my *Theravada Buddhism* and many others have done so in more detail.[11]

I suggest that in this period an unusually high proportion of people must have lived relatively free from oppression. It is clear both from the early texts and, a bit later, from archaeological evidence that Buddhism particularly appealed to the new social classes, such as traders. Traders were by no means the only people who were largely self-employed. Kosambi writes:

> The existence of new classes in the Gangetic basin of the sixth century is undeniable. The free peasants and farmers were one. The neo-Vedic pastoral class of vaiśyas within the tribe was replaced by agriculturists for whom the tribe had ceased to exist. ... The existence of free, tenant or land-owning peasants ... is clear from the texts ... [L]arge-scale slave labour was not available.[12]

Trade gave the farmers an incentive to produce a surplus, and because clan organization had broken down there was no obligation to share that surplus; the peasants now had 'private property in farm animals, in land and its produce'.[13]

The canonical texts can give us an idea of the social composition of the Buddha's lay support. The term which constantly recurs is *gahapati,* which literally means 'master of a house', i.e., 'householder'. To this day in Indian villages people think of the population very much in terms of family groups or 'houses', each one with its head. It is far easier to get from a villager an estimate of how many such units there are in an area than of the total number of human beings. It is from these 'householders' that such institutions as village councils have always recruited their membership. A household includes not only close kin but servants and other dependants. When ancient texts mention householders, they are referring to heads of families of the top three *varṇas*; the other families do not count socially. Moreover, since brahmins and *kṣatriyas* can have formed only a small part of the population, the term must refer mainly to heads of families which brahminism classified as *vaiśya.* Indeed, the term *vaiśya* (P: *vessa*) is rare in Buddhist scripture; it occurs only when discussing brahmin classification, not as the natural designation for someone's primary social status. It is clear that the canonical *gahapati* is the head of a respectable family – but not a brahmin, unless specifically said to be so.

Who were these people in terms of class or profession? In the Canon, most of them evidently own land, but they usually have labourers to do the physical work. Sometimes they are also in business. In fact, they illustrate how it is in the first instance wealth derived from agriculture which provides business capital. The average *gahapati* who gave material support to the Buddha and his Saṅgha thus seems to have been something like a gentleman farmer, perhaps with a town house. On the other hand, inscriptions in the western Deccan, where Buddhism flourished in the early centuries AD, use the term *gahapati* to refer to urban merchants. We must distinguish between reference and meaning: the meaning of *gahapati* is simple and unvarying, but the reference shifts with the social context.

I should add that since I first began to write about the socio-economic background to the rise of Buddhism, a large-scale British research project, led by Dr Michael Willis and Dr Julia Shaw, has conducted surveys and undertaken surface archaeology in the relevant parts of India, and their research has helped to fill in the picture I have been sketching. To quote from an abstract of a lecture given by Dr Willis: they conclude, *inter alia*, 'that the appearance of Buddhism and its relic cult in central India coincided with the building of a vast hydrological system which radically changed both agrarian production and the immediate environment,' and 'that a new social class of landed farmers were important instruments in the whole process, functioning both as constituents in a new polity and lay supporters of Buddhism.'[14]

I have been made aware of an even more important line of interpretation too late to do it full justice in this book. This concerns the radical effect on thought of monetization. Richard Seaford was kind enough to write to me, after reading my *Social History*: 'There is a striking similarity with what I have argued to be the socio-economic preconditions for the (roughly contemporary) beginnings of western "philosophy" (in my *Money and the Early Greek Mind*).' I find his book fascinating, and hope I can discuss its wider implications for early Indian thought elsewhere. Here let me just quote the passages which I find most relevant to the Buddha's karma theory. The 'metaphysics of money' involves 'the belief that we are primarily individual agents and only secondarily (if at all) members of a larger [social] entity ...'[15]

> The individual with money, although he may find useful and desirable the personal relations of kinship and friendship (reciprocity) as well as participation in collective sacrifices (redistribution), can frequently do without them, relying instead on the impersonal power of money ... The power of money can increase human independence even from deity; ...[16]

This fits Buddhist karma perfectly.

Since it is explicitly stated in a canonical text,[17] it has often been noted that the organization of the Buddhist Saṅgha was modelled on that of a tribal republic or oligarchy: the only ranking principle was that of seniority, i.e., number of years since full ordination. The Buddha, according to the same text, refused to appoint a head of the Saṅgha, and told monks to rely on themselves, not on external authority. Obviously this fits well with a doctrine of free will: it attempts to put the teaching that everyone is fully responsible for themselves into practice. However, as Obeyesekere demonstrates,[18] Buddhist karma doctrine is just as much for the laity as for the Saṅgha.

In sum, my claim is that this teaching could only succeed because so many people found it did not run counter to their experience. For a modern audience I should perhaps repeat that the 'people' primarily – though not exclusively – involved were the heads of households, those who controlled the economic resources to support the Saṅgha and who also, no doubt, set the religious tone for the rest of their families.

KARMA THEORY'S BEARING ON SOCIETY AND COSMOLOGY

If karma is completely ethicized, the whole universe becomes an ethical arena, because everywhere all beings are placed according to their deserts. If this is generalized into a view of the world, as it has been in Theravādin cultures, it means that ultimately power (including the power to enjoy oneself) and goodness are always perfectly correlated, both increasing as one proceeds (literally) up the universe. Gods are more powerful than human beings, but since they owe their position to their virtue they may be expected to exercise that power justly. Human beings, in turn, are better and also better off than animals, let alone demons. Moreover, even demons are only rationally punitive: they can be the instruments to give people their just deserts, but if they try to go further, like an over-zealous policeman, they will themselves be punished for it. This picture of a universe under control is from one angle reassuring; but in its belief that there is really no undeserved suffering it can also be harsh. Logically it solves the problem of theodicy, but at a price. Many have found this solution as unbearable as the situation it resolves, and it is hardly surprising that Buddhism as it developed after the Buddha's death became rich in ways of obscuring or escaping such an intransigent law of the universe, often at the cost of logical consistency.

Obeyesekere has also shown[19] how it is logical that the ethicization of a society's eschatology should lead to its universalization. Once ethics is reduced to the simple values of right and wrong, and located in the mind, something common to all human beings, distinctions of gender, age and social class become irrelevant. Moreover, Buddhism – like mercantile wealth—was not ascribed but achieved. It appealed largely to new men who did not fit well into the four-*varṇa* system of brahmin ideology.

Buddhism, in origin an Indian ideology, spread over half the ancient world and took root in quite disparate civilizations. Despite huge setbacks, it is still spreading. I would suggest that it acquired this adaptability not by chance, but because the Buddha himself was able to see that local mores were man-made, and could show that what brahmins believed to be ingrained in nature was nothing but convention. In much the same period (though they started somewhat earlier) the Greeks were making the distinction between *phusis*, nature, and *nomos*, man-made rule, and drawing similar conclusions. The Buddha probably began with an advantage in that he was born and bred in north-eastern India on the very margin of Vedic civilization. But he was also addressing audiences among which were men who had acquired the same perception when they had travelled on business. Disputing with a young brahmin, the Buddha points out that in the far north-west and other distant countries there are only two *varṇa*, master and slave (or servant), and it happens on occasion that masters become slaves and slaves masters.[20] As has happened several times in history, awareness of foreign cultures had a truly liberating effect.

Buddhism was attached neither to community nor to locality, neither to shrine nor to hearth, but resided in the hearts of its adherents; it was readily transportable. It suited people who moved around, whether changing residence from village to town or travelling on business. Hence it spread along trade routes. It is striking that though monks were not normally allowed to travel during the rainy season, an exception is made[21] for the monk who is in a caravan or on a ship – presumably accompanying Buddhist merchants. The Buddhist value system can travel and adapt itself to other cultures. For example, the Buddhist layman vows 'not to act wrongly in respect of sense desires'; this can be used in any society, no matter what its sexual mores, for it is just a promise to abide by those mores.

Making the individual conscience the ultimate authority is both a liberating and a dangerous move. What if someone acts on wrong moral reasoning? Society needs a sanction. That is why it was immensely important for the Buddha, and indeed for the whole tradition that followed him, to keep stressing that the law of moral reckoning worked throughout the universe: that good would be rewarded and evil punished in the end. That, I suggest, is also why the Buddha made belief in this law of karma the first step on his noble eightfold path to nirvana. The first step is called 'right view', *sammā diṭṭhi*. What this refers to is precisely accepting this tenet (in Pali: being a *kamma-vādin*).

There is an interesting inconsistency here in the Buddha's presentation. Steven Collins[22] has discussed and explained the fact that while the Buddha often commends 'right views' and condemns 'wrong views', in some contexts the canonical texts have the Buddha say that he has no views (*diṭṭhi*) at all, that only other people have views. He is there talking about metaphysical speculation, and it is not hard to see what he means, even if one finally assesses the claim as disingenuous. But when it comes to preaching to the public, to attracting and perhaps converting laymen, he cannot avoid making clear that there is one 'right view' without which his entire edifice collapses: that the law of karma ensures that there is justice in the world.

When one introduces the Buddha's teaching to a modern audience, one very often stresses at the outset – as indeed I have done – that he asked people to use their own judgement, to go by their own experience and take nothing on trust. One soon has to qualify this, however, by saying that there was one belief which he held himself and relied on in his teaching, the belief in the law of karma; and if that was not to be obviously falsified by every cot death, it had to entail belief in rebirth. One tends to add, perhaps in an apologetic tone, that these were beliefs that the Buddha inherited and simply could not shake off. I hope I have shown that this is the very reverse of the truth. The Buddha's version of the law of karma was entirely his own; but to accept it was the leap of faith he demanded of every follower.

Chapter 3

THE ANTECEDENTS OF THE KARMA DOCTRINE IN BRAHMINISM

In this chapter and the next I shall try to outline the earlier Indian ideas of rebirth and karma which led up to those taught by the Buddha. In this chapter I shall be dealing with brahminism, but only those aspects of it strictly relevant to that theme. Other aspects of brahminism which fundamentally influenced the Buddha are postponed till Chapter 5.

Until very recently, all scholars have agreed that the *Ṛg Veda* shows no signs of a belief in rebirth. Basing themselves on the 'Funeral Hymn', *RV* X.16, scholars have thought that when people (in fact, only men are explicitly referred to) died and were cremated, they went upwards to join their ancestors, who were known as 'fathers' (*pitaras*) and lived in the sky, or more precisely in the sun. Since no more was said about them, it was presumed that they stayed there, having a good time. The idea of a second death, which can be avoided by providing the ancestors with daily libations, is found in the *Brāhmaṇas*, a stratum of religious texts generally thought to be several centuries younger than the *Ṛg Veda*.

By this same agreed account, the idea of a cycle of rebirth first appears in the early *Upaniṣads*, texts which follow the *Brāhmaṇas*. But where did it come from?

The oldest *Upaniṣads* have been tentatively dated to the seventh or sixth century BC. The word *karma* is first mentioned in connection with rebirth in two brief passages in the *Bṛhad-āraṇyaka Upaniṣad*, one of the oldest, if not the very oldest, of the *Upaniṣads*. Towards the end of the text, the *Bṛhad-āraṇyaka Upaniṣad* has a longer passage (see below), known as the 'five fire wisdom' (*pañcāgni-vidyā*), which describes three destinations for men at death. (Women are again not mentioned and it is doubtful whether they are included.) This passage appears with only very slight variation in another *Upaniṣad*, the *Chāndogya*. In this account, people fall into three groups: the best go up to the sun and are not reborn, the middle group go via the moon and are reborn on earth, the third, of whom little is said, apparently are reborn too.[1]

From the agreed account, it is a puzzle to conjecture how the notion of rebirth suddenly appeared in the brahmin tradition. One theory has been that the brahmins learnt it from the royal class, the *kṣatriyas*, whom they served as priests. This theory arose because in the *Bṛhad-āraṇyaka* and the *Chāndogya* the 'five fire wisdom' and some other doctrines are said to be taught to brahmins by kings; but I could never understand how it was imagined that a group of people could develop and transmit such a religious theory while keeping it secret from their own priests. Another theory has held that rebirth was an idea which started among the non-Aryan, indigenous population; but that is an even more desperate guess, because of their religion we know absolutely nothing.

Luckily, we have been saved from such idle speculations, with their uncomfortably racialist overtones, by the wonderful recent researches of Gananath Obeyesekere and Joanna Jurewicz. In this chapter I shall first report the discovery by Jurewicz that the agreed account is wrong: that the Vedic funeral hymn has been misinterpreted and does indeed refer to rebirth. I regard her arguments as conclusive, and consider that they make better sense of the early history of Indian religion.[2] Confining myself to essentials, I shall then show the major stages through which a theory of rebirth according to one's karma developed. This will include a brief account of rebirth in Jainism; in the following chapter I shall explain in more detail why in my opinion Jainism, or something very close to it, must have antedated the Buddha and exercised an important influence on his ideas.

Let me begin by putting Jurewicz's discovery in a wider framework. Gananath Obeyesekere has shown[3] that a belief in rebirth has been found in many small-scale societies round the world, but usually follows a certain pattern. Only a few societies, of which India is perhaps the best example, develop this simpler kind of belief into something more complex, of which the salient characteristic is ethicization.

What exactly does this mean? Though all societies have ethics, most theories of rebirth, in societies as far apart as West Africa, the Trobriand Islands, and the far north-west of Canada, believe that rewards and punishments come only in this life, and that by and large the ethical quality of one's conduct has no bearing on one's rebirth. In such societies, rebirth is a matter of moving between this world and another very much like it: when one dies here, one goes there, and when in due course one dies there, one is reborn here. The theory of karma, introduced as the scale of society greatly expanded, ethicized this process; and this in turn led to further new ideas, notably a theory of how one could escape from the cycle altogether.

In the rebirth theories of small-scale societies,

> The fundamental idea of reincarnation is that at death an ancestor or close kin is reborn in the human world, whether or not there has been an intermediate sojourn in another sphere of existence or after-world. I may die or go to some place of sojourn after death, but eventually I must come down and be reborn in the world I left.[4]

Typically, one oscillates between this world and another very like it, which may, for example, be just over the horizon. Sometimes the other world is known as 'the world of the ancestors'. In principle such a cycle of rebirth, alternating between two worlds, may go on forever. Moreover, when one comes back to this world, one is usually expected to rejoin the same family or clan.

In such theories rebirth has nothing to do with ethics. In such small-scale societies people sooner or later come to know of each others' good and bad deeds, so that rewards and punishments are meted out in this world.

> Although the idea of a world of ancestors (paradisical or otherwise) is omnipresent, this is not so with the idea of a hell or a similar place of punishment. Occasionally there is a place where violators of taboos and those guilty of heinous acts such as incest and sorcery are confined, but there is no hell to which the bad are condemned. Most often ... such persons are punished by being denied a human reincarnation. Entry into the other world rarely depends on the ethical nature of one's this-worldly behavior. With the exceptions already noted, entry

> into that other world is a privilege available to all, and this entry is achieved by the correct performance of the funeral rites.[5]

It is only when societies transcend a certain scale, Obeyesekere argues, so that often justice is *not* seen to be done in this world, that enforcing moral rules becomes a worry. Then there arises the theory that some other, unseen, force in the cosmos will ensure that people's crimes do not go unpunished. That is what he calls the ethicization of rebirth.

> I use the term *ethicization* to conceptualize the processes whereby a morally right or wrong action becomes a religiously right or wrong action that in turn affects the person's destiny after death. Ethicization deals with a thoroughgoing religious evaluation of morality that entails delayed punishments and rewards quite unlike the immediate or this-worldly compensations meted out by deities or ancestors.[6]

This is where the karma theories of Buddhism and Jainism come in.

❧

Let me turn to Jurewicz's discovery of rebirth in the *Ṛg Veda*.[7] Her argument begins with a radically new translation of a verse in the 'Funeral Hymn', X.16.5. All previous translators took the word *pitṛbhyo*[8] as a dative and understood the verse as a request to the funeral fire (personified) that he send the dead man again 'to his ancestors'. Jurewicz begins by asking, why 'again'? She then takes *pitṛbhyo* as an ablative, which grammatically is equally possible, and translates 'Release him down, Agni, from [his] fathers, [him] who, poured into you, wanders according to his will. Let him who wears life come to his offspring. Let him join his body, Jāta-vedas[9]!'[10]

This fits Obeyesekere's pattern for small-scale societies to perfection. The dead person goes to join his ancestors – we learn from other verses in the *Ṛg Veda* they live in the sun – but this has nothing to do with his moral qualities. When he comes back, and takes a body, he will rejoin his family (offspring). Jurewicz then goes on to show that the form in which the dead person returns is the rain, which is 'sown' and produces barley. This perfectly accords with part of the earliest full account of rebirth, the 'five fire doctrine', in the *Bṛhad-āraṇyaka Upaniṣad*, referred to above (see below for further details).

There are two fundamental differences between rebirth in the *Ṛg Veda* and all the later theories of rebirth. In the *Ṛg Veda* one oscillates between just two worlds, this one and the other one; and the process has nothing to do with one's good or bad actions, one's karma, on any interpretation of what exactly that term refers to. Nor is any end to the process envisaged.

When rebirth is first ethicized, the basic model remains simple. This world is the arena of action, the other world is the arena of pay-off. When the pay-off is complete, you come back to this world and start again. Let me call this a binary cosmology. There are Sanskrit terms for the two arenas in this model: this world is called *karma-bhūmi*, the sphere of action, and the other world is *bhoga-bhūmi*, the sphere of experiencing [the results]. This looks like an unending cycle. However, what characterizes all the Indian soteriologies – brahminical/Hindu, Jain and Buddhist – is that they add to rebirth the idea that one can escape from the cycle; in fact, it is precisely such an escape that constitutes salvation. So to the binary cosmology is added the idea of escaping from the cosmos altogether. There are two special dimensions to the Indian developments, of which this is the first.

Obeyesekere suggests (p.79) that once the world is thus ethicized, 'There can no longer be a single place [after death] for those who have done good and those who have done bad. The other world must minimally split into two, a world of retribution ("hell") and a world of reward ("heaven").' The 'minimal split' describes traditional Christianity (at least, if we ignore purgatory). But Indian religions have seen three possible destinies at death: heaven, hell and neither, which is to say escape from rebirth, and the different religions have arranged these in different permutations.

While each religion has its own terminology, the cycle of rebirth is generally called *saṃsāra*, a word which suggests the meaning 'keeping going'. By a different but equally common metaphor, this is felt to be a kind of slavery or imprisonment, so that release from it is called 'liberation'; the cognate words *mokṣa* and *mukti* are the commonest Sanskrit terms. All traditions agree that since a good rebirth will inevitably come to an end, the best solution – because the only final one – is liberation.

The second special Indian dimension concerns the relationship between ethics and ritual. Perhaps the most important characteristic of both Buddhism and Jainism was that they made an absolutely clear-cut distinction between the two. For them, only what we call morality was relevant for soteriology, for determining one's destiny: ritual *per se* was utterly irrelevant. Brahminism and Hinduism, by contrast, never decisively took this step. Although the word basically means 'act', in brahminical literature 'karma' refers first and foremost to a ritual act. One could even claim, I believe, that to this very day ritual and ethics have not been entirely disentangled in the mainstream of Hindu tradition. The theory underlying the commonest category of rituals is that they are necessary in order to purify human beings of impurities which inevitably arise from their very nature as animals, impurities connected with bodily functions such as excretion and menstruation.

The binary cosmology remains the underlying Hindu model. It is humans and the higher animals who are moral agents, and when they die they go to a heaven or a hell to be rewarded or punished. On the whole the inhabitants of heaven or hell (which may be subdivided and multiplied, but that does not affect the basic system) only experience the results of what they did on earth, and return once that process is complete. There are exceptions in mythology: gods commit sins (typically out of lust) and are cursed to suffer for them, or conversely an *asura* (an anti-god) may do something virtuous and be blessed for it; but that is not what people envisage for themselves. Most people aim for a rebirth in a heaven or a good station on earth; to escape rebirth altogether is seen as extremely difficult, but ultimately the best destiny. (In the monotheistic sects, this escape from rebirth is brought about or helped by one's God, and the distinction between heaven and escape from rebirth becomes blurred.)

The same binary pattern characterizes early Jainism, but in a remarkable variant. As Will Johnson demonstrates, the earliest form of Jain doctrine considers all karma to be bad, for almost all action is liable to involve injury to living beings. The karma will then stick to the life monad (the *jīva*) and weigh it down, preventing it from attaining liberation by floating to the top of the universe. (This will be further explained in the next chapter.)

> The prospect of a better rebirth in heaven or on earth, as a result of good activity which attracts good karma, is hardly admitted .... [T]hat any rebirth is relatively undesirable remains a constant component of [Jain] doctrine. However, what is largely absent from the earliest texts is the idea that there is any gradation or progression through a series of births to ultimate liberation. Instead, what is emphasised is the critical nature of the present birth and, necessarily (since these texts are addressed to ascetics), those kinds of ascetic restraint which will ensure that there is no further rebirth. The *Āyāraṅga Sutta* 1.6.2, for instance, apparently considers that there are only two possibilities at death: 1) birth among hellish beings and animals, and 2) *mokṣa* [liberation]. The latter will be the condition of the *jīva* of the ideal monk, and the former that of the *jīvas* of everyone else, whether householder or monk.[11]

It is only in Buddhism that the binary model of the sphere of action and the sphere of experiencing the results is superseded, and the whole universe is ethicized. In other words, according to the Buddha's teaching all sentient beings throughout the universe are morally responsible and can be reborn in a higher or lower station because of the good and evil they have done. There are in fact some minor exceptions to this, inconsistencies in the general pattern, but they are of no importance for our present purposes. However, it is interesting to note in passing that the Pali Canon here and there preserves a verse which still assumes the old binary model of 'this world and the next'. For instance: 'He grieves here, he grieves after death, the evil-doer grieves in both places (*ubhayattha*)' (*Dhammapada* 15ab). This begins a series of four verses with the same structure and the same word 'in both places'. Similarly, 'Just as one welcomes the arrival of a beloved relative, his good deeds welcome the man who has done good when he passes from this world to the other' (*asmā lokā paraṃ gataṃ*) (*Dhammapada* 220). And again: 'The man who understands both worlds (*ubho loke*) is therefore called a sage' (*Dhammapada* 269cd). This is evidently so embedded in the idiom that no doctrinal shift can quite dislodge it.

Indeed, the same old model is found in prose discourse, for the Buddha characterizes as 'wrong view' (*micchā-diṭṭhi*) the denial that 'this world exists, the other world exists'; conversely, to accept this is 'right view' (*sammā-diṭṭhi*).[12] The context of this idiom always concerns karma: to accept that this world and the other exist is to accept that good and bad karma performed in this life will surely bring results sooner or later.

The main exception to the total ethicization of the Buddhist universe does not impinge on the moral teaching. There is a widespread belief that the gods in the heavens cannot or do not make merit, and similarly those suffering in a hell are not generally considered to be active as moral agents. This is clearly a relic of the archaic binary cosmology which I have expounded above, according to which it is only this earth which is the arena of moral action; the other parts of the universe are there for pay-off. Some Buddhists hold that the gods do not make merit because life in heaven is too comfortable, so they forget about the Noble Truth of suffering.

However, I know of no textual evidence (though there may be some) that the Buddha himself exempted denizens of heaven from moral agency. I think that the Buddha probably only concerned himself with the morals of those on earth and that the idea that gods too are moral agents only become operational once the so-called 'transfer of merit' had invaded Buddhist practice. (I think this began to happen around the time of the Buddha's death.) Transferring merit to the gods was then justified by the archaic theory that they could not make merit for themselves.

❧

In the next chapter I shall present my hypothesis that the Buddha was deeply influenced by the Jain doctrine of karma and *saṃsāra*, but precisely reversed the original Jain view that karma consisted in action, not intention. First, however, we must revert to tracing the history of these ideas in the brahminical literature.

A detailed account of rebirth, and rudimentary references to karma, are found in the *Bṛhad-āraṇyaka Upaniṣad* (*BĀU*). One can trace a development within this rather long and varied text. One might say that the central concept of this text, and indeed of all the *Upaniṣads*, is that of the *ātman*, the 'self' or 'soul'; that will be further explained below.

I start with a passage which is still based on a clear binary cosmology. It begins by equating the self, *ātman*, with the 'person', *puruṣa*, who transmigrates.

> [The self] is this person, the one that consists of perception among the vital functions (*prāṇa*), the one that is the inner light within the heart. He travels across both worlds, being common to both. Sometimes he reflects, sometimes he flutters, for when he falls asleep he transcends this world, these visible forms of death. When at birth this person takes on a body, he becomes united with bad things [*pāpman*], and when at death he leaves it behind, he gets rid of those bad things.
>
> Now, this person has just two places – this world and the other world. And there is a third, the place of dream where the two meet. Standing there in the place where the two meet, he sees both those places – this world and the other world. Now, that place serves as an entryway to the other world, and as he moves through that entryway he sees both the bad things and the joys.[13]

The text goes on to give an account of dreaming. This sounds much like the non-ethicized, *Ṛg Vedic* idea, because the other world, which is unitary, seems to be a happier place than this one. No mention of karma here.

The first mention of karma in the *Bṛhad-āraṇyaka* is tantalizingly brief. The sage Yājñavalkya takes his questioner Ārtabhāga aside to tell him, 'A man turns into something good by good action and into something bad by bad action' (3.2.13). Here we cannot tell whether good/bad action (karma) refers to ritual or ethical goodness; it is possible that 'bad action' refers to incorrect performance of sacrifice. Possible, but I think rather unlikely; for in a second passage, 4.4.6, Yājñavalkya says (in verse),

> A man who's attached goes with his action
> to that very place to which
> his mind and character cling.
> Reaching the end of his action,
> of whatever he has done in this world –
> From that world he returns
> back to this world,
> back to action.

This looks like the old binary cosmology. But with a difference; for the passage continues:

That is the course of a man who desires.

Now a man who does not desire – who is without desires, who is freed from desires, whose desires are fulfilled, whose only desire is his self – his vital functions do not depart. *Brahman* he is, and to *brahman* he goes. On this point there is the following verse:

> When they are all banished,
> those desires lurking in one's heart;
> Then a mortal becomes immortal,
> and attains *brahman* in this world.

Here then we have not only rebirth but the possibility of escape from it. Even if 'action' refers primarily to ritual action, we have here a very simple ethicized theory of rebirth, in which this world is the scene of action and the other the scene of reaping the results (see above), and when the results have been reaped one repeats the cycle. This idea that a good action is one performed without desire was to be of crucial importance in the history of Indian religion. But what about '*Brahman* he is, and to *brahman* he goes'?

Though it does not use the word 'karma', the 'five fire wisdom' found in the last book of the same *Upaniṣad* gives a much more elaborate ethicized account of rebirth. Almost the same text occurs in the *Chāndogya Upaniṣad,* but my exposition will take the *Bṛhad-āraṇyaka* version as primary, because I believe it to be the older. (The reasons for this will appear in due course.) This text describes people acting in this life and finding an appropriate destiny hereafter; it does not envisage any further good or evil action in the next world, merely either repetition of the cycle or escape from it. Escape comes through gnosis: that is, understanding and totally internalizing the realization, 'I am Brahman.'[14] This is the same as realizing that 'My self (*ātman*) is Brahman.' To understand the central message of the five fire wisdom, we therefore first need to understand the concepts of *ātman* and *brahman.*

MACROCOSM AND MICROCOSM

Brahmin speculative thought had for long been playing with the fundamental supposition that there was a systematic correspondence between the human individual and the universe, the cosmos. This idea has been found elsewhere in the world, and it is customary to refer to the human being as the microcosm, i.e., the ordered system on a small scale, and the world as the macrocosm, i.e., the same ordered system on a large scale.

In the brahminical development of this idea, the same ordered system was also to be found at an intermediate level; this mesocosm was constituted by the sacrifice. The mesocosm, so far as I can see, is not relevant for understanding the Buddha. However, it is worth mentioning here, because anyone inspired by this book to read Patrick Olivelle's fine translation of the *BĀU* may well be puzzled by the first words of the text: 'The head of the sacrificial horse, clearly, is the dawn.' What on earth is that about? you may wonder. It is about correspondence between the mesocosm and the macrocosm, because the text begins by explaining the esoteric meaning of the horse sacrifice.

The esoteric knowledge which brahmin teachers passed on to their pupils consisted largely in understanding the correspondences between these ordered systems; and indeed *upaniṣad* was one of several terms for such a correspondence. The idea then grew up that there must be some central principle in both macrocosm and microcosm, something from which perhaps the systems originally grew, but certainly something which was of crucial importance, so that if one understood the whole one could easily grasp the parts. In his *History of Indian Philosophy*,[15] Erich Frauwallner gave a brilliant summary exposition of how this vital principle was variously sought in water, in air and in fire – very much as happened in early Greek philosophy, though the pre-Socratic philosophers were concerned only with the evolution of the world, not with mystical correspondences. Although different schools of thought thus gave primacy to different elements, they produced many ideas, some of which blended and survived while others fell away.

It seems likely, though many philologists do not consider it proven, that the word *ātman* is connected to the German verb *atmen* 'to breathe'. The word *ātman* was from the time of our earliest records the Sanskrit reflexive pronoun, and thus translatable in appropriate contexts as 'self'. As probably happens in every culture, this 'self' was reified and taken as the core of each individual living being.

At the same time, the universe, the macrocosm, was also taken to have a vital principle, as if air were its very breath of life. In the *Upaniṣads* this too was sometimes referred to as *ātman*, though more often the term for it is *brahman*. Obviously the universe has only one *ātman*, as does each living being. Through the equivalence of macrocosm and microcosm, the universal *ātman*, alias *brahman*, and the individual *ātman* were equated, though what exactly was meant by this equation varied from one metaphysician to another – which for us means from one textual passage and its interpretation to another. The message was summarized in the formulation: 'I am *brahma*':[16] to know this was the salvific gnosis.

Moreover, it more or less follows, if the universal *ātman* and the individual *ātman* are the same, that each individual *ātman* is the same as every other. Though this must initially strike us as strange, one way of thinking of it would be to see the *ātman* as something like life: though your life is not the same as my life from a pragmatic point of view, life is a single concept applicable equally to every instance. Though of course one can pick holes in this argument, it seems a good analogy, because in some ancient Indian schools of thought, notably Jainism, the word for the vital principle in each individual was not *ātman* but *jīva*, which means precisely 'life'.

❧

The word *brahman* originally referred, among other things, to the *Veda*, and lengthy monographs have discussed its original meaning, but luckily that is not relevant here. In the *Upaniṣads*, *brahman* is the term for ultimate reality, indeed, the only ultimate reality. *Brahman* is the spirit immanent both in the universe and in individual human beings. All that can be predicated of *brahman* in this sense is being, consciousness and bliss; I shall return to this in Chapter 5. Being beyond duality, *brahman* can of course have no gender, and grammatically is neuter. More or less by definition, *brahman* can also have no plural.

As against this neuter *brahman*, there is a god called Brahman, who is masculine. It has become customary in European books to refer to this god as Brahmā, using the masculine nominative singular, in order to differentiate him from the neuter *brahman*. Brahmā is the creator god, equated with Prajāpati, a name which means 'Lord of Progeny'. While the neuter Brahman is immanent in the universe, permeating it as salt permeates seawater, the god Brahmā transcends the world.[17] Though in principle Brahmā too must, one would think, be singular, he is not always and entirely exempt from a Hindu tendency to multiply gods, turning a single central figure into a plurality, where we would perhaps talk of different aspects or emanations of a deity.

One can regard the god Brahmā as a personification of the supreme principle *brahman*, or one can consider *brahman* to be a more sophisticated expression of the thought that created Brahmā. Indeed, both ways of seeing it are no doubt valid and correct. Presumably the more sophisticated process, abstraction, produced the duality in the first place. But one can also presume that the god was more popular than the ontological principle.

The phonetics of the formula 'I am *brahma*' (*ahaṃ brahmāsmi*) are such that here *brahma* could be either neuter or masculine. Indeed, the formula occurs twice in a short passage,[18] and the first time is naturally read as neuter, but the second time might seem more likely to be masculine (*Brahmā*). This subtle ambiguity is crucial to understanding why the Buddha disagreed with Upaniṣadic soteriology.

We return to the five fire wisdom. Though it does not envisage that people can do good or bad acts in the next world, and in this respect remains archaic, the cosmology has become more complicated. People are divided into three groups. The first and best are those who know and understand the five fire wisdom; they seem (whether all or just some of them is not clear) to live in the jungle, in other words to live as renunciates. When they are cremated,

> they pass into the flame, from the flame into the day, from the day into the fortnight of the waxing moon, from the fortnight of the waxing moon into the six months when the sun moves north, from these months into the world of the gods, from the world of the gods into the sun, and from the sun into the region of lightning. A person consisting of mind comes to the regions of lightning and leads them to the worlds of *brahman*. These exalted people live in those worlds of *brahman* for the longest time. They do not return.[19]

The *Chāndogya Upaniṣad* version, which is very similar indeed, includes in this group those who practise austerities.[20]

The second group consists of those who have offered sacrifices, given gifts and performed austerities. (In the *Chāndogya* version (5.10.3) this group consists of those who, living in villages, make offerings at sacrifices.) At cremation

> they pass into the smoke, from the smoke into the night, from the night into the fortnight of the waning moon, from the fortnight of the waning moon into the six months when the sun moves south, from these months into the world of the fathers, and from the world of the fathers into the moon. Reaching the moon, they become food. There, the gods feed on them, as they tell King Soma, the moon: 'Increase! Decrease!' When that ends, they pass into this very sky, from the sky into the wind, from the wind into the rain, and from the rain into the earth. Reaching the earth, they become food. They are again offered in the fire of man and then take birth in the fire of woman. Rising up once again to the heavenly worlds, they circle around in the same way.[21]

The *Chāndogya* version of this path contains even clearer wording:

> ... [a cloud] rains down. On earth they spring up as rice and barley, plants and trees, sesame and beans, from which it is extremely difficult to get out. When someone eats that food and deposits the semen, from him one comes into being again.[22]

This group perfectly fits the pattern of rebirth found by Jurewicz in the *Ṛg Veda*. As in the *Ṛg Veda*, the version of heaven these people attain is the world of the fathers. We also recall particularly that the dead person returns in the rain and is sown as barley.

The *Chāndogya* then adds a short passage about this second group which has no parallel in the *Bṛhad-āraṇyaka*. This says:

> People whose behaviour here is pleasant can expect to enter a pleasant womb, like that of a woman of the Brahmin, the Kṣatriya or the Vaiśya class.[23] But people of foul behaviour can expect to enter a foul womb, like that of a dog, a pig, or an outcaste woman.[24]

Both the *Bṛhad-āraṇyaka* and the *Chāndogya* then briefly mention a third group. The *Bṛhad-āraṇyaka* says: 'Those who do not know these two paths, however, become worms, insects or snakes.'[25] The *Chāndogya* is a little more helpful: '... those proceeding on neither of these two paths – they become the tiny creatures revolving here ceaselessly. "Be born! Die!" – that is a third state. As a result that world up there is not filled up.'[26]

It strikes one that although so little is said about them, the third class of people must be far the largest, for it comprises those who neither have sacred knowledge, which is evidently confined to very few, nor perform brahminical sacrifices. So it must comprise nearly all those people who are not brahmins or, perhaps, *kṣatriyas*. One recalls Obeyesekere's remark that the basic requisite for rebirth in its widespread non-ethicized form is a proper funeral. Here perhaps a proper funeral would mean a cremation according to brahminical rites, and those who do not have that privilege are condemned to being worms or insects forever.

The *Chāndogya* version is a strange kind of hybrid. Those who make offerings at sacrifices – in other words, high-caste people who follow their ritual obligations – are then sub-divided into those whose behaviour is 'pleasant' (*ramaṇīya*) and those whose behaviour is 'stinking' (*kapūya*, a very rare word), and have better or worse rebirths accordingly. The vague term 'pleasant behaviour' obviously extends beyond ritual; if we take it as approximating to morally good action, then the pattern starts to look something like that of Buddhism: people have good or bad rebirths on earth, while an élite escape from the cycle of rebirth altogether. The third category, those who stay worms and insects forever, is clearly inherited from the *Bṛhad-āraṇyaka* and therefore cannot be dropped, even though it now looks anomalous.

The word 'karma' does not occur in the five fire wisdom. But it is an account of how a man's destiny at death is determined by his karma, if we do not seek to differentiate the meaning of karma as ritual from that as morally charged action; my hypothesis about funeral rites would fit this interpretation well.

❧

We have glimpsed in one passage in the *Bṛhad-āraṇyaka* the idea that a good action is one done without desire, and this is a point that the Buddha would have agreed with. By and large, however, while there are considerable resemblances between his thought and that of the *Bṛhad-āraṇyaka* in certain other respects, his making karma a matter of intention created a vast gulf between his thought world and that of brahminism.

The primary purpose of brahmin ritual was to purify, and for brahmins *puṇya karma* meant 'purifying act', i.e., 'rite of purification'. This term the Buddha redefined as good or meritorious action – the sole criterion for which was morally good intention. Perhaps the commonest of all Buddhist words for vice, *kilesa*, literally means 'defilement', and we are dealing with the same metaphor: a bad person's mind is said to be dirty. Buddhist discourse is permeated by talk of purity and purification, but invariably that is a metaphor which refers to improving one's mind ethically and, in due course, intellectually – for the Buddha considered intelligence to be a virtue.

In ritual, acts are enjoined or prohibited according to the agent: what is right for a man may be wrong for a woman, and *vice versa*; what is right for a brahmin may be wrong for an outcaste; etc. Norms are thus particularized, not universal. If they are universal, the moral value of an act, whether positive or negative, lies only in the act itself, and is not affected by who the agent is. In my opening chapters I have shown that Buddhism both ethicized karma and universalized it. One could claim, however, that these steps had already been taken by Jainism. The next chapter shows how that may have happened.

Chapter 4

JAIN ANTECEDENTS

Though I mentioned Jain influence on the Buddha in my *Social History*, for lack of both time and space I said too little about it there. That is indeed the easy, perhaps even the prudent, way out. Our evidence for early Jainism is distressingly meagre and difficult to evaluate. It is well known and firmly established that the Buddha and Mahāvīra, who is sometimes considered to be the founder of Jainism, lived in the same town, Rājagṛha, now Rajgir in modern Bihar, and were approximate contemporaries: Mahāvīra was younger than the Buddha but died before him, which is hardly surprising given the extremity of his austerities. Certain broad similarities between Buddhism and Jainism are so obvious that the earliest European Indologists to discover Jainism took it for an offshoot of Buddhism.[1]

Since very early times the Jain tradition has been split into two branches, the Digambara, whose monks go naked, and the Śvetāmbara, whose monks wear a white garment. Jain tradition ascribes the split to some historical event, maybe a couple of centuries after Mahāvīra. However, Dundas writes: 'The archaeological and inscriptional evidence suggests that there was a gradual movement among Jain monks towards a differentiation based on apparel, or the lack of it, rather than any abrupt doctrinal split.'[2]

Jainism and Buddhism are alike in claiming that the figures whom modern scholars have considered to be founders of their respective religions were not founders but re-founders: that each was part of a chain of great religious leaders who appear on earth at vast intervals of time to promulgate the truth and the ideal way of life. Jainism calls these leaders Tīrthaṃkara, 'ford-maker', a metaphor that means that they have found, and showed others, how to cross the ocean of *saṃsāra*, the endless cycle of rebirth. Not surprisingly, these leaders tend to have stereotyped biographies. A very early form of this doctrine appears to have held that Mahāvīra was twenty-fourth in the sequence of 'ford-makers', and the Buddhists held that the Buddha was twenty-fifth in their series. Elsewhere I have tried to demonstrate that the doctrine originated with the Jains and was copied by the Buddhists.[3] What is much more important, however, is that modern scholars have come to accept the Jains' own view that Mahāvīra was not really a founder of a religion, analogous to the Buddha or Jesus, but rather a reformer. This is not to say that scholars now accept that there were twenty-four figures like Mahāvīra spanning many centuries before him; but they do think that something very like the Jainism we know already existed before Mahāvīra. In particular, they accept that the ford-maker before Mahāvīra was called Pārśva and that he had a community of followers.

Exactly what changes can be ascribed to Mahāvīra is controversial. I find very convincing the conjecture by Dundas, who writes:

> ... [A]ll biographies of Mahāvīra portray him as, unlike all other fordmakers, renouncing the world alone ... and there is never any suggestion that he entered an already existing ascetic corporation. A tentative explanation might therefore be that early Jainism coalesced out of an interaction between the cosmological [I would add: and soteriological] ideas of Parshva and a more rigorous form of orthopraxy advocated by Mahāvīra.[4]

In particular, Mahāvīra insisted that monks go naked, but Pārśva's followers probably did not.

These facts seem probable, but they have to be deduced by putting together various bits of evidence. This is because, although many Jain texts survive, very few of them, or even parts of them, seem to go back even to within a couple of centuries of Mahāvīra. A passage which occurs in three *suttas* of the Pali Canon records that as soon as Mahāvīra had died, his followers began to disagree about what he had actually preached.[5]

According to the Digambara tradition, the oldest texts preserved are not the original canon: that has been lost.[6] It seems to me highly unlikely that such a tradition would have been invented, whereas one can easily understand the motivation behind the opposite view, taken by the Śvetāmbaras, that the texts preserved do belong to the original canon. Even the Śvetāmbaras, however, hold that some of the original canon has been lost.

At this early stage the Jains had a greater problem than the Buddhists in preserving their texts because they spent all the year except the rainy season as solitary itinerant mendicants. The Buddha's organization of his Saṅgha was, I would argue, in conscious reaction to this. After a while the Jains came to learn from the Buddhists, in this as in other matters. The Śvetāmbaras divided monks into two vocations:[7] *jina-kappa* ('the way of a Jina'[8]), solitary wandering ascetics striving for liberation in this lifetime, and *thera-kappa* ('the way of an elder'[9]), professional monks concerned to preserve the scriptures. The *jina-kappa* monks, they held, went naked like Mahāvīra, but that way of life was now obsolete.[10] The Theravada Buddhists introduced a very similar formal distinction in Sri Lanka, round the turn of the Christian era; from then on Theravada monks have had to choose to be either *vipassanā-dhura* (literally: 'yoked to insight meditation'), taking meditation as their primary duty, or *gantha-dhura* (literally: 'yoked to books'), whose main responsibility is to preserve the scriptures.

In fact much of our best evidence for early Jainism comes from texts in the Pali Canon.[11] Of course, it is the Jain texts themselves that have far the most information, but it is terribly difficult to know how to date that. Moreover, none of those texts is accepted as authoritative by both the Digambara and the Śvetāmbara traditions. The Buddhist texts, by contrast, tell us things about Jainism before that split occurred.

❧

There is some excellent modern scholarly literature on what we can learn about Jainism from Pali Buddhist texts[12] (and indeed *vice versa*[13]), so I shall try not to repeat what can be found there. I believe, however, that I have significant things to add.

My main theme is karma and rebirth. The following teachings, relevant to this theme, are likely to have been as central to Jainism before Mahāvīra as they were to the Jainism attributed to him.

> *Saṃsāra*: all living beings are caught in a perpetual cycle of rebirth, which encompasses heavens and hells as well as many forms of life on earth.

Liberation: in this cycle, suffering outweighs pleasure, so it is desirable to gain release from it; this is most commonly compared to escaping from bondage.

The cycle is ethicized: the quality of one's rebirth is determined by the moral quality of one's actions (karma) in earlier life/lives.

Hylozoism. All matter contains sentient life in the form of *jīva*. This word basically means 'life', but here it denotes something which has certain of the properties of material, for it occupies the same space as the body it inhabits. Paul Dundas calls it a 'life monad'. Even microscopic particles of the four elements (earth, air, fire and water) each contain their own *jīva*. '[T]here is not a single space point ... in which a *jīva* has not entered or left an existence, just as ... there is not one single point in a pen full of goats which has not been covered with droppings and hair.'[14] A *jīva* is naturally pure and buoyant, and if left inviolate will float to the top of the universe, where it can remain in eternal bliss.

But karma binds the jīva to saṃsāra. Every act attracts something analogous to dust, which clings to the *jīva* and weighs it down. So to gain release one has to scrub off all the old dust and not let any new dust gather.

I observed at the beginning of Chapter 2 that in general the operation of karma is conceived by analogy with agriculture. I suspect that the idea of karma in Jainism uses the same metaphor and the word itself carries the connotation of 'work'. When one does agricultural work, one sweats and dust adheres to one's body – especially in India!

It is hylozoism that underlies the particular ethical emphasis for which Jainism is famous: the paramount importance of non-violence, *ahiṃsā*. '[G]iven the ubiquity of *jīvas*, almost any activity is liable to be harmful in some way or other.'[15] Even the forms of life generally considered insentient have the sense of touch and hence the capacity to suffer pain. Moreover, even these insentient beings may themselves cause pain, injury and death.[16] No wonder there is more pain than pleasure in the universe! And in order to minimize the harm one does it is necessary to curtail all one's activities, from eating down to mere movement. This lies at the root of Jain asceticism. '[F]or the early Jains physical activity is, by definition, "hurtful" and thus binding.'[17] Thus 'the earliest detectable Jaina doctrine of karma leaves no room at all for the idea of meritorious action.'[18]

This is an extreme doctrine, and indeed an early Jain text boasts that it is the toughest that has ever been taught or will be taught.[19] Only renunciates can aim to lead such ascetic lives – which ideally end in starving oneself to death. In the earliest Jain texts there is little said about good karma, and this must be closely tied to the fact that these texts were composed by and for renunciates. All activity, however well-intentioned, is liable to cause suffering and death; and the law of karma means that this will bring retribution to the agent in a future life, probably the next one. There are, however, a few references to merit (*puṇya*) and gaining a better rebirth, and Johnson suggests that 'meritorious action and a better rebirth on earth or in heaven as a result of it were concepts familiar to the householders with whom the early Jaina ascetics had their minimal contact; such ideas were part of the general cultural furniture' and had to be taken into account, though without 'any systematic doctrinal concessions to that view. For the real possibility of a better rebirth for an ordinary lay person to be theoretically established, some doctrine of intention or motive as being, at some level, more karmically significant than action alone would have been required.'[20]

That crucial doctrinal move was made by the Buddha. I repeat his words: 'By karma I mean intention.' Karma, whatever its instrument, is mental, a matter of the agent's intention (or lack of it – negligence is taken into account), and has its effect through the agent's mental condition, each state of mind influencing the next, even from one life to the next. One effect of this shift to intention is that in Buddhism there is more of a symmetry than in early Jainism between good and bad karma. In Jainism, even good karma impedes liberation by weighing down the soul; in Buddhism good karma is the essential first stage of spiritual progress.

The Buddha most often related his teaching, both explicitly and implicitly, to brahminism. But there are also several passages in the Pali Canon where he argues with followers of Mahāvīra (and of course always wins). I have always stressed in my previous publications that for the brahmins karma primarily referred to ritual; only in the *Bṛhadāraṇyaka Upaniṣad* do we find brief suggestions that it can refer to ethics. This is indeed of paramount importance and I shall have more to say about it in Chapter 6. But there is also another side to the story of the antecedents of Buddhist karma, the Jain side.

There is a passage in the *Sūyagaḍaṅga Sutta,* perhaps (at least in part) one of the two oldest Jain texts preserved, which argues against the Buddhist view that there is no evil action without intention, which is thus represented:

> If his mind, speech, and body are free from evil, if he does not kill, if he is mindless (i.e. without an internal organ or organ of consciousness), and if he is unaware of the workings of his mind, speech, and body, and does not see even a dream, he does not perform evil actions. (2.4.2)[21]

The formulation is indeed very reminiscent of rules in the Buddhist monastic code, which regularly list conditions, such as madness, under which an act does not constitute an offence. The Jain text disagrees.

> Though these beings have neither mind nor speech, yet as they cause pain, grief, damage, harm, and injury, they must be regarded as not abstaining from causing pain, etc. (2.4.9) .... Thus even senseless beings are reckoned instrumental in bringing about slaughter of living beings ... (2.4.10).

In other words, injury is injury, whatever the motive or lack of motive which accompanies it.[22]

To me this suggests that the Buddha's insistence on calling action intention was not a wish to be paradoxical, but was a direct response to Jainism. Though the doctrine that everything that matters happens in the mind is of a piece with the rest of the Buddha's teachings, perhaps at the moment when he made that bald statement he did primarily have the Jains in mind.

Several texts in the *Sutta Piṭaka* show the Buddha interacting with Mahāvīra's followers. To begin with, even the Middle Way enunciated at the beginning of the First Sermon, in which the Buddha condemns mortification of the flesh as unprofitable, evidently alludes to Jains and other ascetics like them. Despite this, scholars seem (so far as I can see) to have treated Jainism only as a teaching contemporary with the Buddha's and not to have considered that it was something older which had an influence – whether positive or negative – upon him. I cannot fully account for this. Maybe it has something to do with the fact that though Jacobi argued in 1880 that Pārśva, said by the Jains to be the 'ford-maker' before Mahāvīra, was a historical figure, T. W. Rhys Davids disagreed;[23] and since then Jain studies and Buddhist studies have tended to go their separate ways. Be that as it may, while my friend Johannes Bronkhorst and I published argument and counter-argument[24] about how to interpret some passages in the Pali Canon which show the Buddha reacting to Jain ideas and practices, we simply treated this as an argument between contemporaries. Though we brought out interesting points of detail, it now seems to me that we both missed the wood for the trees.

I suggest that the positive influence of Jainism on the Buddha was massive. As Will Johnson writes, early Jainism has 'ethical, compassionate roots' in its doctrine of *ahiṃsā*:

> ... injury is bad in the first place because it is injury to *others*. It is only with the development of a consistent theory of bondage and liberation that the stress switches from the fact of injury to others to its consequence, namely, self-injury through bondage.[25]

Indeed, we can go further and suggest that the credit for the first ethicized karma theory should go to the Jains, not the Buddhists. If Will Johnson is right (as I think he is), in the earliest Jain doctrine, that to which the Buddha was reacting, there was no possibility of good karma; one could only aim to eliminate the bad. Buddhism can thus claim to have a better rounded (and indeed more plausible) ethicized doctrine, but not the first. Moreover, Buddhists and Jains were at one in their opposition to the animal sacrifice which was integral to the Vedic ritual system.

Of the five Jain doctrines listed above, the Buddha accepted the first three, but not the fourth and fifth. That is to say, he accepted the doctrines of *saṃsāra*, of the desirability of getting out of *saṃsāra*, and the role that ethics played in making that escape possible, but he did not accept the existence of life-monads. (Indeed, he offered no explanation for life as such.) For the Buddha, plants were insentient, so one could not hurt them. The same was true, *a fortiori*, of what we would call inorganic matter.

On the other hand, the Buddha also reacted against Jainism. He strongly disapproved of the lifestyle of Jain monks and wanted to be sure that his monks were not taken for Jains or similar groups. An amusing story tells that once some monks had their robes stolen by highway robbers and arrived at their destination naked. People took them for Ājīvikas, a group closely associated with the Jains.[26] The Buddha ruled that in such a quandary one should cover one's nakedness with anything, even grass and leaves, and might then ask a householder to supply a robe (such a request normally being forbidden).[27] There is an analogous ruling about begging bowls. Jain monks were not allowed alms bowls but could only receive food in their bare hands – the Digambaras follow this rule even today. Initially there was a *vinaya* rule that monks could not ask for a bowl, so when his bowl was broken a certain monk did not ask for a replacement. The Buddha disapproved of his receiving food in his hands like a member of another (unspecified) sect (*titthiya*) and laid down that under such circumstances monks were to ask for replacements.[28]

Jains seem to have set the standards according to which the public formed their expectations of renunciates, and this had a major influence on the Buddhist Saṅgha, and even on the Buddha himself. We have seen that the Jains believed that all matter was alive.[29] They classified living beings by the number of their sense organs. Gods, humans and other higher animals of course have five. Things we normally consider insentient, including plants, have only one sense organ, the sense of touch. The Buddha, by contrast, was only concerned for the purposes of his moral teaching with whether something was conscious or not. Plants were not. It is therefore quite a surprise to read in a stock list of the Buddha's moral characteristics that he abstains from violence against plants.[30] The same reason lies behind the Buddha's establishment of a rains retreat for the Saṅgha. The *Vinaya* says that originally they kept moving all the year round; but this meant that they trod on lots of fresh grass (the term 'with one sense organ' is used) and killed tiny insects. Other sects, they said, avoided this by settling in one place for the monsoon. The Buddha therefore decreed that his Saṅgha should do likewise.[31] We find that often the reason why the Buddha formulates a *vinaya* rule is to placate public criticism.

Consonant with this, there is a monastic disciplinary rule that monks and nuns should avoid destroying plants.[32] Though the rule itself perhaps tells us nothing new, I shall examine the text, because it is a charming example of how the Buddha, or possibly his followers, adapted inherited material. Each rule is introduced by a story of how a monk or nun did something which was not at that time an offence but which was justly criticized, so that when the Buddha came to hear of it he declared that in future that act would constitute an offence. Scholars think that many of these introductory stories were composed *ex post facto.*

In this case, the story is that a monk was cutting down a tree. The deity who lived in that tree protested, but the monk took no notice, and knocked (a euphemism?) the arm of the deity's baby. Her first impulse was to kill him in revenge, but she thought better of it and decided to complain to the Buddha instead. The Buddha congratulated her on having avoided an evil act, and pointed out another tree to which she could move. However, both members of the public and virtuous monks criticized the monk for depriving a living thing with one sense organ of life. The Buddha scolded the monk for cutting down a tree with the sentence, 'For people think there is life in a tree.' He then laid down that it was an offence to cut down plants.

Let us pause a moment to appreciate the Buddha's subtlety. It seems to be a popular belief throughout the subcontinent that every impressively large tree is inhabited by a deity, who is feminine and generally benign. When I did fieldwork in Sri Lanka, I found that before the village carpenters cut down such a tree, they would go and formally ask the permission of the deity who lived in it, suggesting that she move to another tree. There are quite a few texts in which the Buddha talks to a tree deity. He is therefore being intentionally ambiguous. The words I have translated could equally mean 'People think there is a life monad [to use Paul Dundas's translation] in a tree,' which would be true about Jains, and 'People are aware that there is life in a tree,' which would satisfy Buddhists, who believed in tree deities but not in moral duties towards things with only one sense organ.[33]

I think that there was Jain influence on a much grander scale in the way the Buddha set up his Saṅgha. Positively, he learnt to have an Order of nuns besides that of monks. (I am convinced by the arguments of Ute Hüsken that the story of the Buddha's reluctance to allow nuns into the Saṅgha does not date from his lifetime.[34]) There is particularly interesting evidence in the *Thera-therī-gāthā*, a book in the Pali Canon. This is a collection of poems, most of them quite short, attributed by the commentary to individual monks and nuns (some anonymous), in which each author briefly describes his or her spiritual experiences. At verse 427 in the nuns' section a lady called Isidāsī, who has had the misfortune to be abandoned by three husbands, encounters a nun called Jinadattā, a name which makes it almost sure she was a Jain. Isidāsī, impressed by Jinadattā, declares her intention of expunging her evil karma, using the Jain technical word, *nijjarā*, for this process;[35] however, her father persuades her to become a Buddhist instead. According to K. R. Norman,[36] two of the monks and at least two of the women in the collection are claimed by the commentary to have converted to Buddhism from Jainism. The most interesting case is the author of verses 107–111 in the nuns' section, a lady called Bhaddā, whom the commentary specifically calls a former Jain (*purāṇa-nigaṇṭhī*). Bhaddā begins by saying she used to pull her hair out, be covered in mud and wear only a single garment. She saw fault in blameless things and no fault in blameworthy things. This the commentary explains as meaning that she was attached to pointless physical austerities but neglected moral qualities. Then she met the Buddha, who ordained her as a nun by simply saying, 'Come, Bhaddā.'[37] This is utterly fascinating. The *Vinaya* gives us a picture of how the rules gradually evolved. Ordination by the simple formula of saying 'Come' is the very earliest form, which was soon superseded as the Buddha saw the need to lay down a procedure by which any body of monks could bestow ordination. Moreover, in due course a person who had been ordained in another sect had to undergo a probationary period before full admittance. The commentarial tradition could not possibly have been unaware of these facts, but the text was allowed to survive unexpurgated. This is corroborative evidence for Ute Hüsken's thesis that the story that nuns were allowed into the Order only at a late stage is a forgery.

It is never logically possible, when dealing with ancient history, to convince a determined sceptic. It could be that all these poems come from a period after the Buddha had permitted his own Order of nuns to be founded; it is even logically possible that the Buddhist Order of nuns existed before the Jain one. However, that is a very contorted hypothesis, and it is far more plausible to give the texts the straightforward interpretation that the Jain Order of nuns already existed when the Buddha founded his Saṅgha, not very long after his Enlightenment.

This is not to say that all statements and all silences should be taken at face value without any further exercise of judgement. The Pali record tells us of Jains converting to Buddhism but not *vice versa*. Naturally, such a thing would not be mentioned, but that does not mean that it may not have occurred.

As I have written elsewhere,[38] I think that the very term *pātimokkha* betrays Jain influence. The word refers both to the set of rules governing the personal conduct of each member of the Saṅgha and to the ceremony of its recitation; there is one *pātimokkha* for monks and one for nuns. The *Vinaya* makes it mandatory for all monks and nuns to assemble once a fortnight to confess to each other any infringements of this code. Jain monks and nuns have to confess any transgressions to their teacher. The Jain term for this is *paḍikkamaṇa*, 'going back', 'retracing one's steps'. By confessing a fault one goes back to where one was before one deviated; one gets back on track, we would say. The Buddhist term for this act of confession, *pātimokkha*, means 'purgative', an even more vivid metaphor, but the basic idea is surely the same.

The Buddha perceived, however, that the organization of the Jain Saṅgha was too loose for it to be an effective instrument in preserving the doctrine. He regulated his own Saṅgha accordingly, and linked confession to community: he made it a strict rule that all monks within a given territory had to meet at least once a fortnight in order to recite their disciplinary code, and to confess transgressions against it. The Jains had such an obligatory communal ceremony only when they met at the end of the annual rains retreat.

My reconstruction is of course only conjectural, but I trust it is convincing. Another small piece of evidence in its favour may be that Jain monks and nuns are supposed to confess to their teacher three times a day (first thing in the morning, on return from the alms round, and last thing at night), while it says in the *Vinaya*[39] that the Buddha had to stop certain monks from confessing daily.

I believe that the most striking piece of evidence to show that the Buddha was influenced by early Jainism comes not from the *Vinaya*, but from a basic item of doctrinal terminology. In a standard account,[40] which looks early, the Buddha describes his own Enlightenment by saying that his thought became freed from the *āsava*s. Modern scholars have not reached a consensus how to translate this technical term, but I think that 'corruptions' will do nicely. My choice has no regard for the word's etymology; we are about to see why.

The Pali word *āsava* corresponds to Sanskrit *āsrava*, a noun from the verb *ā-sru*, 'to flow in'. Thus *āsava* has often been translated 'influx', which is literally correct. But the term makes no sense, as in Buddhism there is nothing which 'flows in' on one. On the other hand, that is precisely how the Jains envisage the operation of karma. The Buddha says that his *āsavas* have waned away (*khīṇa*); they are three: sensual desire (*kāma*), the urge to continue in existence (*bhava*), and ignorance (*avijjā*). (Sometimes there is a fourth: speculative views (*diṭṭhi*).) In fact, in the Pali texts *khīṇāsava* becomes a stock epithet of any enlightened person – see below. This idea of an impure 'influx' fits what Dundas says (p.83) is the oldest of many similes for karma, that which likens it to dust which clings to something damp or sticky.

Peter Harvey has kindly drawn my attention to the *Sabbāsava* ('All the corruptions') *Sutta*,[41] in which most instances of *āsava* 'concern relating to what is external with wisdom and restraint. So here one sees a parallel to the move from an emphasis on overt action (Jainism) to inner intention (Buddhism).'[42]

It has been claimed[43] that the use of the word *āsava* in both Buddhism and Jainism shows not direct influence but that both drew on a common background. While this is logically possible, there is no evidence for it, so I prefer the hypothesis that the Buddha was influenced by Jain usage. In any case, this would be an instance of his adopting a term from opponents and infusing it with a new meaning. My view that the Buddha associated the term with the Jains is buttressed by a canonical *sutta* in which the Buddha converts a Jain by making play with two words, *āsava* and *samārambha*.[44]

A similarly suggestive use of terminology concerns the common expression *ñāṇa-dassana*, literally 'knowing and seeing', which refers to attaining nirvana.[45] It is not clear *a priori* why this stock term uses two words, since the knowing and the seeing would seem to be the same. The shortage of reliably ancient evidence again must make this conjectural, but it is striking that in Jainism both this word for 'knowledge' and this word for 'seeing' constitute part of liberation, but there they have distinct referents. According to the classic Jain summary of doctrine, the *Tattvārtha-sūtra*,[46] 'The path to liberation is perfect insight, knowledge and conduct.' 'Insight' is the same word as Pali *dassana*, and 'knowledge' the same word as Pali *ñāṇa*;

but P. S. Jaini explains that what is meant is a combination of 'insight into the nature of reality (along with faith in this view)' with 'critical knowledge as outlined in the scripture'.[47] I conjecture that a technical term has been borrowed by Buddhism even though in its original context it draws a distinction which is not relevant in their own system.

I have an even bolder suggestion. The commonest Buddhist term for an enlightened person is P: *arahat*, S: *arhat*. The strong stem of these words is P: *arahant*, S: *arhant*. These are present participles derived from the Sanskrit verbal root *arh*, 'to be worthy'. If one asks 'worthy of what?' the answer comes 'of worship'. Nevertheless, this has always struck me as a rather feeble term for the highest spiritual status. But there is a grammatical oddity which is even more jarring. There is a perfectly good adjective which would supply the same meaning: P: *araha*, S: *arha*. Why use a present participle? In fact, I cannot think of any other title in Sanskrit or Pali which is a present participle.

In Jainism one of the terms for the same supreme status is clearly related, but has two forms: *arahanta* and *arihanta*.[48] The former is the same as P: *arahant*, and is likewise traditionally interpreted to mean 'worthy (of worship)'.[49] While it is possible for *arihanta* to be just a phonetic variant, another interpretation of the word is not only possible, but is indeed found in the Jain tradition: it can be analysed as a compound to mean 'killer' (*hanta*) 'of enemies' (*ari*). The metaphor is the same one that gives us *Jina*, 'Conqueror', as the title of Mahāvīra and the other Jain spiritual leaders – and hence the very word 'Jain'.

The Buddha occasionally used the title *Jina* of himself. According to the *Khandhaka*, soon after Enlightenment he told a wondering renunciate called Upaka, 'I have conquered evil states of mind; so, Upaka, I am a Conqueror.'[50] (Upaka was apparently not impressed.)

In Jainism, as later in brahminism, the enemies are listed as desire, anger, greed, confusion, arrogance and stinginess. Buddhism lacks this particular list, as the Buddha's metaphor of the three fires (desire/greed, hatred and confusion) was evidently dominant from the first (see Chapter 8 below). Thus the vices were not usually personified as enemies.[51] Maybe the Buddha also found it tasteless to refer to himself as a killer, even metaphorically. So *arihant* was not used in Buddhism,[52] whereas *arahant* was. Moreover, as noted above in the discussion of *āsava*, the words *arahant* and *khīṇāsava* often occur together. I therefore think that *arahant* was appropriated from Jainism.

SUMMARY

Of course, in a sense everyone who knows anything at all about the life of the Buddha knows that he tried Jain practice and then rejected it. In the six years of wandering, between his renouncing home and family and his final discovery of the salvific truth, he learnt meditation under two teachers without reaching his goal, and then practised the most extreme austerities. These included fasting almost to death. It was only when he saw that this was fruitless and began to eat again that he was able to achieve Enlightenment; and his First Sermon, as I have already recalled, began with a rejection both of self-indulgence and of such austerities, and a call for the practice of the middle way between them.

The text does not specifically identify those austerities with Jain practice, nor were such practices necessarily confined to Jains, but we know that they were the kinds of things that Jains did, and indeed even in the texts Jains are described as doing such things. But the Buddha rejected these austerities, as he rejected brahmin rituals, because they dealt with externals. The Buddha's great insight was that everything that matters happens in the mind.

Our particular concern is how the Buddha's ideas of karma and rebirth related to the Jain ideas which he knew. At the very end of the previous chapter I mentioned that Jainism ethicized and universalized karma, and in this respect probably anticipated the Buddha. However, it seems that the Buddha introduced a symmetry between good and evil karma which early Jainism lacked. (In this, he may well have been influenced by brahminism.) Early Jainism had nothing to offer the householder. Even the idea which one readily assumes to be pan-Indian, that giving is meritorious, is called into question by the earliest Jain texts.[53] Had this ideology not been modified, it is hard to believe that Jainism would have survived for long, since renunciates were dependent on the laity for their food. The Jain ethic may thus be universalized, in the sense that it applies to everyone, but it is hardly designed for universal adoption!

The Buddha's great innovation, we have seen, was to make ethical value dependent not on what is overt but on intention. In due course Jain doctrine came to accommodate meritorious action and to envisage karma that would cause one to have a good rebirth, i.e., in heaven or in a favourable position on earth. At much the same time, intention came to play a part in the Jain assessment of what constituted good and bad karma, though not until Umāsvāti's *Tattvārtha-sūtra* was intention given an unambiguously decisive role.[54] I would guess that both these developments, the symmetry between bad and good karma and the importance of intention, were due to Buddhist influence.

On another level, we can contrast Buddhism with Jainism because of the Buddha's capacity for abstraction. The Jains built their ideological edifice on karma, but they took 'action', which is surely an abstract noun, not merely to have a physical effect but also to be something physical itself. One could argue that their reinterpretation of karma was no less radical than the Buddha's when he called it 'intention', but in terms of the history of ideas the Jain concretization of simple abstractions was naïve literalism and a dead end.

The Buddhist handling of abstraction was still sometimes crude. To the normal gamut of five senses, our organs of perception, the Buddha added a sixth, the mind, which we use for perceiving abstractions (*dhamma*); and its perception of those abstractions was held to be on a par with the workings of the other five faculties (*indriya*). It is not surprising that the results of failing to make the mind somehow superordinate to the senses were clumsy and unsatisfactory.

In a nutshell: I wish to argue that the Jain influence on the Buddha's thought and practice has not so far been given enough weight. In many ways the Buddha reacted against Jainism, as he did against brahminism. But his ideas about the cycle of rebirth, karma and non-violence owe a great deal to the Jains, even though he considerably developed and changed their doctrines.

Chapter 5

WHAT DID THE BUDDHA MEAN BY 'NO SOUL'?

Introductions to the Buddha's thought usually begin by highlighting two of his ideas: the First Noble Truth, that 'everything is suffering'; and the teaching of No Soul or No Self. So far I have devoted only a few short sentences in the Introduction to those ideas. There I showed that in my view the key to the Buddha's thought is the doctrine of karma and the idea that we are all responsible for ourselves – an idea that has an important metaphysical aspect but is above all an ethical principle.

The statement, almost a maxim, that 'everything' – which means 'every aspect of life as we normally know it' – is suffering has made those who look for historical parallels compare the Buddha's preaching to Stoicism, and to other western philosophies of a pessimistic tinge such as that of Schopenhauer. The teaching of No Soul or No Self has often been compared to the philosophy of David Hume. These comparisons are by no means stupid; they can be interesting in their own right. But they do not further my present purpose, for, by uprooting the Buddha's words from their historical context, we tend to obscure, not illuminate, their meaning.

In order to make himself understood, the Buddha had to talk in terms with which his audiences were already familiar. The historical record shows that he was adverting almost entirely to brahminical terms. Indeed, he was alluding primarily to teachings in the early *Upaniṣads*, especially the *BĀU*, teachings which are usually known as *Vedānta*, a term which literally means 'Conclusions of the Veda'. With some of these teachings the Buddha agreed; others he criticized, though usually he did so obliquely.

GIVEN TRANSMIGRATION, WHAT IS IT THAT TRANSMIGRATES?

I suppose the most basic questions encountered by every philosophy or system of speculative thought are: What exists? and How do we know anything? In ancient India the belief in rebirth added to these a third question: What is it that continues from life to life? Obviously, great neatness and economy are achieved if the answer to all these three questions turns out to be the same.

In *Ṛg Veda* X, 129, the text often called 'The Creation Hymn', existence and consciousness are considered somehow to originate together, in such a way that each one presupposes the other. 'Then there was neither existent nor non-existent ... Initially there came upon that one desire, which was the first seed of mind. Seers searching with wisdom in their hearts found the connection to existence in non-existence.' This is, of course, paradoxical; but it became fundamental for the entire history of brahminical and Hindu thought. In the *Vedānta*, ontology, the question of what exists, and epistemology, the question of how we know anything, became intertwined.

The answer to the question of what transmigrates had less philosophical origins. In very many cultures, probably the majority, a dead person is thought to linger on in a form which is disembodied and yet – at least under certain circumstances – perceptible to human senses. This is what we call a 'ghost'. Belief in ghosts, even though it finds no place in Christian dogma, is very widespread in Britain and other western countries, so there is no need to explain further. It is significant that in pre-modern English 'ghost' and 'spirit' are often synonyms (remember how a priest was described as a 'ghostly father'), just as *Geist* in German means both 'ghost' and 'spirit'. A ghost, then, is the spirit of a departed person, still individuated by most of that person's characteristics.

If the function of a ghost is to act as a vehicle for the characteristics of someone who no longer exists, being dead, it needs to be at the same time material and immaterial. Since this is a paradox, sophisticated theologians try to find a way round it.

That which is a vehicle for the characteristics of a dead person is also often called a 'soul'. A soul usually differs from a ghost in already belonging to an individual during life – in fact, from the moment of birth, or even from the moment of conception. Christian theologians also tend to say that a ghost is perceptible to the senses but a soul only to reason. However, there is on the whole less agreement about the soul than there is about ghosts. Plato considered the soul to be a transmigrating entity, as in India, and Christians in the Platonic tradition thus see it as separable from body and mind, even though they do not accept Plato's view of transmigration. Aristotle, on the other hand, defined the soul as the formal cause of the individual person. A formal cause is what makes a whole more than the sum of its parts; the soul gives each person their individuality.

In brief, such confusion surrounds our own use of the term 'soul' that to translate the Buddhist concept of *anattā* as 'no soul' is at best uninformative and at worst utterly misleading. In fact it *does*, in my experience, often mislead people, because they tend to understand it as denying a principle of continuity. As explained in the Introduction, that is totally wrong, for in Buddhism there is an extremely strong principle of continuity – which is karma. I therefore try to avoid using the word 'soul' in discussing the topic. What makes it impossible, however, to follow this policy consistently is that Buddhism in India became identified with the teaching of *anattā*, which became a virtual label or catchphrase; and in such a context I must admit that I see no better shorthand expression than No Soul, which is how it has always been rendered in English.

❧

The Jains had a coherent theory of the mechanism of transmigration, which also explained how karma carried over from one life to the next. The essential component of a living being (and we recall that for Jains that includes everything, down to particles of dust) is called the *jīva*, literally 'life'. We have already seen in Chapter 4 that Jains got round various problems with abstractions by making them concrete. Thus karma, action, they reify as a kind of dirt or dust. This clings to the *jīva*, which is sticky, and stays there until it is expunged by austerities. The *jīva*, meanwhile, moves from one being to another as death and rebirth follow in endless sequence. It can manage to do this because it is infinitely adaptable in size and shape, very much like the modern plastic product called cling-film. Once all the karma has been scrubbed away, the *jīva* floats to the top of the universe, omniscient and freed of all negative qualities.

In other ideologies the self which endures through a series of lives which ends only with liberation is called the *puruṣa*, a word which in ordinary Sanskrit simply means 'man'. In *Sāṃkhya*, a system of religious philosophy which evidently has roots approximately as old as the *Upaniṣads*, the *puruṣa* is very like the Jain *jīva*, in that its only true nature is to be conscious, and the individual must strive to rid his *puruṣa* of all other attributes in order to be liberated. The term *puruṣa*, however, is of Vedic origin, and occasionally in the *Upaniṣads* the term is used to refer to the individual *ātman*. An example of this has been quoted in Chapter 3, in the passage beginning: '[The self] is this person, the one that consists of perception among the vital functions (*prāṇa*), the one that is the inner light within the heart. He travels across both worlds, being common to both.'[1] As there remarked, this passage has the archaic binary cosmology.

Brahmins, however, came to regard the *ātman* as something so radically different from the empirical self that it could never be involved with (or sullied by) karma.

ĀTMAN/BRAHMAN IN THE *BĀU*

This dissociation of karma from a transmigrating entity seems to have come about by stages. Straight after the passage just alluded to, in which the self oscillates between this world and the next *via* dreams,[2] the sage Yājñavalkya gives an account of dying. It begins: 'As a heavily loaded cart goes along creaking, so this bodily self (*śārīra ātmā*), saddled with the self of knowledge (*prājñena ātmanā*), goes along groaning as he is breathing his last.' This has two points of interest. Firstly, the word *ātman* is now so qualified as to be clearly used in two meanings: the body, and something like the mind. Secondly, the Buddha was familiar with this passage: I have published a short article to show that he alludes to it when he feels that he himself is close to death.[3]

As the man dies, 'his vital functions throng around him.' They gather in his heart.

> Then the top of his heart lights up, and with that light the self exits through the eye or the head or some other part of the body. As he is departing, his lifebreath departs with him. And as his lifebreath departs, all his vital functions depart with it.

He becomes pure awareness (*vijñāna*).

> As a caterpillar, when it comes to the tip of a blade of grass, reaches out to a new foothold and draws itself onto it, so the self (*ātman*), after it has knocked down this body and rendered it unconscious, reaches out to a new foothold and draws itself onto it.[4]

The text goes on to say that the *ātman* is *brahman* and as such consists of everything (*sarva-maya*) – examples are listed. In Chapter 3 I gave the 'five fire wisdom', which occurs in the sixth and last book of the same text, the *BĀU*, and showed that according to that passage those who have realized their identity with *brahman* go to *brahman* when they die. I there explained that there is some ambiguity about whether *brahman* is a principle, or (a less sophisticated reading) that Brahman is the supreme deity. This account by Yājñavalkya in the fourth book is clearly different, a kind of pantheism: *brahman* is here the world itself, not the principle immanent in the world.

That *brahman is* everything in the world, rather than a single entity underlying the world's apparent multiplicity, was many centuries later to become the view upheld by the theologian Rāmānuja (twelfth century) against the monistic Śaṅkara (probably seventh century AD). The view espoused by Śaṅkara was different. In part he relied on the negative description of the *ātman* given three times in the same *BĀU*:[5] that it is simply 'not thus, not thus', i.e., indescribable. But he also relied on such statements in the *Upaniṣads* as 'I am *brahma*', and the description of *brahman* as 'existence, consciousness, bliss'. For Śaṅkara this implied that everything but *brahman*, including all individuality, was an illusion; but this seems to go further than is intended in the *Upaniṣads* themselves.

Brahman is existence. This reification of existence goes back to the 'Creation Hymn', and is of course found in many philosophies round the world. Similarly, the predication of consciousness to existence goes back to the 'Creation Hymn'; and we have seen that a similar thought survives in the Jain and the *Sāṃkhya* concepts of the soul. For these philosophies, in other words, it is unconsciousness and ignorance, not their opposites, which require an explanation, and salvation lies in returning to one's primeval conscious nature.

Truth (*satya*) is at the same time existence (*sat*). It is of our essence that we exist, but also that we be conscious of that truth. We are what we think we are – if we think truly. That is why existence is conscious (*cit*), or rather consciousness (*vijñāna*). In the excellent formulation of Charles Malamoud, if we realize that we are *brahman*, we shall realize – in the sense of 'make real' – that truth when we die.[6]

Existence, in this ideology, implies absence of change, because once *x* changes into *y* it no longer exists. Existence is a plenum (the opposite of a vacuum), as it was for the Greek philosopher Parmenides. There is a further step which may strike us as rather odd. Suffering and unhappiness are considered invariably to be due to a lack of something. In *brahman*, existence, there can be no lack, and therefore no suffering: hence *brahman* is bliss.[7] The logic of this argument seems so frail that one is tempted to seek the origin of the idea that *brahman* is bliss elsewhere. Maybe it originated in what we might call mystical experience: fully to realize one's identity with *brahman* and hence one's imperishability is presumably blissful.

Once the *ātman* had become so rarefied, how did the brahmin, and in due course the Hindu, traditions explain the mechanism of rebirth? We have seen that in the *BĀU* this mechanism is not clear, but appears to be associated with the life-breath. Very early in that text, the *ātman* is itself said to be breath,[8] but then the term mainly used for breath becomes *prāṇa*, and in the context of death and rebirth *prāṇa* is closely associated with consciousness. Death is minutely described, but the mechanism of transfer into a new body is not.

We can gather from later texts that the function of carrying karma from life to life came to be performed by what the tradition variously calls a *liṅga śarīra* or a *sūkṣma śarīra*, a 'subtle body', which is a ghostly replica of the dead person. (One is again reminded of the Jain *jīva*.) As if aware of the unsophisticated origins of this concept, the famous philosophical texts have little to say about it. We have just seen above that in Yājñavalkya's account of death, the *ātman*, or at least one aspect of it, there called the 'self of knowledge', does just what we would expect the subtle body to do. The subtle body, however, is relevant not only at death, but also for the exercise of magical powers, when it can perform feats which are physically impossible for our more familiar, solid bodies, such as flying, walking on water, or diving into the ground. In the possession cults which are found throughout the villages of South Asia, and indeed far beyond, there is widespread belief that the officiants can leave their bodies and go on journeys by means of ghostly replicas of those bodies. (This is often labelled shamanism.) It seems that the shamanic notion of a duplicate body with miraculous powers may have helped adherents of the great soteriologies to imagine how the mechanism of rebirth is effected.

THE BUDDHA'S RESPONSE

Let me now outline how this influenced the Buddha. We can begin with his title, Buddha, the awake or awakened one. His achievement, and the identical achievement which is one way of expressing what constitutes Enlightenment for any Buddhist, is commonly known as 'seeing things as they are' (*yathā-bhūta-dassana*). This is wide-eyed awakeness.

The *Upaniṣads* construct a hierarchy of conscious states. This begins in the *BĀU*, where dreaming can give one a sight of the next world. Building on that, just as waking is inferior to dreaming, dreaming is said to be inferior to dreamless sleep, and finally later *Upaniṣads* top the hierarchy with what they simply call 'the fourth' state (*turīya*), which is the merging of one's consciousness into *brahman*.

The Buddha will have none of this. It is notable that the Pali Canon has nothing to say about dreaming, except to rule that for a monk to emit semen during a dream, being an involuntary action, does not constitute an offence. One gets the impression, indeed, that the Buddha himself does not dream: references to his sleeping simply refer to his 'lying down'. Asked how he has slept, the Buddha replies: 'The brahmin who has attained nirvana always lies comfortably.'[9] (See Chapter 12 for more on his referring to himself as a brahmin.)

The Buddha also has no interest whatsoever in equivalences between microcosm and macrocosm, though a few such equivalences occur when Buddhist cosmology is modelled on meditative states; however, whether this is to be attributed to the Buddha himself is moot.

WHAT WE EXPERIENCE, AS AGAINST WHAT 'REALLY' EXISTS

The Buddha was influenced by the Upaniṣadic theory of 'being' on two levels. Firstly, he accepted the conceptualization of 'being' as the opposite of 'change' or 'becoming'. On a more abstract or philosophical level, however, he rejects the reification of 'being'. He declares that there are three major fetters (*saṃyojana*) binding us to the cycle of rebirth, and the first of these is the view that there is a category 'being'.[10] Accordingly, the Buddha does not seek for a single essence either in the world or in the living being. We shall see in Chapter 8 what he puts in its stead.

Famously, the Buddha's approach to life's problems was pragmatic. Our problems are urgent, and irrelevant theorizing is as silly as refusing to receive treatment for an arrow wound until you know the name of the man who shot the arrow. Today we see the world as in perpetual motion, and that reminds people of the Buddhist principle of impermanence. True, the Buddha saw our experiences as an ever-changing process, a stream of consciousness – the literal Pali equivalent of that expression does occur. But we are talking physics, whereas the Buddha was talking psychology. In my view, he did not see an object like a stone or a table as changing from moment to moment (see below). Nor did he hold the opposite view. Such an analysis of the world outside our minds was to him irrelevant and a mere distraction from what should be commanding our attention, namely, escape from *saṃsāra*. I shall have more to say about this pragmatic approach in Chapter 11. Here let me just reiterate that it was our experience of the world – of life, if you like – that the Buddha was focusing on, and it was our experience that he considered to be a causally conditioned process.

The Buddhist tradition has various ways of expressing this. The word *loka*, common to Sanskrit and Pali, is usually translated 'world'. But Buddhaghosa explains[11] that this word may refer to the *bhājana-loka*, 'the world as receptacle', in other words the space in which we have our being; or it may refer to *satta-loka*, 'the world as [conscious] beings', the inhabitants of the world in the other sense. (We can compare the use of the French *monde* in such phrases as 'tout le monde'.)

Discussion of 'the world as receptacle' was of no relevance to what concerned the Buddha and should concern us. Thus, when he mentioned such things as duration, it was duration in lived experience that interested him. But it was typical of the Buddha's own mode of expression to use the word *loka* as a metaphor without spelling that out. In the Canon he says:

> I do not say that there is a world's end to be known or seen or reached where one is not born, does not age or die or pass on or reappear. Yet I do not say that suffering can be ended without reaching the world's end. Moreover, I declare the world, the arising of the world, the cessation of the world, and the way leading to the cessation of the world to be in this very fathom-long carcase with its perception and its mind.
>
> Never can the world's end/Be reached by travel,
> But there is no escape from pain/Without reaching the world's end.[12]

THE BUDDHA'S ANSWER TO 'BEING, CONSCIOUSNESS, BLISS'

Where the Buddha is positively influenced by the *Upaniṣads* is in his formulation of the basic conditions of existence. For the *Upaniṣads*, ultimate reality, being, is forever unchanging; and it is bliss, whereas everything else is the opposite of bliss. The Buddha agreed that the world we normally know and experience is forever changing, and that therefore it is not bliss but the opposite, *dukkha.* Hence his first Noble Truth, that all we can normally experience is suffering.

(Of course, the words bliss and suffering are both misleading. They are attempts to translate the pair of opposite nouns, *sukha* and *dukkha. Sukha* covers the whole positive range from being pleasant, or OK, to bliss; its opposite, *dukkha,* similarly covers the range from not being quite OK, somehow unsatisfactory, to extreme pain and suffering. What translation is appropriate depends entirely on the context.)

The Buddha also agreed that such concepts as change and *dukkha* make sense only if they can be contrasted with their opposites. Moreover, he did not agree merely on the logical point; he also agreed that one might even experience their opposites, and that this experience would liberate one from the round of rebirth. For this his name was nirvana.

To do justice to the topic of nirvana, I must postpone its full discussion until Chapter 10. However, I should here indicate why the Buddha did not accept such statements as 'I am *brahman*'.

Brahman is being, consciousness, bliss. The Buddha rejected 'being' as a reified category: for him there is no such *thing* as 'existence'. He likewise rejected the concept of consciousness that went with it: just as being was a process, not a thing, so was consciousness. In fact, consciousness was a process we all experience and one which he analysed. (I shall have much more to say about this in Chapter 8.)

Since the Buddha rejected the Vedāntic concepts of being and its inherent consciousness, he of course rejected the ideas of *ātman* and *brahman* to which those concepts were fundamental. And since he rejected macrocosm/microcosm equivalence, the *ātman*/*brahman* equivalence had to go too. A further problem lay in the serious ambiguity about *brahman*. If it/he is also the Creator, he cannot but be involved with change and becoming; the purity of his 'being' is compromised. In other words, we encounter the paradox of what in the Christian tradition is called 'the unmoved mover'. In fact, this paradox remains throughout the Hindu theistic tradition: God has to be both beyond the world, transcendent and changeless, and immanent in the world he has created and sustains.[13] Moreover, if the highest truth is that *brahman* and *ātman* are one, then the soul too becomes an unmoved mover.

These reasons convinced the Buddha that to convey what he meant by nirvana it was best to keep to negative language. Since the problem was that of each individual person, the Buddha saw no need to bring 'God' into it at all. We need not bother with such theoretical questions as who, if anyone, was or is responsible for the universe; all that matters is to understand that we are responsible for ourselves.

❧

There is what we may think of as a Buddhist answer to the triad 'being, consciousness, bliss'. It is the triad referred to as 'the three hallmarks' (P: *ti-lakkhaṇa*), that is, the hallmarks of phenomenal existence. These are impermanence, unsatisfactoriness, absence of self. The order betrays the Upaniṣadic reasoning. Things are impermanent, i.e., ever-changing, and *by that token* they are not satisfactory, and *by that token* they cannot be the *ātman*.

The third hallmark is very often mistranslated (sometimes by me too, in the past) as 'not having a self or essence'. That is indeed how later Buddhists came to interpret it, but that was not its original meaning – in fact, it is doubly misleading. Both Pali grammar[14] and a comparison with the *Vedānta* show that the word means '*is* not *ātman*' rather than 'does not *have ātman*'. Comparison with the *Vedānta* further shows that the translation 'self' is appropriate, as the reference is to living beings. However, as time went by the term was taken as a possessive compound and also taken to refer to everything, so that it became the one-word expression of the Buddha's anti-essentialism.

IMPERMANENCE

When the Buddha died, Sakka, the king of the gods, pronounced a verse:

> Alas, compounded things are impermanent, of a nature to arise and pass away.
> After arising, they are destroyed; their calming is happiness.

This verse is so famous that whenever someone dies in Sinhala Buddhist society, little leaflets are distributed and displayed all over the community announcing the name of the deceased (sometimes with a photograph) and headed by the first words of the verse: *aniccā vata saṃkhārā.*[15] This merely amplifies the general principle of impermanence, the first hallmark of phenomenal existence, and in the context applies it to all human life, even that of the Buddha.

Like many things that he said, the Buddha's observation that everything in life is impermanent, even such things as mountains, met the fate of being taken more literally than I believe he intended. At *SN* III, 38, he says that it is evident (*paññāyati*) that each of the five *khandhas* arises, passes away, and changes while it is there.[16] There is also a short *sutta*[17] in which he says in the same terms that all compounded things (*saṃkhata*) have three hallmarks (*lakkhaṇa*): arising, passing away, and change of what is there (*ṭhitassa aññathattaṃ*). I would interpret this to mean that at a certain point each thing arises, later it comes to an end, and even in between it changes. However, the commentarial tradition unfortunately took it to mean that things all pass through three distinct phases:

arising, duration (*ṭhiti*) and passing away; in due course this led to a subdivision of duration, and then further subdivisions and attempts to quantify them, producing a kind of atomism of time.[18] I am sure that this is an anachronistic misreading of the Buddha's intention.

ANCESTORS AND GHOSTS

Let me now show what Buddhist doctrine made of earlier concepts of the soul, once it had entirely got rid of the need for positing some entity which would carry karma or other elements of the personality from each life to the next.

It is astonishing how long religious ideas and institutions survive in India after the complex in which they made sense has been superseded; this is particularly true of ideas about death. We have seen that in the *Ṛg Veda* a dead man went to join his paternal ancestors, who were called 'fathers' (*pitaras*). These fathers were to receive daily offerings from their male descendants. The obligation to make these offerings has persisted to this day, surviving for centuries, even millennia, the introduction of the doctrine of rebirth.

Although the Buddha considered all ritual to be meaningless, he did not try to abolish rites to which people attached great significance. He explicitly permitted the laity to continue mortuary rituals known as *śrāddha* (P: *saddhaṃ*).[19] Besides, every culture seems to have a need for ghosts, individual spirits who offer some concrete reminder or reassurance that death is not the end of all. These factors were the ingredients which produced the Buddhist category of living being generally known in English as 'hungry ghost'. In Pali these are known as *peta*, in Sanskrit as *preta*. Both words literally mean 'departed' and are used just as in English: 'departed' can mean dead, in particular recently dead. But the words also carry an important possibility for punning. In Sanskrit there is an adjective formed from the word for father, meaning therefore 'connected to a father or fathers'; this word is *paitrya*. In Pali 'the realm of the departed' is called *petti visayo*. But the double *tt* shows that *petti* is not really derived from *peta*, even though it sounds very much like it: it is derived from *paitrya*. So the realm of the departed is at the same time the realm of the fathers.

Then it turns out that in actual usage, both ancient and modern, although the departed are listed as if they were a general cosmological category, like gods, they are in fact dead relatives, and in particular recently dead relatives. This is quite curious. These recently dead relatives, of both sexes, are in a state of torment, not much better off than if they were in hell; they lurk in dark corners, smell bad, and suffer from a hunger and thirst which they cannot quench, because their mouths are as tiny as the eye of a needle. No one, one presumes, would really like their dead relatives to be reborn in this condition. But in a sense it is the other way round, for the logic of the Buddhist system demands that when funeral rituals are held and merit is transferred, that merit is to accrue to the waiting *peta* or *peta*s, who by the power of the merit will be reborn in a better condition. As I have written elsewhere: 'Although cognitively – and logically – *preta*s can be anyone's relations, the only *preta*s of whom people usually think and with whom they interact are their own dead relations.'[20]

I noted above that the brahminical subtle body also comes into play with the performance of such magical feats as flying. Exactly the same idea survives in Buddhism. A Buddhist who has mastered the four *jhāna* is said to be capable of creating a 'mind-made' (*mano-maya*) body which can perform the standard set of shamanic feats.[21] The Buddha, however, deprecates the use of such powers and in particular deprecates their use for showing off and impressing people.[22] He regards them as having no religious value, so that they remain a kind of dead end.

Though of course karma moves from life to life without any kind of physical vehicle, there is a famous text[23] in which the Buddha says that for conception to take place a *gandhabba* has to arrive. This is the name of a kind of spirit in Vedic mythology; what is it doing here? Perhaps such a concept of a carrier of karma was felt to be needed by the unsophisticated, like the brahminical *liṅga śarīra*.

❧

What did the Buddha himself think about *peta*s? Probably the same as he thought about gods. And what was that? He spoke about these categories of beings and did not demur when others spoke about them, even about interacting with them. The question of whether such beings exist is not among the 'unanswered questions'. But then, the Buddha rejected all questions of the type 'Does *x* exist?' He rephrased it: 'Can we experience *x*'?

Since evidently those around him were experiencing gods and *petas*, he let it go at that, in line with his general pragmatic policy of concerning himself only with matters directly relevant to attaining nirvana (see Chapter 11). I am sure that the fully developed cosmology that can be found in the Pali Canon cannot be attributed to the Buddha himself, if only because that would so flagrantly contradict his deprecating any concern with such matters. I am no less sure that some features of that cosmology arose through misunderstandings, such as taking literally some of the Buddha's humorous references to Brahmā, the brahmin super-god (see Chapter 12).

So did the Buddha privately, in his heart of hearts, 'believe in' gods or ghosts? I doubt that we can ever know. Maybe he was so true to his own principles that he thought it pointless to ask himself the question.

THE INTERPLAY BETWEEN EMOTION AND UNDERSTANDING

Near the beginning of this chapter I mentioned the three basic questions of early Indian philosophy: What exists? How do we know anything? What is it that continues from life to life? It may be helpful if I here give approximate answers to these questions, while leaving much detail to later chapters. The Buddha agreed with most modern philosophers in rejecting the first question as pointless or meaningless; he substituted for it: 'What do we experience?' His answer was what we might also call his answer to the second question, an attempt to describe what experience is like. The answer lay not in objects but in processes. It was not an attempt to find the origin of consciousness, a quest which still baffles modern philosophy. The question of what continues from life to life does not arise for western philosophers today, since they do not believe in rebirth. For the Buddha the answer was likewise to be found in a process: karma. The very word karma, if one goes back to its simple root, means doing rather than being, a process not a thing. The Buddha, as we have discussed at length, singled out the process of ethical intention;

and he made it the principle of continuity not just from one life to the next, but from one moment to the next throughout our lives.

As we have seen, the three basic questions very early gave rise to a fourth: How can one escape from the cycle of rebirth? The Buddha saw that normal experience is vitiated by the transience of all worldly phenomena, a transience which must sooner or later render them unsatisfying. Our experience of their transience can only successfully be handled, he argued, by coming to terms with it: we should not want permanence, for ourselves or our loved ones, because we are not going to get it. We need, of course, to understand this fundamental fact if we are going to stop our vain desires. So we have both to control our emotions and to train our intellect; and Buddhist meditation is designed to achieve both goals. We have to adapt our entire mentality to reality, the reality of what life is like, including the fact that we ourselves and our loved ones all must die.

When the Buddha preached, two rival analyses of life's problems were already on offer. On the one hand the *Upaniṣads* had a gnostic soteriology: our basic problem is a lack of understanding. For convenience I call this the intellectualist approach, though I know that far more than intellectual understanding is involved. On the other hand, Jainism and related sects saw our basic problem as involvement with the world through desire: the answer lies in acquiring total self-control. Let me call this the emotionalist approach. Though the *Upaniṣads* also deprecated desire and Jainism also advocated understanding, it was the Buddha who found the perfect combination of the two approaches. You cannot see things straight because you are blinded by passion, and you allow your emotions to control you because you do not see things as they are. If one wanted to argue with this, it is not easy to see how one would begin – though of course many have tried. The main point, however, is that in outline this position was acceptable to both emotionalists and intellectualists. This versatility has proved to have great value for survival.

Chapter 6

THE BUDDHA'S POSITIVE VALUES: LOVE AND COMPASSION

This is an ambitious chapter, because in it I wish to illustrate simultaneously several different dimensions of the Buddha's thought and teaching; one of them I regard as of central importance. In the next chapter, I am going to set out my method, and above all my justification for claiming that the evidence favours our ascribing these ideas to the Buddha, a single person. As I have already written, the proof of the pudding is in the eating, and I believe that my case will carry conviction if I can demonstrate how my method produces results.

Let me set out the main features of my approach which will be on display in this chapter.

1. My method is *historical.* I shall thus be showing how the Buddha's message should, wherever possible, be understood by setting it within its historical context.

2. I argue that the Buddha's thought is characterized by the importance it gives to *ethics.* I have already argued that ethics are substituted for ritual. In *How Buddhism Began*, especially Chapter 2, I similarly argued that the Buddha often substitutes ethics for metaphysics; of that, this chapter will itself offer evidence.

3 and 4. In the Introduction, I have explained that the Buddha in his preaching made extensive use of *metaphor.* I have also shown his capacity for *abstraction.* Thus, while in crucial respects he accepted the early Jain doctrine of *karma*, the Jains took *karma* to be something physical, whereas he argued that it was intention, an abstract concept. Turning something which other people take literally into an abstraction can be at the

same time to take it metaphorically: the two dimensions, abstraction and metaphor, overlap.

5. A further dimension which I use here is that of *sophistication*, or the lack of it. While this third dimension overlaps heavily with the previous two, I believe that using it will serve to make my meaning clearer.

SOPHISTICATION

Let me take a simple example of what I mean by sophistication. Traditional Christianity has a picture, often conveyed to us by artists, of God in heaven: an old man with a white beard sitting on a golden throne in a beautiful garden. Surely I am not insulting anyone if I say that millions of Christians have taken this picture literally. On the other hand, in modern times Christian leaders have encouraged their flocks to think in more abstract, and thus more sophisticated, terms. Heaven is something much more like a blissful state of mind, and God is not even visible in a form like a human being, let alone with a white beard: that is recognized as a personification of a principle which both transcends and infuses human beings. The wise old man in the garden is merely a metaphor.[1]

Almost throughout the history of Hinduism, a more sophisticated and a less sophisticated view of a supreme god have existed side by side; they have their roots in the two views of Brahman presented in Chapter 3. In the case study that occupies most of this chapter, this has to be kept in mind. When the Buddha was presenting his arguments to brahmins, he took their references to *brahman* as references to a creator-god – something analogous to presenting the Christian God as an old man in the sky. Whether or not this was always entirely fair, it certainly does accurately reflect what is said in *BĀU* 1.4.5–6, a passage with which, as we have further evidence to show, the Buddha was familiar.[2]

❧

This chapter will argue that the Buddha saw love and compassion as means to salvation – in his terms, to the attainment of nirvana. This is no minor claim. For the past two thousand years or so, it has been spread about that the Pali texts present the Buddha as teaching a religion which is selfish. This religion, on this widespread view, provides a guide how to attain one's own salvation, but the path it teaches is essentially a solitary one. Paradoxical though it may sound, this view claims both that the religion teaches one to understand that one has no self, and that the religion is selfish. It is agreed, of course, that the Buddha made ethics the foundation of his soteriology, but that ethics is presented almost entirely in negative terms, as abstention from vice and from other misguided thoughts and behaviour. True, there are a few texts, and undeniably early ones at that, which extol the practice of kindness and compassion. Certainly their opposites, hatred and cruelty, are vices; but the positive virtues of kindness and compassion appear almost incidental. Indeed, even the Pali tradition itself does not make the claim that their practice can lead one to nirvana, but on the contrary specifies in which heaven the practitioner will be reborn. For a Buddhist, rebirth in a heaven, any heaven, falls very far short of the ideal religious goal.

Most, if not all, modern controversies about Buddhism have been anticipated in ancient times, usually within the Buddhist tradition itself; and this one is no exception. There exists a *sutta* in the Pali Canon[3] in which a brahmin called Saṅgārava comes and criticizes the Buddha, saying that the sacrificial rituals which he himself performs and has others perform benefit many people, whereas what the Buddha teaches will only benefit the individual practitioner. The Buddha refutes him by saying that, on the contrary, his teaching causes thousands of people to leave home. He has himself found and dwells in the supreme state of immersion (*ogadha*) in *brahman* conduct (*brahma-cariyā*) and he teaches them how to do likewise. By saying '*brahman* conduct' he is of course taking a term from the brahmin's own religious vocabulary; for the latter, that would be a goal even higher than what could be achieved by sacrifice. The Buddha has appropriated the term to make it refer to nirvana; for detail, see the Appendix.

In this reply to Saṅgārava the Buddha bases his defence on his teaching. Throughout the history of Indian Buddhism the Buddha's 'great compassion' (*mahā karuṇā*) was considered to reside and manifest itself first and foremost in that teaching; this is as true of the Mahayana as of the older traditions. Should adherents of a theistic tradition find this somewhat bloodless, they should recall that the doctrine of karma holds that each person is responsible for his own destiny; in the end, no one can save anyone else. The nearest thing to a saviour that the karma doctrine allows is a teacher who gives good advice – and that was the role the Buddha played.

The Buddha was defined as what we might call a 'Buddha with a capital B', a *sammā sambuddha*, by the fact that he had not only discovered (or rather, re-discovered) the truth but also agreed to teach it, thus re-establishing Buddhism in the world. This being so, I find it a trifle odd that the Mahayana has repeated Saṅgārava's criticism, applying it to the early Buddhists.[4] The earlier Buddhists, technically called the 'listeners' (*sāvaka*), had been guided to nirvana by hearing the Buddha preach and so by definition could not themselves have preached to re-establish Buddhism: it was there already. I thus cannot help finding this Mahayana criticism illogical. But perhaps I should not leave it there. After all, does religion always follow logic? Maybe one should concede that, by saying very little about love and compassion manifested in ways other than teaching, the early Buddhists did allow their religion to appear somewhat lacking in warmth.

What I shall now establish, however, is that this deficiency, if it is one, may be laid at the door of the early Buddhist tradition, but cannot be ascribed to the Buddha himself. My claim is that, so far from teaching a path to salvation which did not include kindness and compassion – what Christians call 'love' or 'charity'[5] – he actually preached that such positive feelings were themselves direct and effective means to the attainment of nirvana.[6] This has, however, escaped notice, and his preaching on the subject has been misunderstood, because he expounded the teaching to brahmins by using their language. In so doing, he was but employing his normal technique of Skill in Means, but on this crucial occasion his own tradition unfortunately failed to understand his use of metaphor and took him literally, with disastrous consequences.

THE FOUR BOUNDLESS STATES

There is a set of four states of mind which the Buddha highly commends: kindness, compassion, empathetic joy and equanimity. How the four relate to each other we can learn from the great commentator Buddhaghosa: one becomes

> like a mother with four sons, namely a child, an invalid, one in the flush of youth, and one busy with his own affairs; for she

> wants the child to grow up, wants the invalid to get well, wants the one in the flush of youth to enjoy for long the benefits of youth, and is not at all bothered about the one who is busy with his own affairs.[7]

These four states have two names: they are called 'the boundless'[8] and the *brahma-vihāra*. Why they are called 'boundless' will appear later. A *vihāra* came to be the word for a Buddhist monastery – hence the name of the Indian state of Bihar. It means 'monastery' because it means 'a place to stay'. The noun derives from a verb which simply means 'to spend time, to stay', and the noun can just mean 'staying, being there'.

I have explained above that *brahman* is a name for the religious goal of the brahmins, the monistic principle posited in the *Upaniṣads*. As the monistic principle *brahman* is neuter, but there is also a masculine Brahman, a supreme god, whom one might regard as a personification of the neuter principle, though historically the development may have been the reverse. The Buddhist term *brahma-vihāra* thus carries an inescapable reference to brahminism, for it means 'staying with *brahman*'. Whether one regards that *brahman* as personal or impersonal, masculine or neuter – since the form of the word allows either interpretation – for a brahmin 'staying with *brahman*' is the ultimate goal, the state of salvation.

The *locus classicus* for this idea of salvation has been quoted in full in Chapter 3. In that passage the *Bṛhad-āraṇyaka Upaniṣad* proclaims a special fate after death for those who have achieved gnosis. What does that gnosis consist of? The passage seems to be saying that the content of the gnosis is the five fire wisdom itself. From other passages in both this and other *Upaniṣads*, however, we gather that the gnosis is starker and simpler: it can be expressed as 'I am brahman'. What does this mean? That the essence of the individual and the essence of the universe are but one and the same. If one realizes this in life, one realizes it – makes it real – at death, by joining brahman.

But this is ambiguous. Does one somehow fuse into a neuter principle, or meet and stay with a god called Brahman? The answer to this question, I believe, depends on the level of sophistication of the inquirer. The text recounts how such people, when cremated, embark on a complicated journey. Its last stages are:

> from the world of the gods into the sun, and from the sun into the region of lightning. A person consisting of mind comes to

> the regions of lightning and leads them to the worlds of *brahman*. These exalted people live in those worlds of *brahman* for the longest time. They do not return.

Unfortunately, no English translation can preserve the full ambiguity of the Sanskrit. In the Sanskrit the exalted people are led to the worlds of brahman, *brahma-lokān*, a compound noun. The word 'worlds' is definitely in the plural. The word *brahma*, however, could be either neuter or masculine, and could even be plural – so that the phrase could mean 'the worlds of the Brahma gods'.

At this point the *Chāndogya Upaniṣad* reads simply '*brahma*', unambiguously neuter singular, with no mention of 'worlds'. However, as with the other differences between the two versions mentioned in Chapter 3, this looks like an attempt to tidy up. Moreover, though it is clear that the destination of joining brahman is a final escape from rebirth, that there is no return is explicitly mentioned only in the *Bṛhad-āraṇyaka*, not in the *Chāndogya*. (The significance of this point will appear below.) Since several other allusions by the Buddha to the contents of the *Bṛhad-āraṇyaka* have been traced, but far fewer with certainty to the contents of the *Chāndogya*,[9] I think we can assume that it was the *Bṛhad-āraṇyaka* version that the Buddha knew and responded to.

❧

The four *brahma-vihāra* occur in several canonical texts, but the *locus classicus* is the *Tevijja Sutta*.[10] We shall see that this must be the context in which the concept and the term originated. In that text, the Buddha is talking – it seems a better word than preaching – to two young brahmins. The very term *te-vijja* in the title of the *sutta* is an example of the Buddha's revalorization of terms which lies at the core of my argument. Literally *te-vijja* means 'having three knowledges'. For brahmins in those days, the only thing that counted as true knowledge was the *Veda*, and indeed that word literally means 'knowledge'. The three knowledges, for the brahmins, were the *Ṛg*, *Sāma* and *Yajur Veda*s, and to know all three by heart (necessarily by heart, since there was no writing) entitled a man (it was always a man) to be known as 'having three knowledges'. To this day many brahmins bear surnames such as Trivedi, which has in effect become a heritable title. The Buddha had, however, redefined the three salvific knowledges as knowledge of one's former births, knowledge of the rebirths of others, and knowledge that one's corruptions had been eliminated.[11] There is nothing inherently triple about these accomplishments; that he formulated them as 'three knowledges' was surely no accident.

The two young brahmins in the *Tevijja Sutta* have been arguing about the direct way to what they call 'companionship with Brahma', and decide to ask the Buddha. This leads to a long conversation, in which the Buddha teases them; he makes fun of brahmins for claiming to teach the way to a goal they have never seen, and compares this, among other things, to declaring one is in love with a beauty queen without having the faintest idea what she looks like, who she is or where she lives. The Buddha says that though they can see the sun and moon, they do not even know the way to joining them – let alone the way to Brahmā. I suspect that his remark about the sun and moon is a jocular allusion to the Upaniṣadic two paths at death; jocular, because the Buddha must have known that to take those paths one had to have one's corpse burnt first. He contrasts the moral imperfections of real live brahmins who claim to know the three Vedas with the picture they draw of Brahmā, whom they claim they will join because they resemble him. Brahmā, by the brahmins' account, is morally pure, but they are not, so how can they claim to match him?

The Buddha then tells his brahmin interlocutor that he knows the *brahma*-world and the way to it as well as if he had lived there all his life. The young brahmin replies that he has indeed heard that the Buddha teaches the way to companionship with Brahmās (note the plural); he asks to hear it. The Buddha proceeds to describe the way. He gives a standard account of how someone comes across the Buddha and his preaching, renounces the household life, and keeps all the rules of conduct and morality. It is worth noting that this 'someone' is described as a householder (*gahapati*) or a householder's son or someone of some lower status;[12] to a brahmin this would carry a pointed message that the way was open to anyone, regardless of birth. Then he describes how this person – now referred to as a monk – pervades every direction with thoughts of kindness, compassion, sympathetic joy and equanimity; in the usual repetitious style of the *sutta*s, the same description is repeated for each of the four kinds of thought. The four (in Pali *mettā*, *karuṇā*, *muditā* and *upekkhā*) come to be referred to in other texts as *brahma-vihāra*, obviously because of this context, but that actual term is not used here. The text does, however, allude to being in those states as *evaṃ-vihārī* – 'staying like that'.[13]

Three words based on the word for 'all' (*sabba-*) are used to stress the entirety of the pervasion, and the thought is said to be 'extensive, magnified, boundless, without hatred or ill will' (*vipulena mahaggatena appamāṇena averena avyāpajjhena*). These five adjectives amount to saying that it is pure unalloyed kindness and infinite in extent. It is compared to the noise made by a powerful conch-blower. The point of this is that sound, unlike the objects of the other senses, is considered to be infinite and to pervade all space.

Then kindness (followed by the other three in turn) is described as 'release of the mind' (*ceto-vimutti*); when it has been thus developed, no bounded (i.e., finite) karma remains there. The text repeats the last point for emphasis.[14] This is the way to companionship with Brahmās (plural). A monk who lives like that (*evaṃ-vihārī*) matches Brahmā (singular, but still masculine) in his moral qualities, so that it is possible (*ṭhānaṃ etaṃ vijjati*) that he joins him at death. Convinced by this, the two young brahmins convert to Buddhism. In another *sutta*, the *Aggañña*, which I shall discuss in Chapter 12, we meet them as monks, evidently rather recently ordained. We can assume that once converted they are no longer interested in joining Brahmā, whether singular or plural.

❧

Any gnostic soteriology is bound to envisage salvation as a two-stage process. The salvific realization, the gnosis, can obviously only occur while one is alive. One is then assured of salvation, and can indeed be said to have attained it, but final salvation comes at death.

The Upaniṣads taught a soteriology of this type. One's aim in life was to realize one's essential identity with *brahman*; once realized, that identity became a more literal reality at death. In exactly the same way, nirvana for the Buddhists was a realization attained during life, and having attained it guaranteed that at death one would experience something which was also known as nirvana, though it could be differentiated from the first nirvana by adjectives.[15]

The Buddha's two young brahmin interlocutors, however, interpreted Upaniṣadic doctrine in the unsophisticated way: taking the ideal destiny after death as 'companionship with brahman' (*brahma-sahavyatā*) is obviously an unsophisticated understanding of the five fire doctrine. (The *Bṛhad-āraṇyaka* version, with its mention of '*brahma* worlds', easily allows for this interpretation; the *Chāndogya* wording does not.) This interpretation did not leave an obvious role for the gnosis during life. But the Buddha presented such a gnosis to them in terms that they could understand despite their lack of sophistication.

The Buddha has described the attainment of total love, compassion, empathetic joy or equanimity as 'liberation of the mind'. The term for liberation is *vimutti*, a word which in all religions indigenous to India, so far as I know, refers unambiguously to salvation consisting of escape from the cycle of rebirth. The word for 'mind' is here *ceto* (S: *cetas*), which could just as well be translated 'thought'; it is derived from the root *cit*, which may mean either 'to think' or just 'to be conscious', the prerequisite for thinking.

The Buddha is responding to the brahmin ideology of the *Bṛhad-āraṇyaka Upaniṣad*. In the narrative context of this *sutta*, which may possibly reflect a real event, he is responding to it in its unsophisticated form, but his real target is the sophisticated version. According to that ideology, every significant act, karma, brings its result, but that result is finite; even life in heaven does not last forever. To escape this finitude requires gnosis; then one may join *brahman*, infinite in space and time. Brahman pervades the entire universe as consciousness (*cit*).

Here the Buddhist monk is pervading the universe with his consciousness, but it is an ethicized consciousness. In enlarging his mind to be boundless (metaphorically, of course) he is emulating the brahmin gnostic who identifies with universal consciousness – or rather, going one better, showing the brahmin what he really should be doing. (His consciousness, moreover, is not a thing, but a process, an activity; this will be the topic of Chapter 8.) It is karma, but not the kind of karma that is finite: that he has transcended. Having transcended the finitude of normal ('typical') karma, he is fit, like the brahmin gnostic, to join *brahman* at death. Even the vacillation between the singular and the plural of Brahmā seems to echo the *Bṛhad-āraṇyaka Upaniṣad*.

If one thus understands the context, one will see that joining *brahman* at death is not to be taken any more literally than is the Buddha's introductory teasing promise to show the way to the *brahma*-world. The way to the *brahma*-world is just Upaniṣadic language, borrowed from the interlocutor, for the way to nirvana in this life; and by the same token joining *brahma* at death is a metaphor for the nirvana which follows the death of an *arahant*.

However, this was not understood by the compilers of other *suttas*, let alone by the commentators. This probably is due quite simply to the fact that they did not know the *Bṛhad-āraṇyaka Upaniṣad* or the five fire wisdom. The *ceto-vimutti* they took as a metaphor, whereas joining Brahmā at death they took literally: they got it precisely the wrong way round. Thus, though the text clearly says that the kind monk is released, the tradition said no, he was reborn at a specific level in the universe, that inhabited by Brahmās.

I think that probably later generations were also confused by the text's failure to conform to the standard dogmatic pattern. Spiritual progress, in the Buddhist formulation, has three components: morality, concentration, understanding (*sīla, samādhi, paññā*). Each is a prerequisite for the next, though none is perfectible alone. Even if one can argue that the *brahma-vihāras* transcend this pattern by incorporating something of all three, this flouts the traditional systematization. In particular, the tradition holds that these states cannot be considered to be understanding, *paññā*. Why? Because in this context understanding has a very limited and specific meaning: it refers to 'seeing things as they are', which means seeing all empirical phenomena as impermanent, unsatisfactory and devoid of essence.

On the other hand, Alex Wynne has found another argument in favour of my interpretation.[16] The *Tevijja Sutta* is the thirteenth *sutta* in the *Dīgha Nikāya*, the last in the first section, which is known as the *Sīla-kkhandha* or 'Section of moral rules'. All thirteen contain a long passage – often occupying more than half of the *sutta* – identically worded, which begins with a Buddha being born in the world, a person hearing him preach and deciding to leave the world and follow him, and then how that person follows a path which leads finally to his attaining nirvana. In the first twelve *suttas*, i.e., all the others in the section, what follows the long catalogue of moral rules is that the person starts to practise meditation, and his progress through the four meditative stages called *jhāna* is described. But in this *sutta* the four *jhāna* are not mentioned and the practice of the boundless states precisely takes their place.

In brief: I am claiming that the Buddha used his customary Skill in Means to persuade brahmins that what they had been taught to regard as the supreme goal of life was indeed that, provided that one gave quite new values to the key terms and reinterpreted what was meant by 'staying with *brahman*'. While his twisting of language was certainly audacious, it was no more audacious, I submit, than his saying that by karma he meant intention.

HOW THE FOUR EMOTIONS ARE RELATED

Before I adduce more textual material to bolster my argument, a brief reflection on how the four boundless states are related. I introduced them above by quoting the commentator Buddhaghosa (fifth century AD). Strangely, however, while there are some unimpressive attempts in canonical texts to rank the four states, with love at the bottom and equanimity at the top, I am not aware of any discussion in the Canon of how the four states relate to each other qualitatively.

The Pali word for the first state is *mettā*. It has become customary to translate this as 'loving kindness'. Though this is certainly defensible, for me it is an example, albeit a minor one, of the tendency to invent a kind of Buddhist technical vocabulary which makes the subject retain an alien flavour in English. Obviously, this is non-erotic love, like St Paul's *agapē*, so for an audience of theologians, 'love' is appropriate; but for a wider public, 'love' is an overused word with too wide a range of meanings. On the other hand, the word *mettā* is the abstract noun derived from *mitto*, 'friend', so that 'friendliness' is a possible translation; but to some that may sound too weak. This only goes to show again that a set of English terms may not precisely match the closest Pali equivalents. Thus I prefer to follow my policy of inconsistency,[17] and to use 'love' and 'kindness' indifferently.

To our way of thinking, kindness and compassion are almost the same, and Buddhaghosa's insistence that compassion refers only to feelings towards people who are suffering seems a bit pedantic. I think our instincts in this matter are correct, because the Theravada tradition stresses the kindness, whereas the Mahayana stresses the compassion, and yet this reflects no difference in substance.[18] To single out the third state, empathizing with the happiness of others, is distinctive to Buddhism, and I think became even more so after the Buddha's lifetime. I am referring to the transfer of merit: the apparent recipient of merit is not in fact playing a passive role, but is gaining merit by empathizing with the satisfaction of those who have done something meritorious. The word used is not identical[19] but the emotion is.

It is the relation between the first three states and the fourth which we probably find the most puzzling. I am completely ignorant about early Christianity, but I understand that some of the early church fathers were likewise concerned about the relation between love, *agapē* in Greek, and equanimity, *ataraxia.* The ideal, apparently, is that the love and compassion must be not merely unselfish, but purged of any element of attachment. I think that our culture may offer a parallel in the professional ethos expected of doctors, and particularly perhaps psychiatrists, who must do everything for the patient that benevolence would dictate and yet maintain detachment. It is for this reason, after all, that doctors by tradition never treat seriously ill members of their own family: their emotions would be too much involved.

OTHER TEXTS EXTOLLING KINDNESS AND COMPASSION

To claim that love or compassion can be salvific does go against the Theravadin tradition, and I shall return to what that tradition made of the *Tevijja Sutta.* First, however, let me show that that message is not confined to the one text.

In the Pali Canon[20] there is a poem called the *Metta Sutta,* a title which one could translate 'The Text on Kindness'. This text both exemplifies and extols having kind thoughts towards the whole world. It has traditionally been used by Buddhist meditators, and in modern Sri Lanka it has become for Sinhala Buddhist schoolchildren a kind of functional equivalent to the Lord's Prayer, because they recite it every day at school, usually (I believe) at the end of the school day just before going home.

Most of the poem prescribes how one should love all living beings as a mother loves her own child. We have already mentioned how Buddhaghosa expands on this idea to cover all four of the boundless states. The climax of the text reads:

> Towards the whole world one should develop loving thoughts, boundless: upwards, downwards, sideways, without restriction, enmity or rivalry. Standing, walking, sitting or lying, one should be as alert as possible and keep one's mind on this. They call this divine living in this world. Not taking up ideas, virtuous,

with perfect insight, by controlling greed for sensual pleasure
one does not return to lie in a womb.

This conclusion to the poem surely corroborates that the whole poem is about how one may become enlightened. Moreover, it is natural to interpret 'not returning to lie in a womb' as meaning that one will have escaped altogether from the cycle of rebirth, which is to say that one will have attained nirvana. A scholiast familiar with the full development of Buddhist cosmology could object that there are forms of life, higher than us in the universe, in which rebirth is not via a womb but spontaneous. Thus it is possible to interpret the end of the poem, if it is taken in isolation, as referring only to escape from the grosser forms of rebirth. But there is no such scope for ambiguity in 'the peaceful state', the phrase at the beginning of the poem. So it seems clear that the purport of the whole poem is that kindness is salvific.

The poem does not clearly state that kindness *alone* will produce salvific results. There is a list of other virtues mentioned at the beginning, and the last verse too speaks of other qualities of great importance, notably insight and self-control.

Presumably the most famous of all Pali canonical texts is the *Dhammapada*, the collection of more than four hundred short stanzas on morality. I find it strange that number 368 has not attracted more attention. It says: 'The monk who dwells in kindness, with faith in the Buddha's teaching, may attain the peaceful state, the blissful cessation of conditioning.'

As philologists of Sanskrit or Pali will know, one need not attach much weight to the fact that the verse says 'may attain' (in the optative) rather than 'will attain' (in the indicative). Moreover, in the version of this verse preserved in the *Mahāvastu*,[21] a text of another school, which is generally considered to date from before the Christian era, the verb *is* in the indicative (*adhigacchati*). The verse is in fact saying that kindness is salvific, and it is surely no coincidence that the term for nirvana, 'the peaceful state', is the same as that used at the opening of the *Metta Sutta*. Thus the author of the *Dhammapada* verse apparently interprets the *Metta Sutta* to mean that it is kindness which will get one to nirvana. Tradition holds, of course, that the author of both poems is the Buddha himself.

There is yet another text in the canon in which the Buddha preaches the importance of kindness by making a playful allusion to a passage in the *Bṛhad-āraṇyaka Upaniṣad.* This is the conversation between the sage Yājñavalkya and his favourite wife Maitreyī.[22] Maitreyī asks her husband to tell her what he knows, knowledge which will make her immortal. He begins his teaching: 'It is not for the love of a husband that a husband is dear, but for the love of self (*ātman*) that a husband is dear. It is not for the love of a wife that a wife is dear, but for the love of self that a wife is dear.' A series of parallel statements leads on to the conclusion that to know the self is to know everything.

In a short canonical sutta[23] King Pasenadi reports to the Buddha a conversation which he has had with his wife, Queen Mallikā; they have agreed that no one is dearer than the self – which is what Yājñavalkya said. The Buddha replies in a verse which concludes that because everybody loves themselves one should do no harm to anybody. The verse depends on wordplay, which makes it too cumbrous to explain in this context; readers who want the details can read my explanation elsewhere.[24] The Buddha is again turning brahmin metaphysics into universalizing ethics.

THE TRADITIONAL, LITERAL INTERPRETATION OF THE *TEVIJJA SUTTA*

Despite all this, the Buddhist tradition took the *Tevijja Sutta* literally and henceforth built it into their dogma that someone who successfully practised the *brahma-vihāras* was reborn in the Brahma world, but no higher. This being so, *a fortiori* there had to exist a part of the universe that was the Brahma world! I am by no means sure that the Buddha believed in the existence of a *brahma*-world in any literal sense at all; but it was by this literalism of his interpreters that Buddhist cosmology was given its final shape. Elsewhere I have shown the inconsistency of the efforts then made to line up the four boundless states with levels of the cosmos in which the practitioner would be reborn.[25]

Since this is canonical material, it is binding on Buddhaghosa to accept it. But he is clearly not at ease with such a devaluation of kindness and the rest. He devotes Chapter IX of the *Visuddhi-magga* to the four *brahma-vihāras*, and some of it is very dry indeed. But after he has explained, on canonical authority, exactly how high in the universe each of the four states in turn can take you, he seems to change gear in an eloquent final paragraph. These states, he says, 'bring to perfection' all the other good qualities of a Buddha (here called a 'Great Being'). He writes: 'For the Great Beings' minds retain their balance by giving preference to beings' welfare, by dislike of beings' suffering, by desire for the various successes achieved by beings to last, and by impartiality towards all beings.'[26] And he goes on to apply this to each of the Ten Perfections, the moral qualities which every Buddha is held to bring to their highest pitch. In effect, Buddhaghosa is bypassing the problem of exactly what role the four divine states play in the spiritual development of an ordinary practitioner and saying that for a Buddha they are fundamental.

The *brahma*-worlds have to be situated above the *deva*-worlds, the ordinary heavens, which are within the sphere of desire (*kāma-dhātu*). What is the sphere of desire? A historian's answer must be that it is the Buddhist version, ethicized and elaborated, of the old binary cosmology. The fundamental idea is that good karma in this world will bring you a rebirth in heaven, and you stay there until its effect is exhausted; then you are reborn somewhere lower down. However, the *brahma*-world – which in due course itself came to be subdivided – is not one of those heavens, but a kind of super-heaven. This could be described as overcoding the cosmology of the five fire wisdom. But how seriously, how literally, was it originally intended to be taken?

This is one of those cases where to pose a question is halfway to answering it. I think that the *brahma*-worlds, and the functions they perform, rose from the Buddha's dialogue with brahmins in which he took their cosmology literally – but only for his own didactic purposes. And I would like to push this a bit further. In what are evidently early canonical *suttas* it is mentioned that those who have entered on the Buddhist path have four grades of attainment. The lowest of these grades, the stream-enterer, has at most seven more lives to live and will never be reborn lower than as a human being; the highest, the *arahant*, has attained Enlightenment and will not be reborn. But just below the *arahant* is the non-returner (*anāgāmī*). He will never return to life on earth, but somehow has a guarantee that he will be reborn in a situation from which he will attain nirvana directly.

I suggest that the non-returner comes from the same source as the entire *brahma*-world: the five fire wisdom in the *Bṛhad-āraṇyaka*

Upaniṣad. I have mentioned that the account of the person who reaches the *brahma-loka* after death ends by saying that he will not return. The Buddhist non-returner is said in post-canonical sources to be reborn in worlds still higher than the *brahma*-worlds, but that does not strike me as a blow to my hypothesis. By that time the *brahma*-worlds themselves had been banalized and made much more like ordinary heavens;[27] the non-returner needed something better, and the weirdly abstract strata of the so-called formless worlds, named after states of advanced meditation, were added on to accommodate him. Since those worlds are formless, their inhabitants can have no bodies. So how do bodiless beings have locations? One begins to suspect that the non-returner began his career as a figment of satire.

If the monk described in the *Tevijja Sutta* is reborn in a *brahma* heaven, he obviously cannot be an *arahant,* and it follows that when the text says that by practising kindness and the rest he attains liberation, it cannot really mean that. I have already published something on how the question 'When is liberation not liberation?' led to the invention of a liberation which is only temporary – which is what is needed to explain away this passage. It comes as no surprise to find that this inauthentic liberation plays no part in the rest of the system.

CONCLUSION

These evasions of the true meaning of the text are, however, of interest mainly to the specialist.[28] We must not allow them to detract attention from the positive message: that the Buddha declared love, compassion, empathetic joy and equanimity to be direct routes to nirvana, the supreme bliss and the escape from rebirth.

It has to be admitted, I think, that by misunderstanding this *sutta* the early Buddhists missed the boat. The Buddhist tradition was always clear that non-aggression, *ahiṃsā,* was of paramount importance, and never lost sight of that. But non-aggression, however admirable and important, is a negative virtue. Indeed, the systematizers, the compilers of the *abhidhamma,* do actually define love (*metta*) as absence of hatred.[29] Although the same passage says[30] that *metta* is a component of every skilful (*kusala*) thought, that *metta* need have no specific object, so in principle it is unfocused benevolence. On the one hand the systematizers felt that *metta* had to be given a fundamental role, but on the other they rendered it somewhat bloodless.

The later tradition in India obviously felt this too. Stories became popular in which the Buddha performed great acts of self-sacrifice out of compassion, such as throwing himself off a cliff so that a hungry tigress could feed herself and her starving cubs. The Buddha's followers were exhorted by the Mahayana to follow a path, the *bodhisattva* path, which would make them too become Buddhas and therefore equally compassionate. The rationale for this in the Mahayana becomes tangled, however, because on the one hand a Buddha is no longer a mortal human being, and on the other hand the very existence of benefactors and those they benefit is problematized by their doctrine of emptiness. Perhaps – an audacious thought – none of this attempt to improve Buddhism by giving it more heart would have been felt necessary if the *Tevijja Sutta* had been understood.

Chapter 7

ASSESSING THE EVIDENCE

A BOGUS SUBJECT

Unfortunately, nowadays students are taught that when they embark on research they first have to learn methodology, and that when they write up that research they should start by explaining their methodology. Even worse, they are often led to believe that there is such a subject as methodology. This needs to be unravelled.

There is no such subject as methodology. Mediocre academics like using long words, and at some time in the past generation someone decided it would be more impressive to call method 'methodology'. Obviously, it is true that when one tries to find something out, one uses one or more methods, and it is often appropriate to explain which method or methods one is using. When the police want to find out who committed a crime, they use various methods, such as taking fingerprints or appealing to the public to provide information. But what method or methods they use will depend on the circumstances of the case.

This is always true: the method one uses to try to find something out must always depend on the particulars of the case. Thus I have written at the beginning of the previous chapter that my method is historical. But there is no such thing as a general study of 'methods' which will reveal to one which method is appropriate. Naïve people hope that such a study might reveal to them how to take a short cut or, even more alluring, guarantee success in their quest. But alas, there is no guaranteed road to success; that is a dream, and a childish dream at that.

In case any reader thinks that my view is idiosyncratic, let me quote the views on this topic of a couple of people whom the world has honoured for their distinction. I begin with Professor Max Perutz, OM, the Nobel Prize-winning biologist who for many years headed the Cambridge laboratory where many great discoveries were made, including the discovery of the structure of DNA by Francis Crick and James Watson. Of Crick and Watson Perutz wrote:

> I thought they were wasting their time. However, like Leonardo, they sometimes achieved most when they seemed to be working least. And their apparent idleness led them to solve the greatest of all biological problems, the structure of DNA. There is more than one way of doing good science.

Elsewhere he wrote:

> ... creativity in science, as in the arts, cannot be organised. It arises spontaneously from individual talent. Well-run laboratories can foster it, but hierarchical organisation, inflexible, bureaucratic rules, and mountains of futile paperwork can kill it. Discoveries cannot be planned; they pop up, like Puck, in unexpected corners.[1]

That was from a great scientist. Now let me refer to the famous art historian E. H. Gombrich, my father. Most of his career was spent at the Warburg Institute, in the University of London. In her obituary of him Elizabeth McGrath wrote:

> Questioned ... about the 'Warburg method', his response, 'asking and receiving help from one's colleagues', was not a frivolous one ... when the notion of colleagues is extended to the broad scholarly and scientific community, and the expectation and provision of help is translated into a mutual one ....
>
> His students never formed a 'school'. They neither shared a subject area nor felt bound by a line of approach ... [I]t was enough for Gombrich that a prospective candidate was seriously committed, academically competent, and had chosen a topic of real interest; he had a refreshing aversion to programmatic imposition in scholarly research, as in life.[2]

One more brief quotation, yet again from an obituary.

> Dorothy DeLay, who has died aged 84, was one of the world's foremost violin teachers, with a pupil list which reads like a *Who's Who* of today's top performers. 'Her method,' observed ... [a] star pupil ... 'is that there really is no method.'[3]

CONJECTURE AND REFUTATION

There are, on the other hand, certain principles, which transcend methods and apply to all of them. Most of these principles are simply virtues: one should try above all to be truthful and honest. If one is less talented than Crick and Watson, it is also a good idea to work hard. These principles apply at all times. However, there is one which applies particularly to research. It is using what Karl Popper has called 'conjecture and refutation'.[4]

What this means is that knowledge advances by making conjectures and then testing them against the evidence. It does not matter whether you call the conjectures hypotheses, theses, theories, or simply guesses – the principle is the same. The origin of a conjecture has absolutely no bearing on its value. Some people fancy that you should form your conjecture only after assessing all relevant evidence, but Popper, following David Hume, has shown that this is ultimately wrong, because this principle of induction, as it is called, cannot yield foolproof results. You can never know that you have access to all relevant evidence. You may think, on the basis of seeing thousands of swans, that all swans are white, but then you find black swans in Australia. Or you may think, on the basis of your experience every day of your life, that the sun rises every morning, but then you travel to the Arctic Circle.

What has happened is that on the basis of any number of examples you have built a hypothesis, but a single example is then enough to refute it. This is not to deny that a refutation may itself be refuted, for instance, by discovering that what was believed to be a black swan is in fact no swan at all.

Some scholars in the humanities have drawn a wrong deduction from this. They gather a body of data, for example, about Sanskrit texts, but are then unwilling to extrapolate, which they tend to call 'going beyond the facts'. On the one hand, even the apparently well-established data themselves depend on theories – such as that the texts are not modern forgeries; on the other hand, extrapolation is but another term for a theory which attempts to make a deduction from available evidence, and is thus necessary if knowledge and understanding are to advance.

People seem unwilling or unable to take in that there is a basic asymmetry here. What people think of as 'facts' or 'data' are themselves theories. The weight of evidence, as it accumulates, may make them more and more probable, but their certainty can never be finally established. Take the matter of translation. Let us leave aside the problem that, since hardly any words have a perfect equivalent in another language, there are very few examples of possible perfect translations; let us stick to what an examiner, for example, considers a candidate to have translated correctly or incorrectly. There is a literally infinite number of possible incorrect translations of a sentence, and a very few which have a high probability of being correct. In many cases, when dealing with Sanskrit or Pali, there may seem to be two possibly correct translations, or even more, and which to use becomes a matter of judgement, or indeed of indifference. But the very idea that there exists one correct translation, if one could only find it, and its correctitude will endure forever, is fallacious.[5]

Rather than be unwilling to make bold guesses, we should simply understand that in an empirical subject, be it philology, history or physics, there is no final certitude: all knowledge is provisional. But this is not relativism. It is evident that knowledge does advance: for this modern medicine and technology stand as sufficient proof. If you try to build a computer or a rocket on the basis of nineteenth-century physics, you will get nowhere. So the fact that our theories may always turn out to be wrong should not at all depress us, but on the contrary make us realize how exciting intellectual work can be.

What I have just written is much more important, in my eyes, than what I am going to discuss in the rest of this chapter. I know that most readers will expect me to discuss the evidence for the picture I draw of the Buddha's ideas, and indeed they may well have expected me to start with that. But it is rather a hackneyed topic. And I find it fairly futile to discuss such matters in the abstract without giving examples of how one's approach works in practice. That is why I have already presented many ideas and the evidence for them before proceeding to discuss my method – which is to say, in this case, before assessing the evidence I use.

COPING WITH SCEPTICISM

The first issue to deal with is scepticism. It is as easy as falling off a log to tell students that ancient texts are untrustworthy and perhaps even to poke fun at a professor who joins pious believers in considering that the ancient texts they venerate may be telling the truth about certain historical matters. But this is not worthy of serious scholarship. I have had too much experience of this facile scepticism during my career. When I claimed to have discovered the date of the Buddha, and published a full account of the admittedly rather complex evidence and reasoning which had led me to my conclusion,[6] no one found anything wrong with that evidence – and I suspect that few have bothered to scrutinize it in detail. On the other hand, I found the world in general and colleagues in particular reluctant to accept my claim, simply because they took the lazy attitude of general scepticism. 'The sources are unreliable so the date is not discoverable,' they chanted. But surely intellectual honesty demands that we take each case on its merits. Like citizens, sources must be considered innocent until proven guilty.

I cannot *prove* that the chronicles which supplied my evidence are telling the truth: there is no ultimate defence against scepticism. But the same weapon can be turned on all our sources. Let us recall, among a vast array of possible examples, how very tenuous are our sources for Alexander's invasion of India and his meeting with Candragupta Maurya, events I do not think it reasonable to doubt. Facile scepticism is a boomerang. As a man of scruple, I must say that the Pali chronicles do not enable me to *prove* the date of Buddha: they merely allow me to put forward a theory which has a better chance of being correct than any other propounded so far. Moreover, since they build up through many details a consistent story which seems to have been compiled over a long period, to disbelieve them is at the same time to have a theory that their authors have conspired to hoodwink their audience.

Thus it comes about that I have heard contemporary American scholars recommend that we approach the ancient Buddhist texts with what they call 'a hermeneutic of suspicion' – a term they have misappropriated from Paul Ricoeur.[7] I hope I have said enough to explain why I agree with Alex Wynne in calling this 'a hermeneutic of laziness'.

It should go without saying that we are not bound to take what a Pali text – or any other text in the world – says at face value. But our initial working hypothesis has to be that the text is telling the truth, and in each case where we do not believe it, or doubt it, we must produce our reasons for doing so. There will be innumerable such cases and all kinds of reasons. But if we just dismiss what the texts tell us *a priori*, there is no subject. If there is no subject, no one should be employed to teach it – and good riddance.

I know that among scholars of Buddhism I have sometimes been labelled an extreme/naïve/eccentric conservative, because – it is alleged – I accept what the texts say. Let me make clear once and for all that that is not my position. My position is that I accept what the texts say as an *initial working hypothesis*, and am as interested as anyone in finding out where the tradition cannot be correct and why.

IS THERE BETTER EVIDENCE FOR THE EARLIEST BUDDHISM THAN THE PALI CANON?

In recent times some scholars of Buddhism have decried the value of texts for our study and urged us to turn to inscriptions instead. At one point Gérard Fussmann took a strong line on this, and Gregory Schopen has made the same point. This puzzles me: inscriptions are texts too, and I do not know of any *a priori* reason for assuming them to be more veridical than other texts. Inscriptions do have the advantage that we usually know where they come from, and sometimes they are also dated or at least roughly datable. So of course we should make full use of them. However, the only inscriptions which can have any bearing at all on the Pali canonical material are those of Asoka. Since this book concerns the Buddha and his antecedents, relevant inscriptions do not exist. The same goes, alas, for works of art and architecture.

There are no references to the Buddha in non-Buddhist texts which can plausibly be dated to less than half a millennium after he lived. As I have already mentioned in Chapter 4, there are some references to Buddhist ideas in early Jain literature, probably impossible to date with any accuracy but nevertheless carrying an air of authenticity. I believe that Buddhist ideas began to exert an influence on brahminical ideas not very long after his death. Just as is the case with the influence of earlier ideas on the Buddha himself, some influence was positive, amounting to tacit acceptance, while much of it was negative. It has been very plausibly argued, for example, that there are famous passages in the *Bhagavad-Gītā* which are framed as a reply to Buddhism.[8] However, there is nothing in these non-Buddhist texts to show that the influences to which they are responding emanate from the Buddha himself rather than from his followers in later generations.

For information on what the Buddha said and did we are thus dependent on the Buddhist texts, namely, what western scholarship has called the Canon. There is a complete version of this Canon in the Pali language, and the great majority of texts in this version survive also in Chinese translation, some of them in more than one version. The Chinese translations were made from Indian languages, but most of them probably not from Pali. The largest body of Chinese translations dates from the fifth century AD, though there are a few earlier and many later ones. One substantial part of the canon, the *Vinaya,* has survived not merely in four Chinese versions but in a Buddhist Sanskrit version and a Tibetan version closely related to it. Very few of the old *sutta*s were translated into Tibetan. So, although the Tibetan Buddhist canon, known as the *Kanjur,* is vast, its importance for evaluating the earlier canon is negligible.

A few manuscripts containing versions of *sutta*s found in the Pali Canon survive in other Indian languages. Most of these have been discovered quite recently in the area known in ancient times as Gandhara, which stretched from the Kabul valley in the west to the Indus valley in the east. These may date from the second century AD and thus be the oldest Buddhist manuscripts ever found. Scholars are currently working on them. So far as I can tell, however, these new finds will have no effect on our view of the Buddha and his ideas. Scholars are much given to emphasizing how important it is to compare the Pali versions of canonical *sutta*s with other extant versions, whether they be Gandharan manuscripts or Chinese translations. They are perfectly right to do so. Moreover, I would be the first to agree that to have all this material to hand in a form which makes comparison easy should be a top priority of Buddhist scholarship. But it is easy to convey a misleading impression of what such comparisons have so far achieved. True, literally thousands of differences between versions come to light. But an overwhelming majority of these differences, so far at least, have been rather trivial. Texts are differently arranged, both with regard to each other and internally. The locations at which the Buddha is said to have delivered specific sermons are very often different. But I have yet to see another version of a Pali text which makes me interpret it differently. One thing that has struck me is that when a Pali expression is obscure to us, the Chinese version tends to omit it. One also finds that doctrinal lists tend to be slightly longer in the Chinese; often I would attribute this to the influence of the *abhidhamma,* with which I suspect the Chinese translators tended to 'correct' the *sutta*s.

THE PALI CANON AS WRITTEN EVIDENCE

On my view of the subject, therefore, the Pali version of the *suttas* and *Vinaya* stand unrivalled as our oldest evidence, and if we are seriously interested in how Buddhism began, and hence in how it developed, it is absurd not to give these our fullest attention.

How did these documents originate and how well have they survived the passing of time?[9] Let me tackle the latter question first. Most of the Pali manuscripts that survive in Sri Lanka and Burma were copied as late as the eighteenth and nineteenth centuries. In northern Thailand there are many manuscripts dating back to the sixteenth century, most of them unstudied by modern scholars. Very few Pali manuscripts anywhere are older. In Burma in the twelfth century grammarians systematized Pali grammar and prosody, thus exercising considerable influence on how the language was written thereafter, both in Burma and elsewhere. However, analysis of the only Pali manuscript to antedate those grammarians shows a language identical in most respects to that preserved by the later manuscripts. This oldest witness consists of four leaves of a canonical text; it is in Kathmandu and scholars have dated it to *c.* 800 AD. It seems, however, to have been copied from a north Indian original some centuries older.[10]

This may give the impression that our evidence for the readings in Pali canonical texts is alarmingly modern. Does this impugn their reliability? Scholarship has not yet advanced far enough to give a full answer to this question; I wonder whether it ever will. There are vast numbers of manuscripts of the Canon, especially of the *suttas*, but so far as I know we are still quite unclear about how many archetypes the extant manuscripts are derived from and when those archetypes are likely to date from. It is some consolation that most of the text is supported by two kinds of testimonia: firstly, an enormously high percentage of the text is repeated and found in more than one place in the Canon, and secondly very much of the text is quoted in commentaries and subcommentaries. Of course, once a text is corrupted, misguided scribes may carry the corruption over into parallel texts. The situation is far from satisfactory. Still, we must remember that we are worried here about points of detail, not about whether whole texts and doctrines have been added or changed.

According to the Pali chronicles of Sri Lanka, the Canon as a whole was first committed to writing in Sri Lanka in the first century

BC.[11] It is reasonable to assume that some texts may have been written down earlier, either in India or in Sri Lanka, but exactly in what language we cannot know. The act of writing down the Canon presumably played a part in stabilizing it, particularly as it drew a line between what counted as canonical[12] and what did not. There are a few texts which at various times and places have been either included or excluded from the Canon, but this is not the case with any of the *sutta*s or *vinaya* rules.

THE EARLIEST ORAL TRADITION

Whatever the precise date at which the Pali canonical texts were first written down, what matters most to the historian who wishes to find the Buddha is to what extent he thinks he can trust the transmission of material before that date. To put it slightly differently, when were these texts composed, and do we have anything like the original compositions?

The texts that record the Buddha's sermons are for the most part narrations in which the Buddha plays the leading role, though in some cases the sermon is ascribed to a leading monk. The tradition holds that the texts of the sermons were formulated at the meeting which the monks held soon after the Buddha's death. This meeting is known in English as 'the First Council', but the term translated 'council'[13] really means 'communal recitation'. The *sutta*s were first recited, in response to questioning, by Ānanda, the monk who had been the Buddha's personal attendant during the latter half of his forty-five-year preaching career. The *Vinaya* was similarly recited by Upāli, who as an ex-barber had had the task of shaving ordinands and thus had presumably been present at all the early ordination ceremonies. When Upāli and Ānanda had formulated the texts, they were rehearsed by all the monks attending the council, thus beginning the tradition of oral preservation of the teachings.

Each Buddhist tradition preserves its own version of exactly what happened at this First Council and there is little agreement on who did what or other details. However, all do agree that there was an event of this kind, and I do not see how any coherent body of literature could have come into being without some such event. It is quite clear that, even if we confine ourselves to what we are calling for convenience 'the early canonical texts' (they are listed in 'Basic

Information' at the front of the book), these were not all created in their present form at the First Council. A few sermons even mention people who are known to have lived after the Buddha. The *Vinaya Khandhaka* concludes with the Second Council, which is alleged to have taken place a hundred years after the First; about sixty years is probably closer to the correct figure,[14] but in the present context the discrepancy is not important.

THE CREATION OF STABLE TEXTS

On the other hand, the texts which were recited at the First Council – whichever they were – must have had some kind of existence before that. There is an episode recorded in the Canon[15] in which the Buddha asks a young monk whom he is meeting for the first time to tell him some *Dhamma*; the monk recites the whole *Aṭṭhaka-vagga* (a section of the *Sutta-nipāta*) and the Buddha commends him. The text does not say who originally composed the poems of the *Aṭṭhaka-vagga*; it could be the Buddha himself; it could be the young monk's teacher, Mahākaccāna, who was a reputed preacher; it could be yet other monks; and it could be a combination of these, since not all the poems need be by the same author. But what is clear is that this set of sixteen poems was collected early, presumably in the Buddha's lifetime, and arranged on the principle followed both in the *Ṛg Veda* and in many other parts of the Pali Canon, namely, by increasing length.

The body of sermons preserved in Pali is very large: the Buddhists themselves count them as 17,505,[16] a greater number than appears to have come down to us. Most of them are short, and the corpus is full of repetitions and redundancies. Even so, it is a massive body of literature, mainly in prose. Either at the outset or very early on, the body of sermons was divided into four collections and monks and nuns specialized in learning by heart one of the collections (or another part of the Canon) in order to preserve it.

At the time of the Buddha, the brahmins had already for centuries been preserving their sacred literature, the Vedic texts, orally.[17] They had also already divided into schools (called 'branches') which specialized in particular texts. Learning the texts by heart was virtually coterminous with their education; and that education could last up to thirty-six years.[18] The Buddhist Saṅgha must have operated in a very similar manner. The cultural similarity did not stop there.

Long after the invention of writing, the brahmins were reluctant to write down Vedic texts and continued to preserve them orally. In their case this was motivated, at least in part, by a wish to keep them away from people not entitled to know them: women and people of low caste. Even without that motivation, Buddhists seem to have tended to do the same, and gone on relying more on memory than on written texts; I even found this to be the case in traditional village temples in Sri Lanka when I did fieldwork there in my youth.

In the case of the Vedic tradition, modern scholars have collected texts orally preserved hundreds, even thousands, of miles apart in India. There are certainly some variants, but astonishingly few, given that the tradition stretches over more than two and a half millennia. In his article 'The oral transmission of the early Buddhist literature'[19] Alexander Wynne presents a series of what seem to me to be powerful arguments for his thesis that improvisation of the kind familiar to us from studies of oral epics played little part in the formation of the early Buddhist texts, but on the contrary every effort was made to preserve them *verbatim* – just as in the case of the Veda, I might add.

❧

Since in the time of the Buddha there was no writing, let alone sound recording, a set of words could only have assumed the status of a 'text' – for example, of a *sutta* – once someone had decided to create such a fixed entity, memorized it, and in due course passed it on to others for them to memorize in their turn. The Buddha's First Sermon can stand as an example of what I mean. It is generally known as 'Setting in Motion the Wheel of the Teaching' (*Dhamma-cakka-pavattana*), but this title is not found before the commentaries. It was delivered to five disciples who became the first five monks after the Buddha himself. No doubt some or all of the six people present on that occasion remembered what the Buddha talked about. This probably blended in memory with what he 'should' have talked about in order to introduce others to the insight he had had which constituted his Enlightenment, a self-authenticating experience.

The first topic in the *sutta* is the Middle Way between indulging and mortifying the flesh, which is the way that leads to Enlightenment; this fits the biographical narrative very well. Logically one could also argue the other way round: that the biographical narrative was shaped to fit the First Sermon; but this is such an uneconomical explanation, which leads into many complications, that it is highly improbable. The Middle Way is briefly stated, not expounded in any detail, and is then said to be the same as the Noble Eightfold Path. The Noble Eightfold Path is, however, a very different concept, more precisely articulated than a lifestyle which finds the happy medium between indulgence and asceticism. Its eight constituents, from 'right views' to 'right concentration', are then listed. In no case is there a word of explanation of what is meant by 'right'. So what we have been given so far is just headings, not content.

The Buddha now enunciates the Four Noble Truths. Each is first given its name or title and then briefly expanded. K. R. Norman has published an article[20] which demonstrates on purely linguistic grounds that each Noble Truth is indeed just being introduced by title, so that it appears to be an allusion to something already familiar to the audience, like 'the axis of evil' or the 'shock and awe' policy. The fourth Noble Truth is the Noble Eightfold Path, but nothing is added: the list of eight items is merely repeated.

When one reads the First Sermon with students or finds it in an anthology, it often ends here, because the second half of it is so tedious. With many synonyms the Buddha says of each truth in turn that he glimpsed it, that he realized he should learn it thoroughly (we might say 'internalize' it), and that he had thoroughly learnt it. Because the three processes are applied to four truths, we are told, the doctrine of the Four Noble Truths has twelve aspects.

This reeks of the systematizers who produced the *abhidhamma* and before that certain other doxological texts like the last two *suttas* in the *Dīgha Nikāya.* In my view, it was remembered that the Buddha began his preaching with the Middle Way, the Four Noble Truths and the Noble Eightfold Path; this can never be certain, but it is perfectly plausible. However, what he said about them on that occasion was not clearly remembered, for surely no one at that stage made a 'text' of it. Moreover, the 'first sermon' that has come down to us is chock full of metaphors and technical terms which the Buddha at that stage had not yet explained. The word *nibbāna* is here with several synonyms, but the Buddha had not yet told anyone why he was using this metaphor, the going out of a fire, to express Enlightenment. Similarly, in presenting the first Noble Truth he uses the expression *pañc' upādāna-kkhandhā,* which modern scholars tend to translate as 'five aggregates of grasping'. I have referred to this in the Introduction, and shall show in Chapter 8 that it is a poor translation, because the term is based on the same fire metaphor as *nibbāna*. But without some explanation (which we find elsewhere in the Canon, because the Buddha did give it later), the disciples who made up the original audience could have had no idea what the Buddha was talking about when he used these terms.

Another problem with the First Sermon is that its content does not match what it says at the end that the Ven. Koṇḍañña understood it to mean and was commended for understanding. This, however, I must postpone to Chapter 9.

The description of the Noble Truths (including the listing of the parts of the Eightfold Path) is thus presented in the form it had acquired once it had come to constitute a 'text'. Such textual passages, following biblical scholarship, we can call pericopes. In building up the larger units we call *sutta*s there was a strong tendency, whenever a topic came up, to describe it with a standardized pericope. Pericopes vary in length from a few words to several pages.

In sum, my view of the composition of the First Sermon is that the version we have probably dates from as late as the Second Council. Why just then? Because it is embedded in the *Vinaya Khandhaka*, in the account of how the Buddha began his preaching career, and there is good reason to think that *that* was composed 'shortly before or after' the Second Council.[21] Exactly the same text, still without its later title, is also found near the end of the *Saṃyutta Nikāya*,[22] which makes me surmise that that collection was not closed until about the same time, perhaps at the Second Council itself. On the other hand, I am sure that there was an earlier, probably shorter, version, which contained the gist of the present version; and that the entire text rested on a memory in the Saṅgha, quite likely buttressed by the Buddha while he was still alive, that those were the topics he talked about on that occasion.

PERICOPES

The Pali Canon is immensely repetitious, because it is largely composed of pericopes; this is exactly what one would expect of oral literature. Another feature due to its oral origins is the fondness for numbered lists. Verse often helps one, through its metre, to realize when one has omitted an item, but prose does not, so numbered lists can serve that purpose.

The monks and nuns who composed the texts with the building blocks of pericopes were not all of the highest intelligence, for sometimes they inserted pericopes inappropriately. I have illustrated this in an article called 'Three souls, one or none: the vagaries of a Pali pericope'.[23] It concerns an expression, a set of phrases nine words long, which occurs in five texts in the Pali Canon. In only one of these does it make perfectly good sense. In fact, I have cited this text in Chapter 6: it is the *sutta* in which a brahmin called Saṅgārava is criticizing the Buddha. Once lifted out of that original context, the expression looks very strange, as it seems to suggest that ascetics can 'blow out' a self – whereas the Buddhist position is that one has no such 'self' in the first place. Not only do the commentaries on this expression in its secondary contexts have trouble in explaining it: their explanations are themselves discrepant. This is important: it seems to be an undeniable case in which neither the canonical corpus nor the commentarial corpus can be made to yield homogeneous authorial unity; in other words, people who did not fully understand the expression have used it in the creation of canonical texts, and other, later people who did not understand it have given more than one interpretation of it in the commentaries.

So what of the commentaries? In interpreting a canonical text, the first thing one must do is to see what the commentary says about it. But that is not to say that one then suspends all critical judgement and takes inquiry no further, as has unfortunately been the practice of some leading Pali scholars even in recent times. The previous paragraph alone suffices to prove that this is simply not a viable approach.

THE COMMENTARIES

The commentaries on the Buddha's sermons and on the *Vinaya* are all ascribed to one man, Buddhaghosa, whom we know to have been active in Sri Lanka at the very beginning of the fifth century AD. Buddhaghosa also wrote a huge book, called *The Path to Purity (Visuddhi-magga)*, which summarizes Theravada Buddhist doctrine in so masterly a fashion that it has remained authoritative to this day. Sometimes the other commentaries refer to *The Path to Purity* for amplification on a topic. Even so, I do not myself think that they are all the work of Buddhaghosa; but that is not relevant here. To what extent Buddhaghosa (with possible colleagues) is the author and to what extent he is the editor of the commentaries may never be fully known, but it is beyond dispute that he often explicitly cites older commentaries, mostly written in Sinhala. These have all been lost, but obviously they take us back earlier than the time of Buddhaghosa himself; one scholar who studied them, E. W. Adikaram,[24] deduced that they were closed in the second century AD. What the evidence seems to show beyond doubt is that they were not closed earlier than that. According to tradition (embedded in those same commentaries), their substance goes back to the First Council and was brought to Sri Lanka in the middle of the third century BC by a group led by Mahinda, son of the emperor Asoka; these were the missionaries who introduced Buddhism into the island. Tradition also holds that when the Canon was written down in Sri Lanka in the first century BC the commentaries were written down too. Whether this is true or not, the commentaries at that stage were probably in Sinhala, the local language.

What emerges from all this is that the Theravadin tradition of exegesis, preserved in the Pali language, claims that it stretches right back from the texts we now have to the time of the Buddha himself, a period of about eight hundred years. I see no reason to consider this implausible. But this is entirely different from positing that over those eight centuries, while the commentaries were transmitted orally (at least to begin with), translated and edited, nothing of importance was added, lost or otherwise changed. For that there would surely be no parallel recorded in human history. Nor was there any cultural scruple to inhibit changing the commentaries, for they do not have the sanctity of being ascribed to the Buddha himself.

SHORTCOMINGS OF THE COMMENTARIES

As has happened in every learned religious tradition, the exegetes homogenized and systematized the founder's message. The brahminical exegetical tradition made explicit the principle that revealed texts had only one purport.[25] No such principle was explicitly formulated in Buddhism, but one cannot too often stress that in ancient India the brahmin culture was hegemonic and deeply influenced all other traditions. The anthropologist M. N. Srinivas called this 'sanskritization'. I contend that in more ways than have yet been explicated, Buddhism was 'sanskritized' over the centuries of its development in India, and this commentarial homogenization could be seen as an instance of that process.

This homogenization is the first of three systematic defects which I find in the Pali exegetical tradition. The second is excessive literalism, a failing that the Buddha himself foresaw and warned against.[26] Once the texts had been formulated, their words were carefully preserved. Sometimes too much was read into them, and a technical significance was ascribed to some quite normal and innocent expression; I have provided several examples of this in my book *How Buddhism Began.*

The third deficiency in the commentaries, from our point of view, is that they have largely lost the memory of the Buddha's historical context. I have been at pains to show above, particularly in Chapter 6, and I shall revert to the topic later as well, that important aspects of the Buddha's message are formulated in terms set by the early brahminical scriptures, especially the *Bṛhad-āraṇyaka Upaniṣad,* both where he agrees and where he disagrees with the brahmins, and that we lose a whole dimension of his meaning if we are unaware of this context and argument.

All these three shortcomings in the traditional Buddhist interpretation of the Buddha's sermons – homogenization, literalism, and ignorance of the Vedic background – are no less prevalent among modern scholars than they were in ancient times.

DISCREPANCIES

It is not merely legitimate but necessary for the student of the Pali Canon to employ the same alert eye as any other textual critic in order to spot discrepancies. Of course, one must not be hasty in jumping to conclusions: an obscurity or difficulty is not necessarily a discrepancy. One must never forget the editorial principle that it is the difficult reading which is likely to be the original, the easy one an attempt by the tradition to smooth over the difficulty.[27]

One sort of relevant discrepancy is when a word or expression in a text sounds odd and seems hard to interpret, but then we find it in another text where it fits the context perfectly; one may then hypothesize that the latter context is the original one and the other is secondary, a later creation. The pericope about apparently 'blowing out the self', cited above, is an example of this. To show that A is later than B, of course, only deals with relative, not with absolute, chronology; it could be later by a month, or later by a century. Moreover, it is usually only sections of texts, pericopes, to which this kind of reasoning can be applied; larger textual units may well contain both earlier and later material.

Sometimes this almost stares you in the face. In some passages it is transparent that the *Mahāparinibbāna Sutta*, the account of the Buddha's last days, juxtaposes earlier and later material. This is one of the few texts of which different recensions, the Pali one and several emanating from other early Buddhist traditions, have been carefully compared,[28] an analysis facilitated by its being the longest of all *suttas*. Even without this comparison, however, the Pali text alone has tell-tale incongruities. The account of the Buddha's actual passing away[29] has him first going through the ranked set of meditative states: from the first *jhāna* up to the fourth, then through the five 'formless *jhānas*' culminating in the extinction of apperception and feeling: a series of nine steps in all. At this point Ānanda says to Anuruddha that the Buddha has passed away (*parinibbuto*), but Anuruddha says not so. The Buddha then retraces all nine steps, going back down to the first *jhāna*. Then he climbs again; and on leaving the fourth *jhāna* he dies. Obviously onlookers could not tell which meditative state the Buddha was in, so the whole account must be an ideological construct. Or rather, two constructs. It seems to me that we must have in the text before us a combination of two versions of the Buddha's death. Normally one would expect the later version to come second, but in this case the content makes that impossible, so the simpler version, that with just the four *jhānas*, is likely to be the older.

Exegetes ancient and modern have homogenized the tradition because people are reluctant to admit that a venerated figure may have changed his mind. This is true even though, as I shall show in Chapter 11, the *Vinaya* tradition is built on the Buddha's changing his mind and adapting to circumstances. I believe that if we are concerned to uncover the Buddha's own views from the canonical material, we must jettison the idea that during a preaching career of forty-five years he never changed the form, let alone the content, of his teachings. This is surely true of no great thinker of whom we have good historical records: it suffices to recall the discussions about early Marx and later Marx. In the First Sermon, we have seen, the Buddha spells out the Noble Eightfold Path in terms which the tradition never changes: the final step is Right Concentration, *sammā samādhi*. Later it seems he was more given to proposing a threefold sequence: morality, concentration, wisdom. Each is the prerequisite for the proper development of the next. This appears many times, for example, in the *Mahā Parinibbāna Sutta*.[30] The ancient commentators therefore had a hard time fitting the three into the eight. They had to say that the first two stages of the Noble Eightfold Path were a kind of preliminary wisdom and that after reaching concentration one comes back to the first two stages to make the wisdom perfect. This may suit the first step, right view, but virtually ignores the second, right intention (*sammā saṃkappa*),[31] which according to this revision should be the climax of the whole career. The whole attempt to harmonize the two formulations, by eight stages and by three, is contorted and indeed pointless. Why should anyone who is not blinded by piety not accept that the Buddha first formulated the path as culminating in concentration and then, as his ideas developed, decided that it would be better expressed as culminating in gnosis?

In this case there does seem to have been a temporal sequence: in other words, the Buddha appears to have changed his mind – though on a formulation, not a matter of substance. There are other cases where his formulations seem to be somewhat inconsistent but I would not argue for a change of mind, because I can see no reason why the inconsistency or change of metaphor would have mattered to him or to anyone else. By calling the Noble Eightfold Path a path, he uses a metaphor which implies that its constituents form a sequence; and some formulations of the threefold practice of morality, meditation and wisdom carry the same implication. On the other hand, he also agrees with the brahmin Soṇadaṇḍa that morality and understanding go together and enhance each other, as when one washes one's hands, using each hand to clean the other.[32] For me this very inconsistency is a virtual guarantee of authenticity: no imitator would have dared to innovate like that.

Let me summarize my view on stratifying canonical material by coming at the topic from a slightly different angle. Earlier attempts at finding strata in the Canon have been so crude that they have earned the very idea of stratification a bad name. Certainly, this can turn into a wild-goose chase, if one allows some prejudice about what the Buddha must have originally said to run away with one, regardless of logic or evidence. But it is no less absurd to insist *a priori* that stratification is impossible. The form and language of the texts have probably been reworked so often that formal criteria are in my view likely to be of very limited use: we must rely on content. But I see no reason why in principle we should not be able to produce plausible hypotheses that certain ideas must have preceded or followed certain other ideas.

On some matters, particularly matters of formulation, the Buddha may well have changed his mind. But where two flatly contradictory statements are ascribed to him, we may well be able to reason out that only one is authentic. An example would be his both claiming and denying that he is omniscient; this will be briefly discussed in Chapter 11. But there may also be cases where we can trace the evolution of a doctrine and be able to infer from internal logic which thought must have come first and which later. My analysis of the Chain of Dependent Origination in Chapter 9 concludes with a clear-cut hypothesis of this character.

❧

To conclude this chapter on how I set about my research on the Buddha, I return to its opening theme: conjecture and refutation, and the provisional nature of knowledge. Popper writes of his theory of knowledge: 'Though it stresses our fallibility it does not resign itself to scepticism, for it also stresses the fact that knowledge can grow, and that science can progress – just because we can learn from our mistakes.'[33] So finally let me once again quote from Elizabeth McGrath's obituary of my father. 'While he habitually expressed his views with great firmness, Gombrich liked to remark that one advantage afforded by a long life was the opportunity to change one's mind.' That also applies to me, the Gombrich of the next generation. More important, I have suggested that it applies to the Buddha himself.

Chapter 8

EVERYTHING IS BURNING: THE CENTRALITY OF FIRE IN THE BUDDHA'S THOUGHT

This chapter is about how the Buddha reacted to Vedic ideas and practices concerning fire, and how this focus may have led him to what is perhaps his most important philosophical idea, the substitution of non-random processes for objects. It will provide more examples of how the Buddha reused brahminical religious terms, turning them to his own purposes.

FIRE AS THE CENTRAL METAPHOR IN THE BUDDHA'S SOTERIOLOGY

According to all Buddhist traditions, the Buddha's third sermon (*Vin.* I, 34–5) entirely concerns fire; in fact, the sermon is known in English as the 'Fire Sermon'. In Pali it is called the *Āditta-pariyāya*, 'The Way of Putting Things As Being on Fire', which indicates that fire is being used here as a metaphor. The sermon begins: 'Everything, O monks, is on fire.' The Buddha then explains what he means by 'everything'. It is all our faculties – the five senses plus the mind – and their objects and operations and the feelings they give rise to. To paraphrase, 'everything' refers to the totality of experience. All components of our experience in this world, the Buddha declares, are on fire. They are on fire with the fires of passion, hatred and delusion.

In reading the above it is easy to overlook that it is not only our faculties but their objects and operations that are said to be on fire. We shall return to this point below.

Everyone knows that the ultimate solution which the Buddha offered to the sufferings and dissatisfactions of life was the attainment of nirvana (P: *nibbāna*); and most people likewise know that *nibbāna* is a metaphor connected to fire. But what exactly that metaphor means or refers to has often been misunderstood. The word comes from the Sanskrit verbal root *vā*, 'to blow'; with the prefix *nir*, the basic meaning is 'cease to burn, go out' (like a flame). As the verb is intransitive, the noun S: *nirvāṇa* means 'going out', without implying any agent who causes that going out: it just happens. In the 'Fire Sermon' the Buddha preaches that our experience is on fire with three fires, the fires of passion, hatred and delusion; our aim must be for all of them to go out. Sometimes in the Canon the first fire is called passion, sometimes greed, but this variation is of no importance: the reference is the same and the fires are always three. Why?

The answer lies in Vedic culture. The brahmin householder had the duty to keep alight a set of three fires, which he tended daily. The Buddha thus took these fires to symbolize life in the world, life as a family man. This is not a hypothesis of recent scholarship: it is stated clearly enough in a *sutta* in the *Aṅguttara-nikāya* (IV, 41–6). In this sermon the Buddha first juxtaposes the three sacrificial fires with the fires of passion, hatred and delusion. Then, with the aid of puns, he metaphorically reinterprets the fires: the eastern fire, *āhavanīya* in Sanskrit, he says stands for one's parents; the western (*gārhapatya*) fire for one's household and dependents; the southern *(dakṣiṇāgni)* for holy men (renunciates and brahmins) worthy to receive offerings. It is in this sense, he tells a fat brahmin, that a householder should tend the fires: by supporting *people.*

Here the Buddha, for all that he imposes on the fires a novel meaning, is evaluating them positively. When he equates them with passion, hatred and delusion, he is evaluating them negatively. This little point may seem obvious, even banal, but it is important to bear it in mind. The Buddha expressed himself in a great variety of ways, some positive, some negative. It is often said that the concept of nirvana is negative. Of course, the way that the metaphor of fire is used here is indeed negative. But the same thing is sometimes expressed positively. The Sanskrit word *nirvṛti* means 'bliss', and the related word *nirvṛta* means 'blissful'. In Pali phonetics these two words are *nibbuti* and *nibbuta* respectively. Both *nibbāna* and *nibbuti* are used in the Pali Canon to refer to the Buddhist goal, and one who has attained it is referred to as *nibbuta.*[1] Because of the phonetic similarity – more striking in Pali than in Sanskrit – people have often failed to realize that the words are unrelated. To put it differently: *nibbāna* and *nibbuti* refer to the same thing, but have sharply contrasting meanings, the one negative and the other positive. When the fires of passion, hatred and delusion die out within one, one experiences bliss.

Similarly, in this metaphor, which is so central to his soteriology, the Buddha gives fire strongly negative connotations, but that does not mean that all his other references to fire in a metaphorical context have to be negative. For example, the very narrative which leads up to the 'Fire Sermon' shows ambivalence towards fire. The Buddha preaches the sermon to a thousand newly converted brahmin fire-worshippers, all of whom are said to achieve Enlightenment as a result. The Buddha has procured their initial conversion by producing a bigger and better fire than they could (as well as performing other miracles). It is unlikely to be mere coincidence that in the verses[2] describing the contest to produce heat, at the point when multi-coloured flames come from the Buddha's body, he is called Aṅgirasa (*Vin.* I, 25). The Buddha is called Aṅgirasa or Aṅgīrasa several times in the Pali Canon. In the *Ṛg Veda* Aṅgīras is a class of supermen, standing between men and gods, and Agni, the personification of fire, is the first and foremost Aṅgīras (*RV* I.31.1). In other Pali texts too the Buddha is called Aṅgīrasa when he is said to shine very brilliantly: at *SN* I, 96, he outshines the world; at *AN* III, 239 (= *J.* I, 116) he shines and glows like the sun. So in this passage he is virtually impersonating Agni, the brahmins' fire god. This looks less like a debate than a takeover bid.

Later generations of Buddhists had no reason to be interested in Vedic brahmins or in the Buddha's debate with them, so the origin of the metaphor of the three fires was forgotten. So far as I know, it is not mentioned in the commentaries. In the Mahayana, the metaphor was so thoroughly forgotten that passion, hatred and delusion came to be known as the three poisons.[3] Since even the core of the fire metaphor was thus early forgotten by Buddhist tradition, it is not surprising that its extensions were forgotten too.

❧

When, in Chapter 7, I introduced the content of the Buddha's First Sermon, as it has come down to us, I mentioned that *dukkha* was defined as the five *upādāna-khandhā*, and that this compound noun is usually translated as something like 'the aggregates of grasping', which in normal English is meaningless. In fact, the term conveys the same message as the Fire Sermon, using the same metaphor.

The five *khandha*, from form to consciousness, are so often referred to in the texts that one can hardly imagine a summary of the Buddha's teaching, however brief, that omitted them. While they have usually been understood to be the five components of a living being, Sue Hamilton's research has clearly demonstrated that this is inaccurate: they are the five components of all experience.[4] What we normally think of as a person or living being is in fact a set of five processes: physical processes (typically but not only visible processes), including the five senses and their objects; feelings, as of pain or pleasure; apperceptions (perceptions in which we put a name to what we perceive); volitions; and consciousness. Note again that the first *khandha* includes the objects of the senses; obviously this goes beyond what we can consider to be part of a person, whereas it fits into what we consider to constitute personal experience.

In my opinion the term *khandha* too was a part of the fire metaphor. The word *upādāna* has both a concrete and an abstract meaning. In the abstract it means attachment, grasping; in this sense it is much used in Buddhist dogmatics. Concretely, it means that which fuels this process. The *PED*, *s.v.*: '(lit. that [material] substratum by means of which an active process is kept alive and going), fuel, supply, provision'. So when the context deals with fire it simply means fuel.

There is a short text in the *Saṃyutta Nikāya*, *SN* III, 71, which states that the five *khandha* are ablaze (*āditta*), so that one should stop caring for them.[5] Pali has a common expression for a blazing fire, *aggi-kkhandha*.[6] In the compound *upādāna-kkhandha* I believe the word for fire, *aggi*, has been dropped, being felt to be redundant when the word for fuel is present. I therefore translate *upādāna-kkhandha* as 'blazing masses of fuel', and consider it to be a coherent part of the same metaphor as the word *nibbāna*.

My hypothesis is surely confirmed by another short text centring on these words, *SN* II, 84–5. To establish this point is so important that I shall go into detail. The text has been translated by Bhikkhu Bodhi;[7] his footnotes show that, as usual, he has scrupulously followed the commentary – but he has missed the metaphor. In my summary, I shall give his translation of the key terms in italics. (Otherwise the translation is my own.)

The text begins:

> If one lives in expectation of enjoyment from things *that can be clung to*, one's thirst increases; through thirst, *clinging*; through *clinging*, becoming; through becoming, birth; through birth, decay and death, grief, lamentation, sorrow, sadness and torment come into being. Thus there comes about the arising of this whole *mass of suffering*.

This is like when a great *bonfire* of many loads of wood is blazing away, and a man from time to time throws onto it dry grass, cow dung and wood, so that it goes on blazing a long time, *sustained by that material, fuelled by it*. Conversely, if one considers the risks in things that *can be clung to*, one's thirst for them is destroyed, and this leads to the destruction of the rest of the chain. 'Thus there comes about the destruction of this whole *mass of suffering*.' This is like when the same *bonfire* is not given any more *fuel*: when the original *fuel* is consumed, *lacking sustenance* it *would be extinguished*.

The word for 'bonfire' is *aggi-kkhandha*, mentioned just above. 'Mass of suffering' translates *dukkha-kkhandha*, so it is a blazing mass: we have not just a simile but also a metaphor. This is extended by punning on *upādāna*, the word translated as 'fuel' in the simile but as 'clinging' when referring to a person. Both translations are of course correct; but the point has been lost. Similarly, at the beginning the translation 'that can be clung to' is correct, but conceals the fact that the word, *upādāniya*, can also mean 'potential fuel'. There is a parallel metaphor in 'sustained by that material', which translates *tad-āhāra*, and 'lacking sustenance', which translates *an-āhāra*; *āhāra* means 'food', and in English too we talk of 'feeding' a fire. The last words in my summary translate *nibbāyeyya*, a form of the verb which gives us *nibbāna*. So the parallelism shows that if we stop giving it fuel to feed on, the blazing fire of our suffering will likewise go out.

❧

Once one understands that the five processes that constitute our experiences are being compared to burning bundles of firewood to feed either the fire of our suffering or the fires of passion, hatred and confusion (it makes no difference which way you look at it), this also makes sense of the old terms for the two kinds of nirvana: *sa-upādi-sesa* and *an-upādi-sesa*.[8] As the *PED*, *s.v. upādi*, tells us, *upādi* = *upādāna*. The attainment of nirvana during one's life (the only time when it is possible to attain it!) is called *sa-upādi-sesa*, but this does not mean that one still has a residue of grasping – just a little bit of vice! If we follow the metaphor, we understand that at the moment when we extinguish the fires of passion, hatred and delusion we still have the five *khandha*, the potential to have experiences, so we still have a residue (*sesa*) of fuel (*upādi*); however, it is no longer burning. When the five *khandha* cease to exist, i.e., when we die enlightened, we have no more potential for experience; we have run out of fuel.[9]

FIRE IN VEDIC THOUGHT

Vedic religion centred on worship of fire and sacrifices made into fire, which is something entirely positive. The fire here on earth is equated with the fire in heaven, the sun, and we depend on both forms for light and warmth and hence for life itself. Like other forces of nature, Fire can be personified as a god. The very first verse of the *Ṛg Veda* begins 'I worship Fire, the *purohita*'. *Purohita*, which literally means 'placed in front', refers to an officiating priest, particularly one who officiates for a ruler; the name 'placed in front' indicates that the priest, the brahmin, has precedence even over the ruler, as the sacred takes precedence over the worldly. So the fire can be a symbol summarizing all that is sacred.

Fire can also stand for consciousness, which in this context is seen as the very essence of life: to live is to be aware, or at least to have the potential for awareness. When I write that fire can 'stand for' consciousness, what exactly does 'stand for' mean? Is fire just a metaphor for consciousness, or is consciousness literally some kind of fire? In describing the *Ṛg Veda* and the ideology that flows from it, it would be wrong to choose either alternative. The Buddha, like Aristotle, clearly distinguished between the metaphorical and the literal,[10] but the *Ṛg Veda* did not. It thought of consciousness *in terms of* fire without drawing a boundary between what was to be taken literally and what was not. Joanna Jurewicz has demonstrated[11] that the approach of George Lakoff and his followers, who recognize that our entire patterns of thought and language are built on primitive metaphors, which vary to some extent from culture to culture, can wonderfully elucidate for us the world of Vedic thought. The Vedic poets did not just think *about* the salient elements of their physical surroundings, such as cattle, soma and fire; they thought *with* them, by means of them.

The link between fire and thinking in the *Ṛg Veda* is in a superficial sense well known. Probably the most famous, and certainly the most used, verse in the entire text is a three-line verse known as the *Gāyatrī*, after its metre, or the *Sāvitrī*, after its topic, Savitṛ, the Sun. This verse has to be recited daily at twilight worship[12] by every male initiated into the Vedic community – which should be the same, very approximately, as saying by every brahmin male who has reached puberty. The verse may be translated: 'Let us think of that excellent brilliance of the Impeller God, that it may animate our thoughts.' The word 'Impeller' translates Savitṛ and this is a frequently used name of the sun. (In Oxford I used to begin my annual series of lectures on Indian religion by reciting this verse and hoping that a little sunshine might dispel the usual dank Oxonian gloom and make our minds less sluggish. Though the Indians are less starved of sunshine, they too regarded the daily appearance of fire in the sky as the precondition for mental activity.)

The connection between Agni and consciousness or cognition extends far beyond the Sāvitrī verse.[13] For example, Jurewicz shows that in *RV* 9.27.24 Agni is invoked to purify his worshippers by stimulations of their prayers or Vedic utterances, *brahma-savaiḥ*. Here again we have the verbal root *sū*, as in Savitṛ; and in fact in the next two verses, 25 and 26, a very similar invocation is addressed to Savitṛ under that name. Agni and Savitṛ are here being identified.[14]

Jurewicz writes:

> The description of Agni as the cause of mental activity is not only metaphorical. It can be understood as expressing a real experience of physical heat under the influence of Soma. There are at least two other stanzas in the *Ṛg Veda,* 8, 4, 86 and 1, 52, 6, which seem to express this experience. There is however one further dimension to its literality: the image of Agni causing cognition expresses the idea of mental heating, which is the experience of the fiery creative principle. In other words Agni, being the efficient cause of the vision, is its ultimate subject who manifests himself in the human individual, the originator of the vision. Manifesting himself, he causes internal heat.

She then quotes 3.1.8, part of which reads: 'The streams of clarified butter trickle to the place where the bull has grown thanks to his poetic art.' The bull is a common metaphor for Agni. Having discussed at length the metaphorical use of 'streams of clarified butter', she concludes:

> On the metaphorical level, this image expresses mental concentration on fire as the object of cognition. The poetic art, which causes the growth of fire recognised and experienced in the vision, can be originated by the poet and by Agni himself; in the latter case it is Agni who is the ultimate originator of the vision.

Agni can therefore stand for both the subject and the object of cognition. As Jurewicz remarks: 'A similar idea is expressed in the *Mokṣa-dharma*[15] and the *Bhagavad-gītā*: that the *ātman* functions as both subject and object of yogic cognition.'

That Agni can stand for both the subject of cognition and its object, sometimes separately and sometimes together, Jurewicz has shown in her discussion of many different passages in the *Ṛg Veda.* Most of the verses she discusses are at first blush quite obscure, and it is her analysis of the metaphorical structure through piling up examples which at the same time makes her argument so convincing and means that no brief attempt to summarize it can do it justice.

Agni, then, can be manifested as consciousness, both the activity itself and its objects. What our discussion so far has not clearly expressed is the appetitive nature of that consciousness. This, however, is at the centre of the picture in a passage to which Jurewicz has drawn attention elsewhere,[16] the cosmogonic myth at *Śatapatha Brāhmaṇa* 2.2.4.1ff. This states that the world begins when Prajāpati, the Creator God, begins by creating Fire from his mouth, 'and because he generated him from his mouth, Agni is an eater of food.' But then Prajāpati is terrified because Fire, finding no other fuel, wants to eat him. He solves the problem by creating milk for Fire to eat; from milk, plants also arise. There is a close homology between milk and Soma; indeed, *BĀU* 1.4.6 says: 'The whole world is nothing but food and eater. Soma is the food, Agni the eater.'

In *Ś.Br.* 2.2.4.3, Prajāpati plans in his mind to create plants and trees as fuel for Agni so that the latter should have something other than his own creator to eat.[17] Jurewicz argues: 'So the eating part of Prajāpati can also be interpreted as representing the subject of the cognition, the eaten one – its object.'[18] The identity of subject and object, she writes, 'is confirmed in the act of eating, in which food becomes one with its eater.'

FIRE AS A MODEL FOR APPETITIVE CONSCIOUSNESS

Let us return to the Buddha. *Sutta* 38 of the *Majjhima Nikāya* is called the *Mahā Taṇhā-Saṅkhaya Sutta*, 'The Major Text on the Destruction of Thirst'. It is an important text for the teaching of dependent origination (*paṭicca-samuppāda*), a topic reached via a discussion of the nature of consciousness, which is compared to fire. Again, it was Professor Jurewicz who drew my attention to the full significance of this comparison.

The *Mahā Taṇhā-Saṅkhaya Sutta* begins with a misguided monk, an ex-fisherman called Sāti, who holds what is called an 'evil view'. It is that the Buddha has taught that 'this same consciousness, and no other, transmigrates' (*tad ev' idaṃ viññāṇaṃ sandhāvati saṃsarati, anaññaṃ*). The correct view is that 'the Buddha has taught, putting it in many ways, that consciousness originates from causes; it cannot arise without a cause' (*aneka-pariyāyena paṭicca-samuppannaṃ viññāṇaṃ vuttaṃ Bhagavatā, aññatra paccayā n'atthi viññāṇassa sambhavo*) (*MN* I, 256–8). When he is brought before the Buddha, Sāti adds something to his evil view. The Buddha asks him what he means by consciousness, and he replies: 'This speaking, feeling one [masculine] who experiences the results of good and bad actions' (*yvāyaṃ vado vedeyyo tatra tatra kalyāṇa-pāpakānaṃ kammānaṃ vipākaṃ paṭisaṃvedeti*). So he has a naïve view of consciousness as a transmigrating soul or essence.

In terms of Buddhist dogmatics, as the commentator reminds us (*Papañca-sūdanī* II, 305), Sāti is propounding eternalism (*sassata-diṭṭhi*), an error which the commentator says he fell into because his speciality was *jātaka* stories and he was misled by the Buddha's saying things like, 'At that time I was Vessantara.'[19]

The Buddha then proceeds to show that indeed Sāti has got it wrong: that consciousness is not a *thing* which can move from body to body, but a *process*, and a causally conditioned process at that. However, he does not do so by using such an abstract formulation. After saying that Sāti is an idiot who will long suffer for his error, the Buddha launches into an extended comparison of consciousness with fire. Consciousness, he says, is classified – indeed, one might say named – according to what has brought it about. If it arises on account of the eye and visible forms it counts as 'eye consciousness'; similarly, there arise ear consciousness, smell consciousness, tongue consciousness, body consciousness (from the sense of touch) and mind consciousness, the last being due to the mind and ideas.[20] Just so, a fire is classified according to its cause, whether it be a stick fire, a splinter fire, a grass fire, a cowdung fire, a chaff fire or a rubbish fire.

This is easy for us to understand. The Buddha is saying that consciousness is always consciousness *of* something. This is the opposite of the Upaniṣadic doctrine that consciousness is inherent in the world spirit, *brahman*, and hence in the individual soul, *ātman*, which is ultimately identical with *brahman*. The *Upaniṣads* tend to use the term *cit* for consciousness, but also *jñānaṃ* (*Taittirīya Upaniṣad* 2.1.1 says: *satyaṃ jñānaṃ anantaṃ brahma*, which I would translate: 'Brahman is reality, awareness, infinite') and *vijñānaṃ*, the very word of which we have the Pali form here. Brahman is defined as *vijñānaṃ*, for instance, at *BĀU* 3.9.28 and *Taittirīya Upaniṣad* 2.5.1.

The point is twofold: that for the Upaniṣads consciousness is not consciousness of anything outside itself, but the prerequisite for such consciousness; and that it is inextricably bound up with true being, so that ontology and epistemology are merged. Whether or not we agree with the Buddha in considering that consciousness must always be consciousness of something, there is no doubt that in separating ontology from epistemology he is taking a point of view with which we feel at home.

❧

The next passage in the text has been a puzzle. Let me translate it as literally as I can. The Buddha is speaking. 'Monks, do you see that this [neuter] has come into being?' 'Yes, sir.' 'Monks, do you see that it originates in its food?' 'Yes, sir.' 'Monks, do you see that what has come into being is of a nature to finish through the finishing of its food?' 'Yes, sir.'

The question is, what is 'this'? The commentator says it is the set of five *khandha*, the five processes which constitute a living being; but that concept has not been referred to in the text and I do not believe him. The neuter thing that has been referred to in the previous paragraph, and was indeed the topic of that paragraph, is consciousness, and the simple solution would be to take 'this' as referring to consciousness. Why then did the commentator not propose this solution? I suppose that like me he finds it very odd to talk to an audience about consciousness by saying, 'Do you see that this has come into being?' Of course, seeing can always be a metaphor for understanding. But the word for 'this' (*idaṃ*) is deictic, and one cannot point to a piece of consciousness.

My hypothesis is that the deictic pronoun here refers to a piece of action not mentioned in the dialogue. Patrick Olivelle has convincingly shown that this is how we have to interpret some passages in the early *Upaniṣads* in which deictic pronouns are used.[21] There is even a passage early in the *BĀU* (1.4.6), a cosmogonic narrative, which reads: 'Then he churned *like this* and, using his hands, produced fire ...' I shall produce evidence below (Chapter 12) that there is a direct connection between that passage and this. I think, therefore, that at this point the Buddha either lit a fire or had one in front of him. The word for 'fire', *aggi*, is masculine, but fire is also an element, *bhūta*, which is neuter.[22] So there is also wordplay: the Buddha is saying, punningly, 'Do you see this element which has come into being?' The passage continues with sets of rather strange questions, such as whether one could doubt the existence of 'this' and its dependence on its fuel, now referred to as its 'food'; to go into these here would be tedious, but I think they too make far better sense if they refer to something happening before the audience's eyes.

❧

The Buddha then says that there are four kinds of food (*āhāra*) to maintain those living beings that already exist and to help along those that are coming into existence. The first is the food made into mouthfuls (i.e., what we normally call food), the second contact (*phasso*), the third intention (*mano-saṃcetanā*) and the fourth consciousness. All these four, he says, owe their origin to thirst – the commonest of all the Buddha's many metaphors for desire. This thirst in turn owes its origin to feeling (as of pleasure or pain); feeling to contact; contact to the six senses. In thus tracing the origin of thirst to feeling, of feeling to contact, and of contact to the six senses, the text has become banal, in that it is simply reproducing the standard formula of dependent origination (to be expounded in the next chapter), which indeed it then takes back, as usual, all the way to ignorance (*avijjā*). The formula is rehearsed in the normal repetitive way, leading to the conclusion that the destruction of ignorance leads to that of each successive link, culminating in putting an end to rebirth and its suffering. This passage justifies the title of the text, 'The Destruction of Thirst', and is further expounded in such a way as to make clear that it is also a rebuttal of Sāti's eternalist heresy.

The four foods – normal food, contact, intention and consciousness – seem to be left high and dry. The commentary is no help at all. I surmise that the mention of the fire's food – as in the bonfire *sutta* discussed above – was the connection that brought in the four foods here. (That this passage with the double causal chain also occurs, by itself with no context, elsewhere in the Canon[23] does not dissuade me; as shown in Chapter 7, pericopes often migrate like this.) The result is a mess: contact (*phasso*) occurs twice, and so, with the two instances further apart, does consciousness. The natural deduction is that an inept editor has cobbled two teachings together;[24] below I shall suggest more precisely why I think this happened.

Consciousness is a food, that is, something that fuels existence, and in an undesirable way at that, since it arises directly from thirst. We shall see in the next chapter that in the full twelve-link chain of dependent origination consciousness arises from volitions, but I do not see an important difference in substance between saying that it arises from volitions and saying that it arises from thirst. I shall return to this below.

Though the *Mahā Taṇhā-Saṅkhaya Sutta* does not say so in so many words, there is obviously more to the Buddha's analogy between consciousness and fire than the fact that they are – or can be – classified according to their fuel. Fire is dynamic and appetitive: it seeks out its objects. If we read the text as a whole, we see that the Buddha himself is saying that fire and consciousness are alike in this crucial respect. His familiarity with Vedic thought surely guarantees that he had this in mind.

To sum up so far, in Vedic tradition consciousness and its objects are thought of in terms of fire. In the *Mahā Taṇhā-Saṅkhaya Sutta* the Buddha draws on this idea but is more analytical. He sees consciousness as being like fire in that it is an appetitive process, which cannot exist without having something to feed on. Moreover, the analogy with fire can provide a model of how a process can be dynamic and seek out its objects without being guided by a seeker.

ETHICIZING CONSCIOUSNESS

All this seems coherent and illuminating. But how does it square with the picture of consciousness found elsewhere in the Canon?

Among the five *khandha*, the fourth group, volitions, includes *cetanā*, intention. This the Buddha declared to be what constitutes karma and therefore lends an action its ethical quality, whether good or bad. The other four *khandha* do not have an ethical quality and by the same token are not a matter of intention. Consciousness, *viññāṇa*, is on this view ethically neutral, and merely a necessary component, along with the sense organs and their objects, of the functioning of the senses, and analogously of the mind.

In the Vedic way of seeing consciousness in terms of fire, both have a will of their own. By contrast here, in the list of the *khandha*, consciousness has been separated from volition. True, the separation is only analytical, because in life the five sets of processes always operate together to create experience. But we have seen that the same separation occurs in the *sutta* passage mentioned above about the four foods. Though what had come earlier in the *sutta* prepared us for the idea that consciousness is appetitive and arises from thirst, it turned out to be accompanied by a separate entity called intention. Moreover, the word used there for intention, *mano-saṃcetanā*, is virtually the same[25] as *cetanā*, the word for intention which the Buddha chooses to define karma.

What has happened here? The Vedic thoughts with which we have been dealing concern ontology and epistemology, what exists and how we can be aware of it; for them, the two questions are interlocked. None of this has anything to do with ethics. By contrast, the basic drive of the Buddha's teaching was to ethicize the world and see the whole of life and experience in ethical terms, as good or bad. His analysis therefore simply has to find a place for an ethical element, something which makes a thought, an instance of consciousness, good or bad.

We have just seen, however, that in the *Mahā Taṇhā-Saṅkhaya Sutta* consciousness is appetitive, and that that appetite, like all others, is considered as an aspect of *taṇhā* (thirst) and thus as the prime obstacle to spiritual progress. This should mean that consciousness is ethically bad. Yet if it is separated from intention, surely it should be ethically neutral. I think that the passage may be garbled because it tries to combine the Vedic concept of an appetitive consciousness, which the Buddha inherited and to which the first part of the *sutta* is devoted, with an analysis following that of the five *khandha*, in which consciousness *per se* has no ethical charge. We cannot tell exactly how this occurred, but we may presume that when the editor or compiler became aware of the contradiction, he panicked, and used 'contact' as a bridge to get him back to the standard formula for the chain of dependent origination, leaving a certain amount of chaos in his wake.

THE FIVE KHANDHA ARE PROCESSES

Let me return to the five *khandha* and the 'Fire Sermon'. Both, we have seen, put the objects of sense perception in the same category as the senses themselves. Thus sights, sounds, etc., are said in the 'Fire Sermon' to be on fire with passion, hatred and delusion, just as are seeing, hearing, etc. Another thing to note about the 'Fire Sermon' is that it does not seem to envisage that the senses, their objects, and the other things it mentions could somehow continue to exist when they are no longer on fire. When one realizes that they are on fire one becomes totally disillusioned with them, and through this disillusion one is liberated and realizes that one will not be reborn.

I have mentioned above that the five *khandha* are five sets of processes which fuel our continued existence in *saṃsāra* because they involve grasping, appetite, thirst, desire, whatever you like to call it. I have also shown *khandha* to be a short form of *aggi-kkhandha*, a common Pali compound word meaning 'mass of flame'. So there are not just five heaps of fuel but five fires burning fuel. Like all fires, they are in a sense what they are made of; and this takes us back to the Vedic thought that fire is both object and subject. Moreover, they are not *things* but *processes.*

I have, in sum, suggested that the Buddha made the following uses of fire as a metaphor.

1. From Vedic thought he derived the view that consciousness is like fire in being appetitive, and that like fire it can go out without having an agent to put it out, simply because the fuel is exhausted.

2. He also derived the idea that fire cannot be separated from that which burns. This means that just as there is no such thing as fire without a burning object, so there is no such thing as consciousness without an object of consciousness. More profoundly, perhaps, this can be expressed in a more general way by saying that the subjective and objective presuppose each other and all experience requires both. The thought that subject and object can ultimately not be separated seems to accord very well with the Buddha's statement that the world lies within this fathom-long body (*SN* I, 62), quoted in Chapter 5. Another facet of this same idea is that the Buddha's key metaphysical statements, whether about *anattā* or about the *khandha*, are generally taken to refer to the person – and this seems natural, since it is individual people that he was trying to help escape from suffering – but in fact they apply equally to the world, for the world can only be described in terms of what can be experienced.

3. Most important of all, he deduced something that I think was never explicit either in Vedic thought or in its Hindu descendants: that what we can experience is only process. This may be his most important philosophical idea. Our consciousness and its objects are like fire in that they are not things but processes, unceasing change. Something beyond this is perhaps conceivable, but the very nature of our apparatus for having experiences determines that if it does exist it must lie completely outside our experience.

4. Again like fire, the processes which constitute our experience are non-random. I shall explore this in the next chapter.

5. The Buddha also ethicized Vedic thought, making the whole of lived experience take place in an ethicized framework. Creating the conditions in which the fires with which we are all burning would go out was an enterprise at the same time ethical and intellectual, for the fires were both emotional (passion and hatred) and intellectual (delusion, stupidity). Egotism and belief in an unchanging ego were the fires' essential fuel, so once they were got rid of, those fires would go out.

THE NEW VIEW OF CONSCIOUSNESS HAS KNOCK-ON EFFECTS

If consciousness is itself on fire with passion, etc., the aim of anyone seeking liberation must surely be to eliminate consciousness. This is indeed the implication of the 'Fire Sermon' and even, one could argue, of the basic formula of the five *khandha*. On the other hand, in taking step four, his ethicization, the Buddha apparently wanted to avoid that conclusion. One of the three fires is delusion, so one is liberated by eliminating delusion; but if that were to mean loss of consciousness, how could one go on to be aware that one has been liberated – as the 'Fire Sermon' proposes one can? Even more crucially, if liberation involved loss of consciousness, would this not undermine the moral character of the whole teaching? So the Buddha took the further step of separating volition, which carries a positive or negative ethical charge, from consciousness. Thus the three fires come to represent not any and all forms of consciousness, but negative ('unskilful') volitions. It is the bad volitions which must stop, and to bring that about surely requires consciousness.

I propose that the two views, that liberation requires elimination of consciousness and, against that, that it is a purification of consciousness and character, mirror a great divide in the Buddha's teaching on the mind between what he learnt from his teachers and his own original ideas.

The tradition holds that the Buddha learnt and practised meditation under the guidance of two teachers before finding their methods inadequate and striking out on his own. Some recent scholarship, culminating in the work of Alex Wynne,[26] has shown that this tradition is almost certain to be authentic, and that the two teachers stood in some kind of brahminical tradition. This recent scholarship also agrees with the Buddhist tradition in holding that what the Buddha learnt from his teachers was the kind of meditation preserved within his own teaching as *samatha*, 'calming' meditation. In this kind of meditation the mind becomes less and less active; it moves towards *samādhi*, concentration. The highest point that it can reach is termed by the Buddhists *saññā-vedayita-nirodha*, 'cessation of apperception and feeling'. That is a kind of trance, in which one cannot survive for more than seven days.

Theravadin orthodoxy, as incorporated, for example, in Buddhaghosa's *Visuddhi-magga*, is clear that this state, which lacks all mental activity, is *not* nirvana, but a kind of spiritual exercise, which can be resorted to whether one has previously attained nirvana or not. The Buddha resorted to it on his deathbed (*DN* II,156), but left the state before actually dying. The state is thus neither permanent nor irreversible. The orthodoxy contrasts this with the other kind of meditation, allegedly original to the Buddha, called *vipassanā*, 'insight'; it is this insight which alone culminates in nirvana. Unlike the cessation of apperception and feeling, nirvana is an experiential condition which is irreversible, for it involves 'seeing things as they are', which cannot but be conscious.[27]

Even though this is the settled orthodox position, the texts in the Pali Canon itself are not in fact entirely consistent, and there are a few passages which do seem to equate the cessation of apperception and feeling with the ultimate goal. However, I shall not digress to explore the oddities of this position, because for present purposes I only need to show that it may well have been seen as the ultimate goal by the Buddha's teachers and others around him who practised an older type of meditation, but that it ended up demoted. Other scholars have noticed this already.

I suggest that in the older type of meditation, or at least in the Buddha's presentation of it in his *samatha* schema, consciousness was indeed seen as appetitive, like fire, and therefore something which in the enlightened state one had got rid of. Not only is this the more natural reading of the 'Fire Sermon'. In the chain of dependent origination, consciousness is said to emerge on the basis of *saṃkhārā*, volitions, and in turn to give rise to individuation and individuating thought.[28] Jurewicz has shown in a brilliant paper[29] that in this teaching the Buddha is ironizing Vedic cosmogony, and the fit is better if consciousness retains its Vedic characteristics of being volitional and appetitive.

I think that when the Buddha decided that the only kind of intention that really mattered was moral intention, the beginning of the Noble Eightfold Path, he was careful to choose a word for intention, *cetanā*, which did not carry Vedic ideological overtones. His doctrine that ethical action, good karma, is the only true purification and the foundation of spiritual progress, was utterly radical and new. But older ideas about the character of consciousness lingered, whether in his own mind or those of some of his followers, or both, and left their traces in many texts down the centuries. For example, nearly a thousand years later a major school of Buddhism[30] held that the unenlightened mind was at base an *ālaya-vijñāna*. *Ālaya* in the Pali Canon is a synonym for *taṇhā*, craving, so that *ālaya-vijñāna* means precisely 'appetitive consciousness'.

AN ANALOGY WITH PRE-SOCRATIC PHILOSOPHY

Let me end this chapter with an even more far-reaching suggestion. Though the Buddha did not regard himself as a philosopher, he certainly propounded some notable philosophical ideas; and the most notable among these is probably that for things, as commonly understood, he substituted processes. A salient example is his doctrine of the five *khandha*, according to which what we normally think of as a person is constituted by a set of five processes. Moreover, these processes are not random but conditioned by a set of causes. I hope to have shown that he may have got this idea precisely from considering the nature of fire, which he perceived to be not a thing – let alone a god – but a process, and a causally conditioned process at that.

There is a striking similarity between the Buddha and Heraclitus. Heraclitus, who lived in Ionia (modern Turkey), was probably a slightly older contemporary of the Buddha. Only a few fragments of his work are preserved. His most famous dictum was 'Panta rhei': 'Everything flows.' He also said, 'You cannot step twice into the same river.' In other words, he shared the Buddha's insight that our world is in constant flux; it is a world of processes. He is supposed to have followed in an intellectual sequence from Thales, who said that everything was ultimately made of water, and Anaximenes, who said no, everything was made of air. Heraclitus argued that fire was the basic element, the stuff from which everything came and into which it returned.

Moreover, as I have written in the previous chapter, the Vedāntic view that true reality is eternal and unchanging recalls the view of the pre-Socratic philosopher Parmenides.[31] Heraclitus was probably responding to Parmenides just as the Buddha was responding to the *Upaniṣads*. I do not believe that Heraclitus can have influenced the Buddha, let alone *vice versa*, but it is worthy of remark that in ancient Greece, too, fire apparently provided someone with the vision of a world of perpetual change.[32]

Chapter 9

CAUSATION AND NON-RANDOM PROCESS

For which of the Buddha's ideas was he most famous among the mass of his followers in ancient India? The theory of karma may not have been understood by later followers to be the Buddha's distinctive contribution, because it soon came to have such a great influence on other Indian religious traditions as well. Yes, he was associated with the teaching of 'no soul', but that was a label; the precise idea was probably understood by few. If we look, however, for the idea which provided Buddhists with their popular self-definition, my question has a clear answer. Buddhist institutions in ancient India provided pilgrims and other devotees with thousands and thousands of small terracotta plaques, most of which bore the same words. Those words, with a little phonetic variation, were *ye dhammā hetu-pabhavā*: 'the *dharmas* which arise from causes'. They originated as the first words of a short verse:

ye dhammā hetu-pabhavā tesaṃ hetuṃ Tathāgato āha
tesaṃ ca yo nirodho; evaṃvādī mahā samaṇo.[1]

This can be translated: 'The Tathāgata has spoken of the cause and cessation of the *dhammas* which arise from causes; such is the teaching of the great renunciate.' But what exactly does that mean?

The term *dhamma* here means a constituent of reality according to the Buddha's analysis. If we are correctly instructed and have internalized the Buddha's teaching, also called the *dhamma*, we will analyse our own experience, in accord with those teachings, in terms of *dhammas*, potential or actual components of that experience.[2] The previous chapter has shown that that experience consists of processes, and that those processes are neither random nor rigidly determined. All but one of them have causes; this the

Buddhist tradition often expresses by saying that they not independent.

Just one *dhamma*, in this sense of the term, is not causally conditioned. That unique *dhamma* must be the opposite of everything we normally experience, and for this reason, as I shall explain in the next chapter, it can hardly be described except negatively. That *dhamma* is the experience of the extinction of the fires of passion, hatred and delusion. The verse is therefore saying that the Buddha has described the origin and cessation of all phenomena – except of nirvana, that which has neither origin nor cessation. Moreover, he has explained their cause or causes.

This verse is supposed to have converted the Buddha's two chief disciples, Sāriputta and Moggallāna. The story occurs in the introductory section of the *Khandhaka*, that half of the *Vinaya* which deals with the rules for the Saṅgha as a community.[3] Having renounced the world under another teacher, the two men had agreed that whoever of them first discovered 'the deathless' would tell the other. One morning Sāriputta saw Assaji, one of the Buddha's first five disciples, on his alms round, and was so impressed by his tranquil and controlled deportment that he asked him who his teacher was and what he taught. Assaji replied that as a recent convert he knew little, but this verse gave the gist of it. When he heard the verse, the scales, as it were, fell from Sāriputta's eyes, and he realized that 'whatever is of a nature to arise is all of a nature to pass away'; thereupon he rushed off to share this with Moggallāna.

The very same words – that 'whatever is of a nature to arise is all of a nature to pass away' – are used, earlier in the same text, to describe the realization of Koṇḍañña, the first convert, at the end of the First Sermon.[4] The other four disciples to hear the First Sermon have the same realization shortly afterwards. This realization is tantamount to being on the verge of becoming an *arahat*. In Chapter 7 I have described the content of the First Sermon: the Middle Way, the Four Noble Truths, the Noble Eightfold Path. I venture to observe that this content does not match the description of Koṇḍañña's realization. What is one to make of this?

I also argued in that chapter that the version we have of the First Sermon probably dates from the Second Council. The story of the conversion of Sāriputta and Moggallāna shows us that by that time the Buddha's analysis of reality in terms of causal process was considered, at least in learned circles, to be his greatest discovery. I suggest, therefore, that the description of the realization which constituted their Enlightenment was then applied retrospectively, but somewhat inappropriately, to the first five disciples. Of course, this does not mean that I am taking the story about Sāriputta and Moggallāna as literally accurate either: just as I argued concerning the First Sermon, the words which are supposed to have convinced them are far too concise to be intelligible on their own. But we can here pinpoint a moment in the development of the Buddhist tradition when this idea of the Buddha's was accorded paramount importance.

DEPENDENT ORIGINATION

In the Buddhist tradition, then, the Buddha is credited with having in some sense discovered causation and demonstrated its centrality for a correct understanding of the world. Sometimes this discovery is summed up in the brief phrase *evaṃ sati idaṃ hoti*, meaning 'It being thus, this comes about'; this could be paraphrased as 'Things happen under certain conditions.' This is still so vague as to be virtually meaningless. So what was it that the Buddha discovered?

At one level I have already given a brief answer to this in the previous chapter: using the analogy of fire, the Buddha saw all our experiences of life as non-random processes, in other words as processes subject to causation. Now I must explore this further.

Nothing accessible to our reason or our normal experience exists without a cause. Thus, for example, there can be no origin to the universe, no first cause, no god who is an unmoved mover. Over the centuries Buddhists came to regard the Buddha's teaching as 'the middle way' in this sense: that he proclaimed neither the existence of things in their own right, which we would now call essentialism, nor some kind of nihilism, but that the world of our experience is a world of flux and process. As Paul Williams once put it to me, for Buddhism there are no nouns, only verbs. This process is also a middle way in that it is neither random nor rigidly determined, for it leaves room for free will, as discussed in Chapter 2. This 'middleness' gave its name to the school of philosophy founded by Nāgārjuna (second century AD?), *Madhyamaka*.

The Buddhist term for being causally determined is *paṭicca-samuppanna*. Strictly speaking, this term refers to a highly specific doctrine. In English the doctrine is usually called the Chain of Dependent Origination (though there is no 'chain' in the Pali); in Pali it is the *paṭicca-samuppāda* and in Sanskrit the *pratītya-samutpāda*. In the version of the Buddha's Enlightenment which begins the *Khandhaka* section of the *Vinaya Piṭaka* (referred to just above), it is the discovery of the Chain of Dependent Origination that constitutes the Buddha's salvific gnosis. Though there are variants in the Canon, by far the commonest form of this chain has twelve links: ignorance > volitions > consciousness > name and form > six sense bases > contact > feeling > thirst > clinging > becoming > birth > decay and death (+ grief, lamentation, sorrow, etc.).[5]

At first blush this may not appear too puzzling. It looks as if the Buddha originally began at the end: he asked himself, 'What is the cause of all our sorrow and suffering?' Having answered that question by saying 'It is decay and death,' he then asked, 'And what is the cause of those?', and went on asking the same question until he got back to 'Ignorance'. My friend Hwang Soon-Il has very plausibly suggested that this may be the origin of the common Pali expression *yoniso manasi-kāra*. The dictionary translates this with such terms as 'proper attention'. But literally it means 'making in the mind according to origin', in other words, thinking over the origin of something, and that is just how the Buddha made his breakthrough. Many of the Buddha's sermons begin with his telling his monks to listen to him with *yoniso manasi-kāra*, but that expression does not seem to be a normal idiom in Sanskrit or indeed in Pali literature, so I think that Hwang has been astute in spotting a problem. To put it simply, the Buddha was trying to work out how we come to be suffering, and found the answer in a series of steps, such that reversing those steps would solve the problem.

So far, so good. However, on closer scrutiny the Chain of Dependent Origination is anything but transparent. What it means in detail has been contested among Buddhists from the earliest days; there is no one agreed interpretation. Moreover, in the *locus classicus* for this doctrine, the *Mahā Nidāna Sutta*, the text has a remarkable introduction.[6] Ānanda happily tells the Buddha that he has understood the Chain of Dependent Origination, and the Buddha reprimands him, saying that it is extremely difficult to understand. The Buddha normally is shown in the Pali Canon as doing his very best to make himself clear, and I know of no parallel to his statement here that this teaching of his is profound and difficult to understand. I interpret it to mean that those who first formulated the text and recorded the teaching felt unsure whether they understood it themselves.

One problem with the chain as we find it in the texts is that it appears not to work well negatively. The original form is positive: Why is there the last link (decay and death)? Because of the previous link; and so on all the way back to ignorance. Or you can start at the front: ignorance causes volitions, volitions cause consciousness; and so on. So to put things right, the whole chain must be negated. But, whichever end you start from, that involves getting rid of consciousness.[7] Can that be correct? I have shown in the previous chapter that the Fire Sermon too seems to read that way, and yet that is incompatible with the Buddha's main teaching. For the moment I merely flag up the problem; I shall suggest its solution below.

JUREWICZ'S DISCOVERY

At the conference of the International Association of Buddhist Studies held in Lausanne in August 1999, Joanna Jurewicz of the University of Warsaw showed that the formulation of the Chain of Dependent Origination is as it is because it represents the Buddha's answer to Vedic cosmogony, and indeed to the fundamental ontology of brahminical thought. Though her paper was published in 2000,[8] to my mind it has not yet attracted the attention it deserves. It deals with the chain with twelve links, as set out above. That the chain sometimes appears with fewer links and sometimes even with loops in it seems to me to be no argument against her interpretation.

This book has been accumulating evidence that the Buddha's teachings are largely formulated as a response to earlier teachings. Jurewicz has shown that the Chain of Dependent Origination is perhaps the most detailed instance of that response. The Buddha chose to express himself in those terms because he was responding to Vedic cosmogony, as represented particularly in the famous 'Hymn of Creation', *Ṛg Veda* X, 129, and in the first chapter of the *Bṛhad-āraṇyaka Upaniṣad*, but also in the *Śatapatha Brāhmaṇa* and other *Upaniṣads*.

In this cosmogony (as mentioned in Chapter 3) a close correspondence, amounting originally even to an identity, between the microcosm and the macrocosm is assumed; so the origin of the macrocosm, the universe, is at the same time the origin of the microcosm, the human being. In the Vedic case, one could say that the primary referent is the universe, but the universe is considered to be grounded on a primordial essence which is endowed with consciousness. The Buddha, by contrast, is referring primarily to the living individual, for he has no interest in the world as such – and that is part of his message.

Another significant contrast between the Vedic cosmogony and Dependent Origination is that the Buddha 'in formulating ... the successive links of the chain ... used abstract terminology instead of metaphors (which he made much use of in his own explanations).'[9]

The Pali word *nidāna* has several meanings, of which perhaps the central ones are foundation, origin and cause. All of these could be said to be relevant to the Chain of Dependent Origination and hence to the title of the *Mahā Nidāna Sutta*, the text in which it is expounded. But Jurewicz has shown that there is something further to this title. The hymn following *Ṛg Veda* X, 129, namely *Ṛg Veda* X, 130, is also about cosmogony, and in its third verse it asks about the *nidāna*. A *nidāna*, Jurewicz explains, is 'the ontological connection between different levels and forms of beings';[10] in other words, it can refer to one of the esoteric correspondences between, for example, macrocosm and microcosm, the understanding of which constitutes the salvific knowledge provided by the *upaniṣads*. (I mentioned in Chapter 3 that the word *upaniṣad* can itself bear exactly this same meaning.)

The part of the chain which has caused the most difficulty is the first four links: ignorance conditions volitional impulses, which condition consciousness, which condition name and form.

Ṛg Veda X, 129 tells us that at first there was nothing, not even existence or non-existence. In an earlier article,[11] Jurewicz shows that this is both an ontological and an epistemological statement; in other words, there was no possibility of even ascertaining existence or non-existence and hence no way of making the distinction. So there was originally neither existence nor consciousness. This initial stage corresponds to ignorance in the Buddha's chain.

The Vedic 'Hymn of Creation' goes on to recount that somehow – inexplicably – a volitional impulse initiates the process of creation or evolution. This volitional impulse is there called *kāma*, the commonest word for 'desire'. Like the English word 'desire', *kāma* has a narrow meaning, sexual desire, and a broader meaning, desire in general. The hymn says that desire was 'the first seed of mind'. For desire the Buddha uses a vast range of metaphors, of which 'thirst' (*taṇhā*) is probably the commonest. That term occurs later in the chain. At this point, what arises from the primordial chaos of unawareness he calls *saṃkhārā*,[12] a plural noun. This is one of the five *khandha*, the processes which constitute a sentient being. It is often translated 'formations', but I object that, like the term 'aggregates' for *khandha*, that tells us nothing. Desire, the process which keeps us in *saṃsāra*, is one of the constituents of this *khandha*, so when *saṃkhārā* strictly refers to this *khandha*, I prefer to translate it 'volitions'. More on this below.

Jurewicz illustrates the various ways in which the Vedic texts portray the next step: how desire, as 'the first seed of mind', creates consciousness.

> The most explicit text is *BĀU* 1.4; here the Creator (*ātman*) in the form of a man (*puruṣa-vidha*) realizes his own singularity. He looks around and does not see anything but himself, which indicates not only that there existed nothing aside from himself, but also that he was not able to cognize anything other than himself.[13]

At this stage, according to Vedic thought, consciousness is non-dual, which is to say that it is the ability to cognize but not yet consciousness *of* anything, for there is no split yet into subject and object.

For the Buddha, consciousness, here the third link in the chain, is the fifth of the *khandha*, but it is always consciousness *of*. In the previous chapter I showed how this was a deliberate refutation of the Vedic position. Moreover, I learnt from Jurewicz that from Vedic thought he inherited a view of consciousness as appetitive, but I went on to show that his ethical concern led him to separate consciousness from the will. He thus conceptualized the fourth and fifth *khandha*, which, though they always operate in conjunction (like all the *khandha*), are analytically separate.

Pure consciousness is thus at best reflexive, cognizing itself. From this reflexivity, in which there is still only one entity, develops an awareness of subject and object; this in turn leads to further individuation, until we reach the multiplicity of our experience: individuation both by name (*nāma*), using a linguistic category, and by appearance (*rūpa*), perceptible to the senses.

The later Buddhist tradition did not understand how the Buddha had appropriated this term *nāma-rūpa* from the *Upaniṣads*. Realizing that at this point in the chain there should be a reference to the emergence of the individual person, and knowing that the Buddha identified the person with the five *khandha*, the tradition made *nāma-rūpa* equivalent to the five *khandha* by saying that *rūpa* was the first *khandha* and *nāma* referred to the other four. Since three of these four (*vedanā*, *saṃkhārā* and *viññāṇa*) appear elsewhere in the chain under their usual names, this can hardly be correct.

Now I must quote at length what Jurewicz writes about *nāma-rūpa*, because only thus can I convey the full flavour of what the Buddha has done by wrenching these terms out of their Vedic context.

> In Vedic cosmogony, the act of giving a name and a form marks the final formation of the Creator's *ātman*. The idea probably goes back to the *jātakarman* [birth] ceremony, in the course of which the father accepted his son and gave him a name. By accepting his son, he confirmed his own identity with him; by giving him a name he took him out of the unnamed, unshaped chaos and finally created him. The same process can be observed in creation: according to the famous passages from BAU I.4.7, the *ātman*, having given name and form to the created world, enters it 'up to the nail tips'. Thus being the subject (or we could say, being the *vijñāna*), he recognizes his own identity with the object and finally shapes it. At the same time and by this very act he continues the process of his own creation as the subject: within the cosmos, he equips himself with the cognitive instruments facilitating his further cognition. As the father lives in his son, so the *ātman* undertakes cognition in his named and formed self.
>
> But self-expression through name and form does not merely enable the Creator to continue self-cognition. At the same time, he hides himself and – as if divided into the different names and forms – loses the ability to be seen as a whole. Thus the act of giving name and form also makes cognition impossible, or at least difficult.
>
> I think that this very fact could have been an important reason for the Buddha's choosing the term *nāmarūpa* to denote an organism in which *vijñāna* settles. If we reject the *ātman*, who, giving himself name and form, performs the cognitive

process, the division of consciousness into name and form has only the negative value of an act which hinders cognition. As such, it fits very well into the *pratītyasamutpāda* understood as a chain of events which drive a human being into deeper and deeper ignorance about himself.[14]

The remaining eight links of the chain are more straightforward and there is no need to discuss them here. The end of the chain – decay, death, grief and lamentation – shows that all that has gone before is but a road to ruin. For Vedic thought, the Absolute which cognizes itself and so generates the world is the *ātman*, which is at the same time the self of every sentient being. Let me quote Jurewicz for the final time (with a small change to clarify her English):

> The Buddha preached at least some of his sermons to educated people, well versed in Brāhmaṇic thought, who were familiar with the concepts and the general idea of the Vedic cosmogony. To them, all the terms used in the *pratītyasamutpāda* had a definite meaning and they evoked definite associations. Let us imagine the Buddha enumerating all the stages of the Vedic cosmogony only to conclude: 'That's right, this is how the whole process develops. However, the only problem is that there exists no one to undergo a transformation here!' From the didactic point of view, it was a brilliant strategy. The act of cutting off the *ātman* ... deprives the Vedic cosmogony of its positive meaning as the successful activity of the Absolute and presents it as a chain of absurd, meaningless changes which could only result in the repeated death of anyone who would reproduce this cosmogonic process in ritual activity and everyday life.[15]

Usually, when a new interpretation of a famous text is proposed, one does well to pose the sceptical question: 'Why did nobody notice this before?' One of the beauties of Jurewicz's discovery is that the answer to this question is simple and obvious: at a very early stage the Buddhist tradition lost sight of the texts and doctrines to which the Buddha was responding. And, I might add, irony does not weather well.

Note also that this interpretation of Dependent Origination does not subvert the Buddhist tradition or run counter to traditional Buddhist ideas. On the contrary, it enriches them, giving precise meaning to what was previously obscure by adding substance and detail to the Buddha's 'no soul' doctrine.

JUREWICZ'S DISCOVERY COMBINED WITH THOSE OF FRAUWALLNER AND HWANG

'But wait a minute,' the reader may cry. 'Before you presented Jurewicz's theory, you told me that the Chain of Dependent Origination began with the last part, when the Buddha asked himself how suffering arose. How can that be true and Jurewicz's theory also be valid?'

I believe there is a perfect answer to this. Erich Frauwallner argued, many years ago, that the twelve-linked chain is a composite of two lists, the second beginning with thirst, because originally – in his First Sermon – this is what the Buddha gave as the cause of suffering, but that as his thought developed he felt the need to elaborate on this.[16] This perfectly fits such texts as *SN* II, 84–5, quoted early in Chapter 8, which begins by expressing the second Noble Truth, the Origin of Suffering (*dukkha-samudaya*), in precisely these terms. If we combine this with Jurewicz's interpretation, it seems to me that all difficulties are resolved.

My conclusion is that Frauwallner and Hwang are right, and the Buddha's chain originally went back only five links, to thirst. (It could also go back six, seven or eight links – nothing hangs on the difference.) Then, at another point, the Buddha produced a different causal chain to ironize and criticize Vedic cosmogony, and noticed that it led very nicely into the earlier chain – perhaps because it is natural for the creation of the individual to lead straight on to the six senses, and thence, via 'contact' and 'feeling', to thirst.[17] It is quite plausible, however, that someone failed to notice that once the first four links became part of the chain, its negative version meant that in order to abolish ignorance one first had to abolish consciousness!

Let me now further dwell on the Vedic background to the Buddha's thought, and try to get the reader used to what may be an unfamiliar view, by supplementing what Jurewicz has written about the first two terms, ignorance and 'formations' or 'volitions'.

Avijjā

The word for ignorance in Sanskrit is *avidyā*. The Pali form, *avijjā*, stands at the beginning of the Chain of Dependent Origination. This is an abstract noun, and the prefix *a* makes it negative. It goes back to a very common verbal root *vid*, which basically means 'to know'. Indeed, the very word *Veda* is another noun derived from that root. However, there is a second verbal root *vid*, also common, meaning 'to find, to obtain'. A verbal root is a kind of theoretical form used as the basis for deriving real words; but in some actual verbal forms these two roots *vid* continue to coincide as homonyms. Thus the present passive, *vidyate*, can mean either 'it is known' or 'it is found'; the latter means 'it exists', rather like French *se trouve*. My suggestion, therefore, is that *avidyā* can mean not only ignorance but also non-existence.[18] If I am right, this would support Jurewicz's interpretation: by placing *avijjā* at the beginning of the chain the Buddha is exploiting the word's ambiguity, suggesting an identity between existing and being cognized.

Saṃkhārā

Now let us further examine the second link in the chain. The difficulty of translating *saṃkhāra* is notorious and several scholars have written about it at length.[19] The long *PED* article on it begins:

> one of the most difficult terms in Buddhist metaphysics, in which the blending of the subjective–objective view of the world and of happening, peculiar to the East, is so complete, that it is almost impossible for Occidental terminology to get at the root of its meaning in a translation. We can only convey an idea of its import by representing several sides of its application, without attempting to give a 'word' as a definite translation.

I have shown in Chapter 1 that there is nothing strange, let alone unique, about the impossibility of finding a word in our language to convey the precise meaning of a Buddhist term – even if that is what most people expect the hapless lexicographer to do! A meaning requires a context, and if that context contains presuppositions alien to us, it will need to be explained.

Etymologically, *saṃkhāra* comes from the common verbal root *kṛ*, to 'do' or 'make', and the prefix *sam*, roughly 'together'. So the word starts off looking as if it should mean something like 'put together', i.e., 'construct'. It tends to be used in the plural: *saṃkhārā*.

First, let me note that *saṃkhāra* is one of a class of words, abstract nouns based on verbs, which can refer either to a process or to the result of that process. We have many such words in English. For example, 'construction': 'The construction of Durham cathedral took a century' refers to the process; 'Durham cathedral is a magnificent Gothic construction' refers to the result. Notice that the word 'building' is another example, and could be substituted for 'construction' in both those sentences. 'Formation' is yet another example. Thus, even if it is uninformative, 'formation' may sometimes be a suitable translation for *saṃkhāra* because it can fit both when the word is being used to denote a process and when it is being used to refer to a result.

Thus, when the Buddha says on his deathbed that *saṃkhārā* (the plural) are impermanent (*anicca*), he could be saying either that the processes of construction are impermanent (i.e., ever-changing), or that the resulting constructions are impermanent. Or both!

In Chapter 1 I used the accepted translation by Rhys Davids: 'compounded things'. This translation suggests, I am sure correctly, that in the context the Buddha is referring primarily to himself, or rather to his body: that it has been constructed by a process, and therefore cannot be permanent. The argument is here implicit, though obvious: the proposition that what has been put together must sooner or later fall apart has been fundamental to the Buddha's teaching. Note, however, that the translation is misleading because it is too narrow; for it has equally been a part of the Buddha's teaching that everything in our experience – in fact, everything but nirvana – is a *saṃkhāra*.

In short, everything in our lives is a process or the result of a process, so necessarily impermanent. This is by now familiar to us: it was argued out at length in the previous chapter. However, that chapter taken on its own might elicit the objection: if the Buddha held that everything was process, why did he not say so straight out, rather than using a metaphor like fire? To that objection one might be tempted to reply: because he had no word available in his vocabulary which meant 'process'. But I think that would not have been quite accurate. I believe that *saṃkhāra* can mean 'process', but the problem is that it does not do so unambiguously, because it can also mean 'result of a process'.

The passage I have quoted above from the *PED* seems to me to frame a valid insight with a dated prejudice. It speaks of 'the blending of the subjective–objective view of the world', but seems to do so in terms of underlying stereotypes: the mysterious, mystical East and the presumably contrasted rational West. We have said enough of the 'Hymn of Creation', and the brahminical cosmology which can be traced back to it, to show that indeed it does blend the subjective and the objective, refusing to separate existence from consciousness; but this is a position peculiar to brahminism, not to the East as a whole!

Our concern here is to trace the relationship between the Vedic cosmogony and the Buddha's own metaphysics. Adhering to an *a priori* view that there must be an equivalence between macrocosm and microcosm, the brahmin cosmogony claimed to trace the origin of the world and man at one and the same time. The Buddha saw no need to bother about a world 'out there', so he reduced the equivalence of macrocosm and microcosm to a metaphor: the 'world' is our experience.

So what about *saṃkhārā*, processes in general? If he saw the world in these terms, why does the same word label just one of the five *khandhas*, the categories of process that make up our experiences? I hope that this book has by now said enough for the reader to anticipate the answer to this question. For the Buddha, the most important thing about living beings was their moral aspect, their karma. Though he says that by karma he means volition, in fact karma is both a process and the result of that process. It is, moreover, the most important of all processes, for it is the dynamic that moves us through our lives (infinite in number), and is what provides the principle of continuity and coherence throughout those lives. Thus, while all the five *khandhas* are processes, the karmic process – or set of processes – is the most important one: the most important pragmatically, because it does the most to affect our environment and to determine our futures, and the most important theoretically, because understanding the karmic process, conditioned but not random, will give us the only solid foundation for understanding how the world works and our responsibility in it.

THREE CORRECTIONS TO ACCEPTED VIEWS

1. Failure to understand the Chain of Dependent Origination – a failure which I attribute not so much to any obscurity as to forgetting its historical context – may be in large part to blame for many of the developments that the theory of causation underwent in Buddhist tradition. These began with typical scholastic efforts to read significance into every word. In the Pali *sutta*s there are two words for 'cause', *hetu* and *paccayo,* which are regularly used together. It is typical of the oral style of these texts to use two synonyms together. I don't suppose there is a single *sutta* which does not afford an instance of this stylistic feature. But the tradition tried to wrench more meaning out of the terms, making them refer to different kinds of causes and conditions. That interpretation is anachronistic.

2. Among the many interpretations offered by commentators both ancient and modern, some have tried to see the Chain of Dependent Origination as dealing with the macrocosm. I hope it is already clear that in my view that must be wrong. But it is quite possible that this line of thought preserves some memory of the fact that the Buddha was ironizing a doctrine that originally dealt principally with the macrocosm. Jurewicz's interpretation also makes it unnecessary to accept the complicated, indeed contorted, interpretation favoured by Buddhaghosa, that the chain covers three lives of the individual.

3. Our normal common-sense understanding of causation is that it applies through time, with cause preceding effect. Metaphorically, we would think of such causation as vertical. This is so even if there are many causes and/or many effects. However, an interpretation of causality arose in Buddhism which has it that things are also caused laterally, as it were, by other things which occur at the same time – or even at a future time. This interpretation is particularly strong in Far Eastern Buddhism: the Hua Yen school holds that all phenomena are interconnected.

I can find no trace of this doctrine in the Pali Canon. What the Buddha taught was that all the phenomena we experience – or, better, all our experiences except Enlightenment – are causally conditioned. In that particular sense they are not independent phenomena, i.e., they cannot occur without a context. One can perhaps push this a little further, and say that without a context the precise meaning of a phenomenon cannot be ascertained. I am after all following that epistemological principle in this book. But it by no means follows that all phenomena exert causal influence on each other.

Indeed, such an interpretation would subvert the Buddha's teaching of karma. The whole point of karma, as I have stressed from the outset, is that it teaches that all individuals are responsible for themselves. In the words of the Buddha, we are 'heirs of our own deeds'. If we were heirs of other people's deeds, the whole moral edifice would collapse.

Chapter 10

COGNITION; LANGUAGE; NIRVANA

We have seen in Chapter 5 that the Vedic tradition blended (from our perspective: confused) ontology, the question of what exists, with epistemology, the question of what we can know, and how. We have also seen there and in Chapter 8 that the Buddha argued against positing a category of 'being', and altogether substituted for the question 'What exists?' the question 'What can we experience?'

COGNITION[1]

Cognition, for the Buddha, begins with the exercise of the six faculties (*indriya*):[2] the normal five senses, plus the mind. Each faculty has its specific category of objects; the objects of the mind are called *dhamma*, which in this context include all ideas, including abstractions. For a sense to function in cognition, there must be synergy between the sense organ, e.g., the eye, its objects, in this case visible phenomena, and the specific functioning of consciousness (*viññāṇa*) which applies to that sense organ. The same is true of the sixth organ, the mind. This is a somewhat crude system: the differentiation between the mind and mental consciousness seems to us clumsy, whereas ranging the mind alongside the five senses rather than making it superordinate to them (as was done by Sāṃkhya and other later philosophical systems) seems simplistic.

Since for the Buddha cognition comes through using a sense organ, and never, say, from a divine source, some have called this a form of empiricism. I find this label questionable, given that one of the 'organs' is the mind. But it is true that when he wants to give an example of cognition, he tends to choose an external organ.

The first Noble Truth is that our experience is unsatisfactory, so it is not surprising to find that the general attitude towards the senses is negative. It is contact between senses and their objects which, by occasioning pleasure or pain, causes desire, positive or negative, the root of all our troubles. The need to 'guard the doors of the senses' may well be the theme which recurs most frequently in the Buddha's sermons.

In the common understanding, the Buddha analysed what we are into five sets of processes, the *khandhas*. While perhaps it goes too far to call this understanding wrong, it is misleading: the *khandhas* are not so much what we *are* as how we *work*, and in particular how we *cognize*. I repeat: epistemology, not ontology. Thus for cognition to take place requires a sense (in this context, one of the five) and its objects, which fall under the first *khandha, rūpa*; consciousness, the fifth *khandha*: then sensation, whether pleasant, unpleasant, or neutral. The fourth *khandha*, volitions, is inevitably involved because the Buddha held that the senses are appetitive: they seek out their objects. *Viññāṇa* likewise requires volition.[3] This leaves *saññā*, which I translate 'apperception'.

'Apperception' is identifying a perceived object by giving it a name. (In fact, 'name' is the basic meaning of the equivalent word in Sanskrit, *saṃjñā*.) Though there is some confusion in the Pali Canon between *saññā* and *viññāṇa*,[4] the settled Buddhist position becomes that *viññāṇa* just makes the perceiver aware that there is something there, while *saññā* then intervenes to identify what it is. Therefore *saññā* is the application of language to one's experience. This is, however, where the Buddha saw a big problem.

My exposition so far states that the Buddha regards the senses as dangerous because their operation easily leads to 'thirst'. This follows both what I have in Chapter 5 dubbed the 'emotionalist' analysis of our existential problem, and what (following Frauwallner) I have argued (in Chapter 9) to be the earliest form of the Chain of Dependent Origination. But there is also a more sophisticated way of looking at the matter, which follows the 'intellectualist' line and the analysis offered by the twelve-link Chain of Dependent Origination as it came to be understood. This line of argument is that the operation of the senses misleads us not only morally but also intellectually.

Noa Ronkin has explained this far better than I could, and I refer interested readers to her admirable book.[5] The *Brahma-jāla Sutta* discusses a long series of views which are one-sided, mostly because they espouse one of the extremes, eternalism or annihilationism. Near the end of it, the Buddha says: 'When, monks, a monk comprehends as they really are the arising and ceasing of the six contact-spheres, their appeal and peril, and the escape from them, he understands that which surpasses all these views.'[6] Ronkin goes on:

> The Buddha's insight reveals that the causal foundation for one's *saṃsāric* experience is the operation of one's cognitive apparatus. One's experience in its entirety arises from the cognitive process of making sense of the incoming sensory data. Basic to this process is the *khandha* of conceptualization and apperception, namely, *saññā* ... This identification process necessarily involves naming.[7]

THE BUDDHA'S VIEW OF LANGUAGE

The Vedic fusion between cognition and reality embraced language. In other words, to know a thing and to know its name were the same. The Sanskrit name of something is not a matter of convention or chance, but inherent, given by nature. The Sanskrit word for 'cow' and really being a cow were inseparable. The Sanskrit language is a blueprint for reality; things and the words denoting them were created together.[8] 'When the gods utter the names of things, at the time of the first sacrifice, these things come into existence (RV X, 71, 1; X, 82,3).'[9]

This leads easily into magic, since naming an object can be seen as a form of control over it. It also meant that it was believed that analysing words[10] could reveal truths about the objects they denoted – an idea which the Buddha made fun of.[11] The role of Sanskrit in brahmin ideology is in fact so fundamental that for the Buddha to reject it was no less fundamental to his own ideology.[12]

The Buddha said that his teaching should not be conveyed in what he called *chandas*.[13] This term may seem to us somewhat ambiguous, as in classical Sanskrit its commonest meaning is 'verse'. But the Buddha was certainly not forbidding his followers to compose verse, for it is widely used in the Pali Canon. His use of the term *chandas* must have been close to that of the great Sanskrit grammarian, Pāṇini, who probably lived one or two generations after him. By *chandas* Pāṇini means Vedic Sanskrit. Vedic texts were recited in a particular style, with pitch accents.[14] What the Buddha was prohibiting was evidently the use of an archaic, hieratic language which by custom was recited in a style that for most people was difficult or impossible to understand, thus inevitably drawing attention away from content to form.

The occasion for the Buddha's prohibiting the use of *chandas* was that two brahmin disciples of his had complained that monks of diverse origins were spoiling his words *sakāya niruttiyā*. The Buddha's response was to declare that he did permit monks to learn his teaching *sakāya niruttiyā*. The phrase *sakāya niruttiyā* has been the subject of seemingly endless debate. At the risk of slight over-simplification, let me explain that the word *nirutti* can mean either something like 'language, dialect' or something like 'gloss, explanation'. The adjective preceding it and agreeing with it, *sakāya*, means 'his own', but it is unclear whether it here refers to the Buddha or to the monk who is learning the Buddha's words. Buddhaghosa interprets the phrase to mean the language of Magadha as used by the Buddha – in other words, what we now call Pali; this is what we would expect, since Buddhaghosa was the great scholar who made Pali the sole authoritative medium of the entire Theravada tradition.[15] But most modern scholars do at least agree that Buddhaghosa is wrong here. It is much more natural grammatically to take the adjective 'his own' as referring to the pupil monks, not the Buddha. The main argument, however, must in my view be built on the evidence of other texts and what we know of Buddhist usage. The *Araṇi-vibhaṅga Sutta* (see below) shows that the Buddha allowed the use of local dialects (his experience was presumably of a range of dialects rather than languages); even more important, the first few centuries of Buddhist history clearly show that the Buddhists, in contrast to the brahmins, had no problem at all with translating their message into other languages. Is this not exactly what we would expect of the Buddha's Skill in Means?

My translation of the troublesome ruling is therefore, 'Monks, I permit the Buddha's words to be learnt using the learner's own mode of expression.' Inelegant but, I hope, clear. Since we know that monks did learn texts word by word,[16] 'their own mode of expression' would refer primarily to explanatory glosses or paraphrases given in their own dialects.

In the *Araṇi-vibhaṅga Sutta*[17] he gives a series of pieces of advice on how to avoid conflict by being moderate – often, indeed, by taking a middle way. He says that in various places people use a range of different terms for a dish or bowl. However, one should not insist on these terms, claiming that they alone are correct and rejecting the terms which are more widely understood.[18]

Thus, the Buddha's attitude to the use of language was pragmatic: his purpose was purely to convey meaning, and anything that might impede communication was to be discarded.

❧

Underlying the pragmatism, however, lay a theoretical issue: the Buddha's rejection of the fundamental attitude and ideology of brahminism. For the brahmins, each Sanskrit word is a kind of unchanging monolith, expressing its meaning throughout eternity and corresponding to a real entity, whether that entity happens to be manifested or not. Thus an expression like 'the king of France' (in Sanskrit) has, they hold, a meaning which is eternally fixed, whether there happens to be a king of France for it to refer to or not. There is a one-to-one correspondence between word and meaning. But for the Buddha such a correspondence is unthinkable. In practical terms, he may have arrived at this conclusion from his knowledge that there were countries where Sanskrit was unknown and it was not plausible to argue that their languages were just debased derivatives from it.[19]

The Buddha's view of language was, however, also basic to his metaphysics. If there are no unchanging entities but only processes, how can words have a fixed and determinate relationship to reality? All our apperceptions, he says, are empty (*suñña*).[20] This means that they are impermanent and unsatisfactory (*dukkha*), for we have seen that the qualities of being impermanent, unsatisfactory and devoid of an unchanging essence entail each other. In this context, the term 'empty' denotes this lack of an unchanging essence, applying it to everything, not just the living individual: it is the generalization to all phenomena of the 'no soul' principle.

To our familiar 'three hallmarks' we can now add another term: *saṃkhata*. This is intimately related to *saṃkhārā*, a term discussed at length in the last part of the previous chapter. In fact, *saṃkhata* is the past participle of the verb which gives us the noun *saṃkhārā*. So when the latter denotes a 'construction' or 'formation' in the sense of the *result* of a process of constructing or forming, it is synonymous with calling that thing *saṃkhata*. The Buddha says that every apperception is *saṃkhata*;[21] and this means that it must be impermanent and ultimately unsatisfactory. Note that what is being said is that these qualities apply both to the act of apperception, the naming process, and to what is being apperceived: both to what we conceptualize as being 'out there', and also to what is 'out there'. On the other hand, it does not say that there is nothing 'out there' at all![22]

There is one thing – if 'thing' is the right word for it! – to which none of this applies: that is nirvana. This will be explained at the end of this chapter.

To sum up: the Buddha concluded not merely that languages were conventional, but that it was inherently impossible for any language fully to capture reality. We have to express our cognitions through language, using *saññā,* but that imposes on experience linguistic categories which cannot do justice to its fluidity – whether we consider experience subjectively, or prefer to think in objective terms of 'the world as experienced'.

Ronkin writes:

> The Buddha ... unveils not only the dominance of language and conceptual thought, but also their inherent ... inadequacy. Although language is a constant feature of our experience, we are normally unaware of the paradox in the cognitive process: to become knowable all the incoming sensory data must be verbally differentiated, but as such they are mere constructions, mental formations; nothing justifies their reliability because they could equally have been constructed otherwise, in accordance with other conventional guidelines ... He points towards conventionalism in language and undermines the misleading character of nouns as substance-words. What we can know is part of the activity of language, but language, by its very nature, undermines certified knowledge.[23]

(I should add that this refers to cataphatic knowledge – see below.)

For all the differences between them, I cannot help being struck by the coincidence between Karl Popper's view (which I espoused in Chapter 7) that we can advance in knowledge and understanding of the world but never reach certainty, with the Buddha's view here expounded.

The very act of conceptualizing, the Buddha held, thus involves some inaccuracy. His term for this was *papañca.* Here again we have a term over which scholars have spilt much ink, without reaching a consensus even about how to translate it.[24] Noa Ronkin suggests 'verbal differentiation' or 'verbal proliferation', and I hope that what I have written above clarifies what that refers to. Neither term, however, conveys in English the message that what is wrong with *papañca* is that it is false. After all, one can verbally differentiate 'dog' into many kinds of dog, and it is not obvious what would be wrong with doing so. Therefore it may be worth reflecting what lies behind the term; but as the discussion cannot avoid being technical, I consign it to the Appendix.

CATAPHATIC AND APOPHATIC

I discussed in Chapter 5 how the Buddha responded to the Vedāntic teaching that one had to realize that one was ultimately nothing but being, consciousness and bliss. Some of it he accepted, more he rejected. However, I think the most decisive influence on him was exerted by what one may say lies behind that formulation, the experience which transcends language and can only be referred to by negation. It is at this point that the view taken of language becomes crucial.

All the major religions of the world have some form of mystical tradition, and hence all know the distinction between what Christian philosophers call cataphatic and apophatic expression.[25] Cataphatic means speaking positively, saying what something is; apophatic, the opposite, is speaking only negatively, trying to express something by saying what it is not.

I surmise that the earliest piece of apophatic theology on record is the statement in the *BĀU* that the *ātman* is 'not thus, not thus'. As I have mentioned in Chapter 5, this occurs in the text three times. Two of the passages are identical. The other one enlarges on it slightly by adding, 'For there exists nothing else beyond this "not thus".' This passage finally adds something positive: 'Then its name is the real of the real, for the vital functions are the real, and this is their reality.'[26] The word I have translated as both 'real' and 'reality' is *satyam,* which one could also translate 'truth' (on this, more below).

There is a famous verse in the *Taittirīya Upaniṣad*:[27]

> Before they reach it, words turn back,
> together with the mind;
> One who knows that bliss of *brahman*,
> he is never afraid.

This describes the salvific experience according to the *Vedānta*, in which the individual self is felt to merge into *brahman*. It is not, I think, well known that there is a short poem in the Pali Canon (*SN* I, 15) which begins by asking 'From what do words turn back?' The answer (by implication) is *nibbāna*. This has probably been overlooked because the tradition has misinterpreted the question. The Pali word here used for 'words' is *sarā* (from Sanskrit *svara*); but the commentator seems to have interpreted it as a homonym which means 'streams' and assumed a reference to another metaphor, that of rivers merging into the ocean (see *Muṇḍaka Upaniṣad* 3.2.8).

Exegetes do not like an apophatic description: it gives them nothing to get their teeth into. But the Buddha certainly did. According to the Pali canonical texts, after his Enlightenment he always referred to himself as *Tathāgata*. This word, the same in Sanskrit and Pali, is a compound with two parts: *tathā*, which means 'thus', and *gata*, which commonly means 'gone'. The whole word is often translated into English as 'Thus-gone'. The Buddhist tradition has made various attempts to etymologize the term, attempts which I regard as fanciful. The word *gata* when it occurs as the second member of a compound of this type often loses its primary meaning and means simply 'being'. For example, *citra-gatā nārī* is not 'the woman who has gone into the picture' but simply 'the woman in the picture'.[28] So the Buddha is referring to himself as 'the one who is like that'. This is tantamount to saying that there are no words to describe his state; he can only point to it. Moreover, though the epithet *Tathāgata* most commonly refers to a Buddha, and in later texts does so exclusively, in the Pali Canon it can refer to any enlightened person (*MN* I, 140). Similarly, the epithet *tādi*, derived from Sanskrit *tādṛś*, also originally meant just 'such' or 'like that', though the commentators read other meanings into it. This word too could in the Pali texts be applied to any enlightened person (*Thg*. 68). (The word *tādi* had a colourful history, for through phonetic change it was reconstituted, or should I say reinterpreted, in the Sanskrit of Mahayana Buddhists as *trāyin*, 'saving', and so became an epithet of Buddhas and Bodhisattvas, denoting their compassion.)

INEFFABILITY

The fact that the Buddhist tradition lost the original meanings of *tathāgata* and *tādi* bears witness to the anti-mystical (or at least non-mystical) stance of that tradition. The Buddha felt the quality of his salvific experience, his Enlightenment, to be ineffable. He could not describe the quality of his experience because it was a unique private experience with no publicly available referent. This, however, in no way implies either that the truths he discovered were inexpressible, or that he was unable to direct others towards a similar experience.

William James considered ineffability to be the leading characteristic of mystical experience. He wrote:

> The handiest of the marks by which I classify a state of mind as mystical is negative. The subject of it immediately says that it defies expression, that no adequate report of its contents can be given in words. It follows from this that its quality must be directly experienced; it cannot be imparted or transferred to others. In this peculiarity mystical states are more like states of feeling than like states of intellect. No one can make clear to another who has never had a certain feeling, in what the quality or worth of it consists. One must have musical ears to know the value of a symphony; one must have been in love one's self to understand a lover's state of mind. Lacking the heart or ear, we cannot interpret the musician or the lover justly, and are even likely to consider him weak-minded or absurd. The mystic finds that most of us accord to his experiences an equally incompetent treatment.[29]

I surmise that in the days immediately following his Enlightenment the Buddha had a real problem about explaining himself, a problem somewhat different from that recorded in texts by people who had little or no understanding of what we call mystical experience. The problem was that his experience transcended language and he was initially daunted by the consequent impossibility of conveying it to others. As we all know, he found his way out of this difficulty and became a great teacher. But the ultimate inadequacy of language for such purposes left its mark on Buddhism and explains some of its features.

When one wants to convey an experience which eludes denotative language, it is natural to resort to metaphor. This the Buddha was constantly doing. All the terms for the supreme good which he had found and was making available to others are obvious metaphors. Indeed, the use of metaphor and analogy is perhaps even more characteristic of his preaching than the use of the parable is for Jesus. I would even go so far as to surmise that this would be a good (though, of course, not absolute) criterion for determining whether or not a *sutta* goes back to the Buddha himself: if the message is conveyed by an analogy, there is a good chance that it is authentic.

PRACTICAL LIMITATIONS OF THE APOPHATIC APPROACH

The tension between the apophatic and the cataphatic is found in the apparent inconsistency between the texts in which the Buddha says that he has no views and those, rather more numerous, in which he refers to 'right views'. I believe that these refer to different aspects of his experience and teachings. Under the impact of his Enlightenment, and indeed of the brahminical tradition which contributed to his making sense of that experience, he felt he had attained to a reality beyond language. Within the Pali Canon, the apophatic strand is particularly notable in the last two books of the *Sutta-nipāta*. But this is a subtle matter. For example, verse 798 is generally taken to be utterly apophatic: Rahula translates its first half as: 'To be attached to one thing (to a certain view) and to look down upon other things (views) as inferior – this the wise men call a fetter.'[30] But I have shown[31] that the previous verse, 797, should be translated: 'Should one see benefit in seeing, hearing or thinking of the *ātman*, or in external observances, clinging there to that alone, one regards all else as inferior.' In this compressed verse the target is specifically the teaching of Yājñavalkya, both his teaching and his adherence to ritual. So under the guise of saying that one should not depend on what is seen, heard or thought – which would be to agree with Yājñavalkya's apophatic teaching – the Buddha is actually attacking him, in other words, attacking the central Upaniṣadic doctrine.

On the other hand, he had also come to understand certain things which he felt to be true, and indeed of fundamental importance. I have shown in Chapter 2 that the doctrine of karma was the first and foremost of these truths, and that is why the Noble Eightfold Path begins with 'right view', which refers specifically to accepting the teaching of karma, the moral law of the universe.

It was in a somewhat similar spirit that the Buddha listed a dozen frequently asked questions which he refused to answer. True, the reason that he gave for refusing to answer them was that they were of no relevance to the quest for Enlightenment: that people should not waste their time on idle speculation. Thus the list of unanswered questions bears testimony in the first instance to the Buddha's pragmatism. On the other hand, the list does include such questions as whether a *tathāgata* exists after death. Ninian Smart was, I think, correct to say that the Buddha rejected these questions also because their formulation was misleading; but in some cases the formulation is misleading precisely because any linguistic formulation would be misleading, since the truth lies beyond language.[32]

The apophatic/cataphatic distinction also helps one to make sense of the later doctrine of the two truths. In the generations following the Buddha's life, his followers were extremely assiduous in spelling out the results of analysing phenomena in accordance with some of the Buddha's insights. They took these insights in a completely literal sense, so that they acquired a reductionist character. To take the best-known and most important example: they held that the Buddha analysed the individual being into five components: physical, sensations as of pleasure and pain, apperceptions, volitions and consciousness. Accordingly, the statement 'John has left the room', if true in a normal sense, was true only conventionally, because it was an agreed convention that a particular set of the five components passed by the name of John. Ultimately, argued the *Abhidhamma*, what had left the room was this set of five components. Thus there were two levels of truth, the conventional and the ultimate. The great philosopher Nāgārjuna used the same two terms but in a different way. He realized that by giving a more analytic description of what we normally called John nothing much had been achieved: the really important difference lay between that which language was adequate to express and that which it was not. Ultimate reality for Nāgārjuna – as for the *Upaniṣads*, and indeed for all mystics – lay beyond the limits of language. Nāgārjuna could link this view to some of the Buddha's statements recorded in the Canon. Thus his 'ultimate truth' simply continues the Buddhist apophatic tradition, while his 'conventional truth' remains in the cataphatic tradition. Throughout its history, on the other hand, the Theravada has remained overwhelmingly cataphatic.

NIRVANA

I trust that by now I have explained enough about the Buddha's thought to indicate his ideas on nirvana. I find that when I teach a course on Buddhism to newcomers, 'What is nirvana?' is the commonest question to come up in the first meeting. It is easy to explain the metaphor, and say that it is completely getting rid of passion, hatred and confusion; that will do for a temporary answer. But the fuller answer, that it is defined by being the precise opposite of everything in our normal experience, obviously demands patience: the class have to learn how the Buddha sees that normal experience.

We must go back to the beginning, and recall that for the Buddha, 'to exist' means to exist without changing; being and becoming are opposites. Our world is what we experience, and it is a world of change, of becoming, of process. It is constructed, composed (*saṃkhata*), by our cognizing apparatus. There is, however, just one thing that is not composed but does exist in its own right, and that is nirvana. That does not just 'appear': it *is*. Nirvana is the one *dhamma* that does not arise from causes and is therefore not covered by the famous verse on causality presented at the beginning of Chapter 9.

RAHULA'S LACK OF CLARITY

My general principle in writing this book has been to put forward my views without explicitly arguing against scholars with whom I disagree. I do not think that most readers would wish to have the book lengthened by such argument. Here, however, I must make a brief exception. The very title of this book pays homage to the famous book by the Ven. Dr Walpola Rahula, *What the Buddha Taught*. Over the years I have come to think that that book might be more appropriately entitled *What Buddhaghosa Taught*, but this scarcely diminishes my admiration for the cogency, economy and beautiful clarity of the text. But there is one point where the great scholar monk has let us down: his account of nirvana, in Chapter IV, is unclear and, to my mind, even at points self-contradictory.

The *Upaniṣads* do not differentiate between ontology and epistemology. This means that they make no difference between between reality and truth. But for us, reality is a property of things, whereas truth is a property of propositions.

Rahula writes:

> It is incorrect to think that Nirvāṇa is the natural result of the extinction of craving. Nirvāṇa is not the result of anything. If it would be a result, then it would be an effect produced by a cause. It would be *saṃkhata* 'produced' and 'conditioned'. Nirvāṇa is neither cause nor effect. It is beyond cause and effect. Truth is not a result nor an effect. It is not produced like a mystic, spiritual, mental state, such as *dhyāna* or *samādhi.* TRUTH IS. NIRVĀṆA IS. The only thing you can do is to see it, to realize it. But Nirvāṇa is not the result of this path. You may get to the mountain along a path, but the mountain is not the result, not an effect of the path. You may see a light, but the light is not the result of your eyesight.[33]

Let me try to sort this out. We need to make a distinction between the experience of realizing something and the thing realized. When I come to understand something, my understanding is indeed the result of a process, maybe of considerable effort, but the thing understood is not: it was there all along. So when Rahula says: 'There is a path leading to the realization of Nirvāṇa. But Nirvāṇa is not the result of this path,' he may sound paradoxical and hence profound, but in fact the matter is simple. Being given the wrong change in the supermarket and realizing that I have been given the wrong change are perfectly easy to distinguish. In all the early Buddhist traditions, attaining nirvana is achieved only after a vast amount of persistent effort, often extending over many lives.

In proclaiming (in block capitals) that 'Truth is', Rahula has for a moment fallen into Upaniṣadic mode. Since truth can only be a property of propositions, which have subjects and predicates, and nirvana is not a proposition, it makes no sense in English to say that nirvana is truth. The confusion arises, perhaps, because the Sanskrit word *satyam* and the corresponding Pali word *saccaṃ* can indeed mean either 'truth' or 'reality'. But in our language this will not work.

It may be helpful to go back to the formulation of Charles Malamoud: to identify one's *ātman* with *brahman* is 'at the same time the truth to be discovered and the end to be attained'.[34] This, of course, describes salvation according to the *Vedānta*. But it pinpoints a crucial ambiguity in talking about a salvific gnosis: is the act of realizing it the same as the content of what is realized? From the point of view of the person who has that experience, the answer might seem to be 'Yes'. But from the point of view of the observer, the analyst, that will bring confusion. For even if the subject of the experience can describe what he has realized only negatively, he can say positively that he did realize it.

Thus we need to clarify a further distinction: between having an experience (in the present) and having had it (in the past). Enlightened monks and nuns have left us poems in the Pali Canon in which they describe their condition in positive language. They are, however, talking about what it feels like to have attained nirvana, not what it feels like to attain it.[35] The moment of attaining it, if it resembles a wide range of mystical experiences which have been testified to the world over, is beyond words; but those who have such experiences go on living. (The testimony of those who do not is inaccessible to us.) I am not now referring to the way in which they try to give linguistic expression to the crucial experience itself. They may also talk about what it now feels like to have had that experience. It may be impossible to find adequate words to express what it feels like to win the marathon at the Olympic Games; but saying, at some later time, what it feels like to be the person who once won that race is surely quite different and far easier.

Though William James writes (surely correctly) that mystical experiences are feelings rather than thoughts ('states of intellect'), he refers to their 'noetic quality'; by this he means that 'mystical states seem to those who experience them to be also states of knowledge. They are states of insight into depths of truth unplumbed by the discursive intellect', 'and as a rule they carry with them a curious sense of authority for after-time.'[36] Though they are felt to be states of knowledge, it follows from their ineffability that what is known cannot be articulated in words. I suggest that on this last point the Buddha might have disagreed with James, if James meant that in this respect the mystical experience was unlike any other.

WAYS OF USING THE TERM 'NIRVANA'

Let me now put my distinctions to work:

1. To experience salvation, according to the Buddha, was an experience beyond words. In this the Buddha stood in what seems to be a worldwide tradition of mystical experience, but he also more particularly was following in the footsteps of the *Upaniṣads*. One should add, however, that for the Buddha there was nothing so special about this, since language is never capable of fully capturing experience. However, the experiencing of Enlightenment is felt to be totally unlike any other experience. Nevertheless, indications are communicated through metaphors. For example, the experience is compared to waking up, or to feeling that the fires of passion, hatred and confusion, with which one had been burning, have gone out.

2. After experiencing Enlightenment, one can say what one feels like. It seems to be common in India's hot climate to talk of feeling cool and comfortable. As mentioned in Chapter 8, a chance phonetic similarity has associated a particular word for 'blissful', P: *nibbuta,* with nirvana. The Buddha apparently considered the experience of Enlightenment to be irreversible and unforgettable.

3. While having the initial experience of Enlightenment, one is in no condition to describe it; that one can only try to do afterwards. On the other hand, before having the experience one will probably be familiar with the accounts of others, and know much what to expect. Therefore despite the fact that dividing the subjective from the objective aspects of the initial experience may be fatuous from the viewpoint of the experiencer, and although there is certainly nothing objective in the sense of being open to public inspection, a tradition may – and in this case certainly does – have plenty to say about the content. As William James has said, one does

feel that what one experiences has an objective content, even though that too is beyond words. Enlightenment is commonly referred to by the Buddha as 'seeing things as they are' (*yathā-bhūta-dassana*). Beyond that, language can again only be indicative, but in this case it can be profuse, for it can say a lot about all other, normal, experience, as indeed the Buddha did, and then say that what the enlightened person experiences – realizes – is the opposite.

The last distinction I must refer to is one made within Buddhism itself. The nirvana discussed so far is Enlightenment, but the term also refers to the death of an enlightened person.[37] Since it is central to Buddhism that the enlightened person will not be reborn, and since there can obviously be no reports from enlightened people describing their deaths, it is here that the apophatic tradition meets no competition.[38]

❧

Nāgārjuna has caused much confusion by stating that there is no difference between *saṃsāra* and *nirvāṇa*. I am no expert on Nāgārjuna, but he was a Buddhist monk and one may presume that he too was striving for Enlightenment; moreover, he saw himself as merely elucidating the Buddha's meaning. I therefore surmise that he meant the same as did the Buddha in the Pali Canon: 'There is, monks, an unborn, unbecome, unmade, uncompounded; if there were not, there would be known no escape here from the born, become, made, compounded.'[39] In other words, the two concepts of *saṃsāra* and *nirvāṇa* are a complementary pair which make sense only in terms of each other, like left and right, or positive and negative. In this sense we could say – even though it might be confusing to do so – that even the conditioned and the unconditioned condition each other; in other words, the concept 'unconditioned' is unintelligible unless we know what is meant by 'conditioned'.[40] Thus the only way for someone who has not had the experience of nirvana to understand what it is about is to understand just what it is not.

NEITHER EXISTING NOR NOT EXISTING

I close this chapter by trying to dispose of another confusion. Building on some of Nāgārjuna's apparent paradoxes, there is a Buddhist tradition, which started in China, that the Buddha taught a middle way between being and non-being. The origin of this strange doctrine is not difficult to explain. In the *Kaccāyana-gotto Sutta* in the *Saṃyutta Nikāya*[41] the Buddha says that he preaches neither *sabbaṃ atthi* 'everything exists' nor *sabbaṃ natthi* 'nothing exists'. What he preaches is the middle way between these two extremes: Dependent Origination; this is the right view (*sammā diṭṭhi*). Surely the last three chapters have made this idea thoroughly familiar to us. It is presupposed that existence is defined as unchanging existence, which is conceived of as the opposite of change or process. The Buddha is simply reiterating that everything in our world, i.e., in our experience, is process, and causally conditioned process at that. By ignoring both the immediate context of this statement and the broader context of the Buddha's teaching, this perfectly rational proposition has been turned into a charter for far-reaching irrationality and a belief that Buddhism flouts the normal rules of logic. Whether or not this is good religion, it is certainly bad history.

Chapter 11

THE BUDDHA'S PRAGMATISM AND INTELLECTUAL STYLE

TO WHAT EXTENT AND IN WHAT SENSE WAS THE BUDDHA A PRAGMATIST?

Again and again the Buddha emphasized that his goal as a teacher was entirely pragmatic. His followers came to know him as the great physician; the *Dhamma* was the medicine he prescribed, the *Saṅgha* were the nurses whose calling it was to administer that medicine. Though there is no canonical evidence for this interpretation, modern scholars have plausibly argued that the formulation of the Four Noble Truths follows the medical idiom of the time: first the disease is diagnosed, then its origin or cause is established, then it is accordingly stated what a cure would consist of, and finally the treatment to achieve that cure is prescribed. The Buddha described himself as the surgeon who removes the arrow of craving.[1]

His teaching was thus a prescription for action. In the brahminical tradition, the word *dharma* indicates what at the same time is the case and should be the case; the usage is much like that of the words 'nature' and 'natural' in English, when we say, for example, that it is natural for parents to love their children and unnatural to abuse them. The Pali word *dhamma* has a similar prescriptive force. Indeed, in a monastic context it can simply mean 'rule'. When the word refers to his teaching in general, however, the Buddha's *Dhamma both describes* the way that things are, *and* at the same time *prescribes* that we see it that way and act accordingly.[2]

The Buddha was a pragmatist as we use the term idiomatically, but not in the modern technically philosophical sense. This means that, as Paul Williams has written,

> There is no suggestion that [the teaching] is only 'pragmatically true', i.e., [that] it is only a question of it being beneficial in the context of the spiritual path .... The teachings of the Buddha are held by the Buddhist tradition to *work* because they are factually *true* (not true because they work).

Further:

> The 'ought' (pragmatic benefit) is never cut adrift from the 'is' (cognitive factual truth). Otherwise it would follow that the Buddha might be able to benefit beings (and thus bring them to enlightenment) even without seeing things the way they really are at all. And that is not Buddhism.[3]

The Buddha said that just as the ocean has only one flavour, that of salt, his teaching had only one flavour, that of liberation.[4] While the comparison strikes us as a natural one to make, the Buddha and his audiences lived very far from the ocean. It is possible that he was inspired by the *Chāndogya Upaniṣad*, which at 6.10 compares the way that rivers merge into the ocean with the way that all creatures merge into being, which at the same time is the truth and the Self, and then at 6.13 compares how when a lump of salt has been dissolved in water the water is permeated with its taste to how the truth, the Self, permeates the world.

Thus I believe that the Buddha would have entirely approved of what Paul Williams has written:

> [W]henever you come across something new, or perhaps even strange, in the study of Buddhism, ask yourself ... 'How might a Buddhist holding or practising that consider that doing so leads to the diminution or eradication of negative mental states, and the increasing or fulfilment of positive mental states?'[5]

This explains why, when we look at the body of texts in the Pali Canon of which the content can plausibly be ascribed to the Buddha himself – I refer mainly to the main parts of the *Vinaya Piṭaka* and the bulk of the four *Nikāya*s of the *Sutta Piṭaka* – we find that the *Vinaya* is about how monks and nuns are to live and the *Sutta Piṭaka* about how people can and should advance towards attaining nirvana. The latter is expressed in terms of ethics and meditation. Very little is said about the ideas that underpin all this advice; and this of course is why the content of this book is so different from the treatment of the Buddha to be found in most introductions to Buddhism. What the Buddha thought, in the sense of his underlying ideas, has largely to be teased out of the material.[6] He is reported in the Canon[7] to have said that what he has explained compared to what he has not is like a handful of leaves compared to a whole forest. He has explained only the Four Noble Truths, but could have explained so much more!

WAS THE BUDDHA OMNISCIENT?

In the *Tevijja-vacchagotta Sutta* the Buddha is asked whether at all times, both asleep and awake, he has complete knowledge and vision. The Buddha says no: what he has is the threefold knowledge. This threefold knowledge, as we know from many texts, is the recollection of his former births, the power to see how all beings are reborn according to their karma, and his destruction of the corruptions (*āsava*), which means that he is liberated.[8] Though we may read this as a denial of omniscience – which is what we would today expect of a great rational intellect – that is not the interpretation accepted by any Buddhist tradition of which I am aware. 'According to the Theravāda exegetical tradition the Buddha is omniscient in the sense that all knowable things are potentially accessible to him. He cannot, however, know everything simultaneously and must advert to whatever he wishes to know.'[9]

It seems to me that the Pali Canon allows one to reach different conclusions on this point. The last part of this chapter will show that in the context of the *Vinaya* the Buddha is plainly not displayed as omniscient, and to claim that he was just pretending not to know things is special pleading which we cannot find plausible, as mentioned late in Chapter 7. At the other extreme stands, for instance, the *Mahā Sīhanāda Sutta.*[10] At the beginning of this text the Buddha hears that someone is spreading the word that he teaches a doctrine for the extinction of suffering, and it does indeed do the job, but that he has worked out that doctrine by his own powers of reasoning and has had no insight beyond the human norm. At first blush it might appear to us that the Buddha would be quite content to be described in these terms. But it turns out that the Buddha takes strong objection to the allegation that he has had no insight beyond the human norm, and proceeds to list a whole string of his extraordinary powers, which make one think of much later Buddhology.

I hope to write on this elsewhere and to show that this text cannot reflect the Buddha's own words, but must reflect disagreement among his followers about whether he could be regarded as a real human being. He claimed, we have seen, that he could remember all his former births and see the rebirths of all other creatures. But these abilities were an inherent part of becoming enlightened; in other words, all enlightened people, all *arahant*s, had them too. From the Buddhist perspective the interesting question is therefore whether and to what extent the Buddha regarded himself as superior to other enlightened beings – taking for granted the distinction that he had had to find the way for himself, whereas his disciples had had the easier task of following his guidance.

In sum: his followers regard the Buddha as omniscient, and we do not: but what did he think? I suggest that yet again it is best to look at the question pragmatically. Just as we probably cannot know whether he really believed in such beings as gods and other spirits, we cannot know whether he thought he could know anything he wanted to; but he would have found it a silly question, because all that concerned him was whether he knew what was relevant to attaining nirvana.

I have discussed the Buddha's attitude to philosophy, i.e., to theorizing, at the beginning of Chapter 2 of *How Buddhism Began*, and so shall not repeat what is there. But on one important matter I have changed my opinion. I opened my discussion by writing: 'One thing about which I feel rather uncertain is how interested the Buddha himself was in presenting a philosophically coherent doctrine. ... [A]re we misrepresenting him if we attribute to him an impressive edifice of argument?' After some more work and some more thought (and how I wish it could have been even more!) I no longer feel uncertain. On the one hand, I do not think the Buddha was interested in *presenting* a philosophically coherent doctrine: the evidence that his concern was pragmatic, to guide his audience's actions, is overwhelming. On the other hand, I have also concluded that the evidence that he had evolved such a structure of thought and that it underpinned his pragmatic advice is no less compelling.

THE BUDDHA'S STYLE OF EXPOSITION

I have referred already to some important facets of the Buddha's pragmatic attitude. His Skill in Means, the brilliant technique by which he adapted the language of his message to his audience of the moment, is a prime example. This is one reason why his attitude to language was so down to earth: for him, it was just a means of communication. Though he was extremely skilful in reducing an opponent in debate to incoherence by asking clever questions, rather like Socrates, the great majority of texts do show him putting forward a view of his own, and his favourite style of exposition was by analogy, with appeals to common sense. 'My teaching is like a raft. So how would you treat a raft? Then treat my teaching the same.' 'My words are like a snake: if you grasp them in the wrong way they can harm you, just as a snake may bite you if you hold it by the tail; but if you grasp them correctly, like holding a snake behind the head, you will be all right.' The sermons are chock-full of analogies, similes and metaphors. Indeed, what else would one expect of a thinker who had concluded that language could give pointers, but could not by its nature give exact expression to the truth about reality?

Too little, perhaps, has been said about this aspect of the Buddha. It is hard to exaggerate how amazingly different the *suttas* are from most early Indian religious texts. (And it is hardly less amazing that their distinctive character has survived the adulation that followed their composition.) The style of the bulk of Vedic literature is declaratory; statements ascribed to gods or to primeval sages are made *ex cathedra*, and there is hardly a trace of an audience or a context. This remains the style until the early *Upaniṣads*. Here styles begin to vary: there are a couple of formal debates, including a few rebuttals of opponents' arguments, and a few charming passages give us glimpses of some rather eccentric teachers of wisdom. But soon a didactic solemnity returns as the norm, and remains dominant for centuries.

Indeed, to appreciate the Buddha's personal style in the Pali Canon, one could hardly do better than compare it with the Mahayana *sūtras* composed by his followers a few centuries later. In such texts as the *Lotus Sutra* the Buddha appears in glory, with a vast entourage, and speaks literally *ex cathedra*, for he is enthroned – with all that that implies. The tone is not merely authoritarian, but sometimes even strident.

THE SPIRIT IN WHICH THE BUDDHA WISHED HIS TEACHING TO BE TAKEN

Let us look at ways in which the Buddha approached his own teaching activity – I suppose one could call them meta-teachings. Perhaps the most famous and important of all, the *Kālāma Sutta*, has already been presented in Chapter 1; there the Buddha tells his audience not to take his words on trust but to test their validity on the touchstone of their own experience.

❧

There is a well-known Sanskrit proverb that one should not speak unless what one says is both true and pleasant. The Buddha changed this principle: questioned by a prince called Abhaya, he said that he would only speak what he knew to be true and beneficial, and knew the time to say it even if it was disagreeable. Typically, he justified this by pointing to a baby on the prince's lap and asking the prince what he would do if the baby put a stick or pebble in its mouth; the prince agreed he would take it out even if doing so hurt the baby. (Indeed, every *vinaya* rule is prefaced by an incident in which a monk or nun does something for which the Buddha finds it necessary to admonish them before laying down the rule to prevent the same thing happening again.) On the other hand, he assures the prince that he will not say anything which is true and agreeable, but not beneficial.[11]

The result of this self-denying ordinance was that the Buddha condemned all theorizing which had no practical value. Whether we like it or not, he tended to be quite harsh on those who indulged in metaphysical speculation. In the Pali tradition, the very first *sutta* in the entire collection of his sermons is the *Brahma-jāla Sutta*, which spends many pages listing the kinds of speculation that people indulge in concerning both the world and the self, and then saying that the Buddha has himself realized their seductive power and made his escape from them. This is so despite the fact that in these long lists of ideological positions there are a couple which do in fact seem to correspond to the Buddha's own views. The point is, however, that they are not the kind of thing that he thinks it beneficial to talk about, let alone to insist on.

By contrast, it is significant that many sermons are devoted to analyses of how we experience the world – what we would call cognitive psychology.

The Buddha's position on these matters is succinctly stated in his famous reply to Māluṅkyāputta. The latter was a monk who came to the Buddha saying that he felt he would have to give up his robes unless the Buddha could give him answers to the following questions: whether the world was eternal; whether it was finite; whether the soul was the same as the body or different; whether a *tathāgata* exists after death, does not exist, both exists and does not exist, or neither exists nor does not exist. The Buddha replies that he had never promised to answer these questions. Māluṅkyāputta was like a man wounded by a poison arrow who refused to let the surgeon remove it until he knew the surgeon's caste and many other personal details about him, as well as other irrelevant information about the arrow. Just as that man would die before the information could be provided, so would die the person who was waiting for the Buddha to explain these matters. 'So,' says the Buddha, 'remember what I have left unexplained as unexplained and remember what I have explained as explained ... Why have I left [your questions] unexplained? Because they are of no benefit and do not lead to nirvana. What I have explained is the Four Noble Truths, because they are beneficial and lead to nirvana.'[12]

One cannot help wondering what the Buddha would have made of the history of Buddhist philosophy. It is indeed a fine example of how actions have unintended consequences.[13]

In my opinion the Buddha objects to the 'unanswered questions' on two levels. It is not merely that 'liberation simply does not require an answer to these questions',[14] so that they waste valuable time. Some of the questions are also objectionable because they are couched in misleading terms: they could not be answered yes or no until one had at least explained how one was using the terms involved, such as 'world' and 'life' (see also p. 154 above).

Indeed, it is a feature of the Buddha's teaching that he often shows that a question is wrongly put, because it is based on false premises, or at least does not admit of a simple answer in terms of yes or no. For example, in the text quoted above prince Abhaya has tried to trap the Buddha (allegedly at the suggestion of the Jain leader Mahāvīra) by asking him whether he would ever say something disagreeable, and the Buddha's first response is that the question cannot be answered unequivocally (*ekaṃsena*).[15] This, we have seen, turns out to be because he would do so if it were both true and beneficial.

On another occasion,[16] saying again that he cannot answer a question unequivocally,[17] he says that he argues after making distinctions. The term he uses is *vibhajja-vādo*. As Bhikkhu Bodhi points out, in later doxology this term designated the Theravādins, being taken to refer to their analysing things into their constituents – the reductionist programme of the *abhidhamma*. But its original meaning here is that 'the Buddha distinguishes the different implications of a question'.[18]

Such cases have also contributed to the tradition that the Buddha takes 'the middle way'. He is said to have taught 'the middle way' between eternalism, the view that the self lasts for ever, and annihilationism, the view that it comes to an end. The 'middle way' here is, of course, that both are wrong because the question has been based on the false premise that the soul exists in the first place. Here I find the term 'middle way' misleading, but it is used in the Buddhist tradition.

Altogether, the Buddha had a pragmatic attitude to answering questions. He said that some should be answered unequivocally, some by analysing the question, some by asking a counter-question, and some be put aside.[19]

> The Buddha was not a computing machine giving answers to whatever questions were put to him by anyone ... he was a practical teacher full of compassion and wisdom. He did not answer questions to show his knowledge and intelligence, but to help the questioner on the way to realisation.[20]

The famous simile in which the Buddha compares his teaching to a raft is imbued with the same spirit. He is simply stating that his teachings have a particular purpose, to guide people towards nirvana, and once that purpose has been achieved there is no point at all in clinging to his 'particular verbal formulations'.[21]

It is also consistent with his view of language – and no doubt with his experience as a teacher! – that the Buddha shows a lively awareness of the dangers of literalism. In a tantalizingly short text,[22] he classifies people who hear his teachings into four types.[23] As commonly, the list is hierarchic, the best type being listed first. The first type (*ugghaṭita-ññu*) understands the teaching as soon as it is uttered; the second (*vipacita-ññu*)[24] understands on mature reflection; the third (*neyya*) is 'educable': he understands it when he has worked at it, thought about it and cultivated wise friends. The fourth is called *pada-parama*, 'putting the words first'; he is defined as one who, though he hears much, preaches much, remembers much and recites much, does not come within this life to understand the teaching. One could hardly ask for a clearer condemnation of literalism, of elevating form above content.[25]

❧

Let me now consider the Buddha's pragmatism in relation to ethics, meditation and the monastic rules.

ETHICAL PRAGMATISM

There is a strongly pragmatic flavour to the Buddha's ethics. The very fact that his karma doctrine propounded universal values and principles did not merely represent a great step forward in rationality; it was also of practical value.

> Buddhism certainly stands at the point when the old world of village life, of face-to-face relations conducted largely with lifelong acquaintances, was giving way to a more transient and varied experience of life. In an increasingly impersonal world, in which one had to do business with strangers, it may have helped both parties to a transaction to feel that the trader subscribed to a straightforward ethic of right and wrong and believed that a law of the universe would see to it that he was punished for cheating even if he evaded human detection. This universal moral law, replacing the certainty of censure by the community, perhaps helped to create that *prima facie* assumption that the trader was not wholly untrustworthy which is a prerequisite for flourishing trade. It may also have helped to create confidence in the honesty of bureaucrats and officials.[26]

The Buddha certainly did not take a purely instrumental view of ethics: he found many reasons for being good.[27] But in preaching to laymen he sometimes made it clear that honesty is the best policy.

For example, when preaching to his lay disciples at Pāṭaligāma, he told them that there were five disadvantages to immorality. Firstly, because of his carelessness the immoral man lost money. Secondly, he acquired a bad reputation. Thirdly, whenever he went into company he felt embarrassed and ill at ease. Fourthly, he died in a state of confusion. Finally, he had a bad rebirth. The good man enjoyed the five corresponding advantages, from wealth in this life to a good rebirth in the next.[28]

Immorality is frequently associated with carelessness (*pamāda*).

> [King Pasenadi] asked the Buddha one day whether there was one thing which could accomplish the ends of both this world and the next. Yes, said the Buddha: diligence. Diligence can win you longevity, health, beauty, heaven, birth in a good family and pleasures of the senses. The modern salutation 'Take care' would have met with the Buddha's approval. The word here rendered as 'diligence', *appamāda,* could also be translated 'attentiveness'; in psychological terms it is that *awareness* which was the most distinctive contribution of Buddhism to India's (or the world's) soteriological practice.[29]

In life in general it is what we have come to call 'mindfulness';[30] in economic life it is manifested as thrift.

Perhaps the pragmatism of the Buddha's ethics told against its development into an interesting topic of discussion, in other words, against the development of an ethical theory. Very rarely does the Buddha seem to envisage that a conflict of values could create a real problem, and I know of no case in the Canon of an unresolved ethical dilemma. The word *kusala* is the commonest term for something morally good, but (as pointed out in Chapter 1) it literally means skilful, and intelligence is a key virtue. Doing good is thus a matter of practical intelligence. That one person's good might conflict with another person's good on the philosophical level seems never to be envisaged. Of course, such issues frequently arise on the practical level in the *Vinaya,* but the Buddha is always ready with an answer. The king asks the Buddha to stop ordaining soldiers – i.e., deserters – and the Buddha complies and forbids the practice. The Buddha does not often propound absolute moral values without reference to context – though Chapter 6 above deals with a major exception. Truth, for example, is a very important value; but in the standard dilemma whether a mother should tell the truth when her son is hiding from murderous enemy soldiers and they come and ask her where he is hiding, one cannot imagine the Buddha saying that she must tell them the truth: he would say he is a *vibhajja-vādo.*

MEDITATION PRAXIS

So far this book has said next to nothing about either meditation or the *Vinaya*; and this is natural, since it is about the Buddha's ideas. However, when my focus is on his pragmatism, it becomes relevant to make some mention of his praxis. Let me deal with meditation first.[31]

The most general word for meditation is *bhāvanā*, which means 'development'; this is a training of the mind. At a very early stage, before the canonical collection of texts was closed, this had been systematized into two sections, in some contexts called concentration and understanding, in others calming (*samatha*) and insight (*vipassanā*). 'Calming' is supposed to discipline the emotions, 'insight' to sharpen the understanding until one sees the world as the Buddha saw it. In this doctrinal system, 'calming' is in the last resort a training for 'insight'; in the Canon it seems to be considered indispensable, but later a minority tradition appears to have argued that for some people salvific insight might be achieved without that kind of meditation.[32]

The pair 'calming' and 'insight' is a formulation which to some extent took over from another pair: 'awareness' (*sati*) and concentration (*samādhi*). The latter two are the seventh and eighth components of the Noble Eightfold Path which tradition considers the Buddha to have enunciated in his First Sermon; they thus look like the culmination of that path, whatever later tradition may say about it. Similarly, the full description of how one reaches Enlightenment found in the *Sāmaññaphala Sutta*,[33] 'The Text on the Fruits of Renunciation', shows the renunciate first training himself in awareness at every moment before it has him sit down to practise what we would regard as meditation proper.

❧

We must recall the cultural context of early Buddhism. There was no writing, so no reading. Educational institutions in any modern sense did not exist. What did education consist of? Most boys were trained to follow in their fathers' footsteps, girls in those of their mothers. A few brahmins learnt sacred texts by heart, and a tiny number of those even learnt to discuss their contents, but these were quite exceptional in society at large. We tend to forget that schooling does not just teach us specific facts or skills; it teaches us while we are still children to be sensitive to people and things around us and to be able to concentrate on a task or a problem. In the Buddha's social environment there were of course skilled craftsmen, trained to concentrate on their work; and it is notable how they appear in the *Sāmaññaphala Sutta* in similes for the meditator as he acquires control over his mind. But even such people were a small minority in the population. And the Buddha aimed his message at people of all classes and both genders, even if we do find a disproportionate number of brahmins among his disciples.

I suggest, therefore, that we today tend to over-interpret what was meant at one level by awareness and concentration. This over-interpretation began, no doubt, with the professional monks who systematized the Buddha's teachings. I am not denying that in order to achieve Enlightenment, awareness and concentration have to be cultivated to a very high pitch. But what the Buddha was prescribing as mental training must initially have been what we nowadays take for granted in an educated person, a basis for moral and intellectual understanding.

Another mental faculty which the Buddha encouraged people to cultivate was the imagination. Use of the imagination is prescribed in various meditation exercises. For example, the monk is encouraged to visualize his body as composed of thirty-two listed components, all described in unattractive terms. For the somewhat similar exercise of observing the disintegration of a corpse, monks are encouraged to visit actual charnel grounds; but they are also encouraged to apply to their own bodies what can be observed on such a visit, to imagine how their own corpses will rot away.

As Rahula points out, *bhāvanā* extends to the use of reason;[34] and indeed this is crucial, since the Buddha claims that if we use our reason properly we shall come to the same conclusions as he did. The training in concentration, awareness, and the use of the imagination are pragmatically necessary in order to make us better at thinking in general.

THE *VINAYA*: A PRAGMATIC LEGAL SYSTEM

The *Vinaya* is historically inexplicable unless it was started by the Buddha, who had the authority and intelligence to lay down the rules which constituted its basic framework – so successfully, indeed, that the Saṅgha, who live by those rules, today constitute one of the world's oldest and longest-lasting institutions. The pragmatism of the Buddha's character and programme are on display throughout the text. Whenever the Buddha is represented as disapproving of something, he says that it is not conducive to increasing the number of believers. He then pronounces a rule, for which he gives a stock list of ten reasons.[35] They can be summarized as the protection and convenience of the Saṅgha, the moral purity of its members, increase in the number of believers and the good of non-believers. Nor is this empty rhetoric: the occasions for promulgating rules frequently arise from lay dissatisfaction. In fact, the scriptures represent the process of forming the *Vinaya* as a continuous process of meeting exigencies, of solving problems as they arise, often as unintended consequences of previous rulings.[36] This is what Karl Popper called 'conjecture and refutation' demonstrated in practice; it amounts to the same as trial and error, and I have shown in Chapter 7 that it is fundamental to my own idea of how progress can be achieved.

Indeed, the *vinaya* is remarkable as a legal system which is not based on *a priori* principles but gradually built up through case law. I wonder if it is not the oldest such system in the world. Every single one of the rules governing individual conduct, the rules that are then encoded as the *pātimokkha* for monks and nuns, is framed to meet a particular situation that has arisen; and the first offender, the person who occasioned the creation of the rule, is not guilty, because the rule did not yet exist to be broken.

It is true that in the case of many of the minor rules the account of how they came to be promulgated is both stereotyped and implausible, and we may well think it improbable that they were laid down by the Buddha himself – most likely they were created after his time. This does not affect my case. It only shows that later generations scrupulously followed the pattern the Buddha had established of laying down rules only when they had been shown by events to be necessary, and always for the same reasons.

I view the text of the *Vinaya* just as I explained in Chapter 7 that I view the text of the *suttas*: while it cannot be true, as the tradition claims, that the whole text goes back to the First Council, I cannot conceive how it could have arisen if the kernel did not become established in much that way. This applies particularly to the rules for individuals, the *Sutta-vibhaṅga*, which is indeed strictly speaking a commentary on the rules: they are embedded in it. The other main part of the *Vinaya*, the *Khandhaka*, which gives the rules governing the Saṅgha as an institution, is somewhat different, in that the rules are embedded in a shaped work which begins with the Buddha's Enlightenment and ends at the Second Council. As mentioned in Chapter 7, this makes me think that the *Khandhaka* was probably composed at the Second Council. But I am not at all sure that the origins of the *Sutta-vibhaṅga* and of the *Khandhaka* need to be contrasted. On the one hand, it could be that the *Sutta-vibhaṅga* as we now have it was given its shape at the Second Council; on the other hand, the Buddha's procedure in forming the rules by trial and error is just as much in evidence in the *Khandhaka* as it is in the *Sutta-vibhaṅga*. Moreover, many passages are found in both texts.

Before I illustrate the Buddha's procedure with a lengthy example from the first book of the *Khandhaka*, I must deal with an initial difficulty. As explained, my view of the Pali *Sutta Piṭaka* means that throughout the rest of this book I have been able to use it as my source for the Buddha's ideas. The *Vinaya* situation is different. There are five versions of the *Vinaya* extant in Chinese and one of them (the Mūlasarvāstivādin) is also extant in Sanskrit and Tibetan (but is incomplete in Chinese). One cannot assume that the Pali version is throughout older or more authentic than the rest. This is a major reason why there is so little modern scholarship on the *Vinaya*: to do a thorough job, one needs to be able to use and compare the texts in all three languages.

I do not know Chinese, but I have found a practical way forward. My doctoral student Jungnok Park had the great kindness to check for me the relevant passages in the Chinese text of the Dharmaguptaka *Vinaya*.[37] All that matters for my present purposes is the process of making and changing the rules, and since Mr Park assured me that everything I say about that applies equally to the Dharmaguptaka version, I think we can take my remarks as valid for the whole *Vinaya* tradition. There are, however, some differences between the Pali and the Dharmaguptaka versions of the passages I am about to discuss, and I refer those interested in such detail to my article in the *Festschrift* for Ernst Steinkellner.[38]

My example describes how the institution of having novices (*sāmaṇera*) in the Saṅgha became established.

There was a boy called Upāli, the leader of a group (a gang?) of seventeen boys.[39] His parents were worried what would happen to him after their deaths. They had heard that Buddhist monks lived in comfort: they ate well and slept under cover. Upāli heard his parents discussing this and went and told his friends, whereupon they all decided to go for ordination with the Buddhists. The parents all gave their consent, so the boys went and took ordination. Though the text has them asking only for the lower ordination (*pabbajjā*), they received both that and the full ordination (*upasampadā*). But in the night towards dawn they got up and cried, demanding food and drink. The monks asked them to be patient until dawn; then they would get whatever there was available, and would get the rest on their alms round. They, however, then used their cells as toilets.

The Buddha heard the clamour and asked Ānanda what was going on; apparently he did not know that the boys were there. When he had ascertained that monks had knowingly ordained people under the age of twenty, he rebuked them, saying:

> A person under the age of twenty cannot put up with heat and cold, hunger and thirst, with insects' bites and stings, with wind and sun, with contact with creepy-crawlies, with harsh and unwelcoming speech. He cannot bear the whole range of physical discomfort and pain, up to the lethal. But a person aged twenty can. This will not make people who do not trust in us have such trust, nor strengthen the trust of those who do.[40]

He then laid down the rule: 'One may not knowingly ordain a person aged under twenty. One who does so is to be penalised according to the rule.'

The rule referred to is in the *Sutta-vibhaṅga*.[41] It lays down that the monk who has conducted this ordination is guilty of a *pācittiya* offence. So far as we know, this means only that he has to confess to it before the *pātimokkha* ceremony, though in this case the rule adds that the monks (presumably all those who participated in the ordination) are to be reprimanded. The rule also says that the ordination is invalid, a point not referred to, though perhaps implied, in the *Khandhaka*.[42] The introductory story about Upāli and his friends is identical, word for word, in the two texts.

Using the cells as toilets sounds extraordinary. Had we no other version of the text we would be left to guess: were these very small children, or was it a kind of 'dirty protest'? The answer is, however, that again the text has become corrupt. The Dharmaguptaka version lacks this detail; but (unlike the Pali) it mentions bedwetting as a problem a little later in this set of rules.

The next episode (section I.50) is that a whole family were wiped out by a disease, leaving only a father and his small son. The two of them joined the Saṅgha (*pabbajitvā*). When they went begging and the father was given something, the little boy would ask to share it. People grumbled because they suspected that the little boy was the child of a nun. Thereupon the Buddha ruled that no one under fifteen was to be admitted to the Order. Note that the previous rule is about full ordination, this one about admission (*pabbajjā*). Even so, the story and the rule do not seem to me to match very well.

Now (section I.51) comes a modification to the previous rule. A family who used to look after Ānanda died of the same kind of epidemic (perhaps the same one?), in this case leaving two boys. These, when they saw monks on their alms rounds, approached them for food, as they had previously been allowed to do; but now the monks rejected them and they cried. They were under fifteen, so Ānanda wondered how to save them, and put the case to the Buddha. The Buddha asked whether they were capable of making crows fly away. On hearing that they were, he decreed that a boy aged under fifteen who could shoo crows away could be admitted to the Order. This is the rule still in use today; in Sri Lanka it is interpreted to mean about seven or eight years old.

The next section (I.52) is very brief. Two named Sakyan boys who were novices under the same monk had sex with each other. (Though Horner calls this 'sodomy', masturbation is surely more likely.) This caused the Buddha to forbid a single monk to take on two novices. We must understand that novices were the responsibility of the monk who admitted them to the Order and presumably also lodged with him.[43]

There is then a long section (I.53) which concerns a different topic. The next section (I.54) tells the famous story of how the Buddha's son Rāhula entered the Order. The Buddha goes to Kapilavatthu – presumably, though the text does not say so, returning for the first time since his Enlightenment. Rāhula's mother – the text gives her no other name – tells him to go and ask his father for his inheritance. When he does so, the Buddha tells Sāriputta to admit him to the Order.

Sāriputta thereupon asks how he is to do that. The Buddha then explains that novices are to be admitted by giving them the Three Refuges. They are to be shaved and clothed in yellow robes. Putting his robe over one shoulder, the postulant is to worship the feet of the monks present, squat with his hands together in the gesture of reverence, and be told to say three times, 'I go to the Buddha for refuge, I go to the Dhamma for refuge, I go to the Saṅgha for refuge.'

What follows is fascinating. The Buddha's father, Suddhodana, comes to see him and asks him for a favour. He vividly describes the pain he suffered when the Buddha left home as a renunciate, and then when Nanda, the Buddha's cousin, did; now Rāhula's leaving is the worst of all. He asks that in future no boy be admitted to the Order without the permission of his parents. The Buddha grants his request. In doing so he in fact corrects himself, for he decides that what he did to his own father, and what he has just repeated with his own son, should never again be inflicted on any parent.

Sāriputta now has Rāhula as his novice. However, a family who support him ask him to accept one of their boys as a novice (I.55). Aware that this has been forbidden, he asks the Buddha's advice. The Buddha in effect rescinds his previous ruling, saying that a competent monk may take as many novices as he is capable of educating.

Whether or not the *Vinaya* is here historically accurate, it does give us a picture of the Buddha's character which is not only attractive but matches fundamental features of his teaching.

THE PRACTICAL COROLLARY OF CONJECTURE AND REFUTATION

We have noticed how the creation of the *Vinaya* corpus of rules is a process of trial and error, and remarked how this anticipates Karl Popper's epistemology of conjecture and refutation. The similarity is in fact even closer than I have so far explained. In writing about politics and society, Popper explained that from his basic stance it follows that the affairs of state (or indeed of any other organization) are best conducted not by making grandiose plans or blueprints, but by what he called 'piecemeal engineering'. By this he meant observing what went wrong and trying to fix it. We have seen that that was indeed exactly the method applied by the Buddha to running the Saṅgha.

To conclude this chapter, I wish to suggest that this draws our attention to something fundamental and distinctive about how the Buddha's mind worked, something which shaped both his style and much of the content of his teachings. Like Popper's social philosophy, the Buddha's approach is not to start from grand theories and ideals but to see what is going wrong and try to put it right.

Indeed, where did the Buddha start? That his starting point was suffering has often drawn the criticism that his teaching is negative or pessimistic. But if your life is perfectly satisfying, why would you need any religious teaching at all? As the wise saying has it: If it ain't broke, why fix it?

Popper's philosophy leads, indeed, to a constant emphasis on the asymmetry between right and wrong. Just as we cannot expect simply to gain the whole of truth, what we can and should do is try to eliminate error and learn from our mistakes. In the sociopolitical sphere, this means that aiming to make everyone happy is an absurdly impractical goal; what we must do is try to eliminate the things that certainly cause unhappiness.

In just the same way, the Buddha proceeds in the overwhelming majority of texts by setting out the negatives. It is by making them clear that he convincingly deduces the positives. The positives, one could say, tend simply to appear as corollaries. This may be satisfactory as oratory, but it does sometimes seem rather banal when one reads the text.

❧

It seems to me that in this respect, as in so many others, the Buddha had a vast effect on Indian thought. In this case I am referring to the presentation. In every Indian prescriptive or philosophical text (*śāstra*), the author sets out the view of his opponent, the view he wishes to refute, at the outset, and gives his own opinion last. This convention is so set that it does not need to be made explicit. I suspect that it derives from the Buddhist *sutta*s.

NEGATIVE FORMULATIONS CAN MISLEAD

The Buddha's ethics are almost entirely expressed through negatives. The sets of precepts[44] are all formulated as vows of abstention: I undertake not to take life, etc. There is a list of 'ten good deeds' (*dasa kusala kamma*), but it is formed on the basis of the list of ten bad (*akusala*) deeds, so again it consists of abstentions. Much the same goes for countless sermons with an ethical content.

Of course, many great Buddhist exegetes and preachers have not been misled by this, and have presented negatives in a positive light. I have mentioned above the importance of the virtue of *appamāda*, literally 'non-carelessness'; it is not difficult to see that diligence and scrupulous attention are positive virtues, not mere negatives. Nor does a negative presentation always have to be colourless. When the Buddha compares a bad monk to a unskilled cowherd and says that the monk who neglects to nip evil tendencies in the bud is like a cowherd who fails to pick out flies' eggs,[45] the simile is vivid and memorable.

Nevertheless, I think I have already shown in Chapter 6 that the Buddha's tendency to present ethics in negative terms did have an unfortunate effect on how his message was interpreted, not least by the later Buddhist tradition itself. As I mentioned in the conclusion to that chapter, the *abhidhamma* actually defined love in negative terms, as lack of hatred. This is too bloodless. Who could guess from that that the Buddha also said[46] that true friendship may even involve sacrificing one's life?

Chapter 12

THE BUDDHA AS SATIRIST; BRAHMIN TERMS AS SOCIAL METAPHORS

THE REPRESENTATION OF BRAHMINS

Buddhist popular literature regularly presents brahmins in a most unfavourable light. The *Vessantara Jātaka*,[1] the account of the Buddha's last birth on earth before this final one, is probably the best-known story in the entire Theravada tradition, and has been important in other Buddhist traditions too.[2] In this story, the future Buddha achieves the highest possible pitch of generosity by giving away his children to an old brahmin called Jūjaka, who follows him to his mountain retreat in order to ask for them. What impelled Jūjaka to make this monstrous request? Having acquired wealth in old age, he married a young wife. When she went to the village well to draw water, the other young women taunted her with having such a decrepit old husband, who could be no fun in bed. On her return home, she told him that he must provide servants for her, to save her from exposing herself to such public humiliation. Having heard that Vessantara was the very paradigm of generosity, he went in search of him. Thus the root cause of his outrageous behaviour was lust, the absurd lust of an aged lecher: Jūjaka's very name suggests decrepitude.[3]

He had other vices too. On his journey to find Vessantara, he displayed both cowardice and mendacity: in order to get past a forester who, suspecting that he was up to no good, tried to stop him, he said he had come with the message that Vessantara's sentence of banishment had been revoked. Worse, he was cruel: having met Vessantara and made his heartless request, he rubbed salt into the wound by beating the children within their father's sight. Finally, he met his end through avarice and gluttony: he sold the little boy back to his grandfather, Vessantara's royal father, for his weight in gold, and then, on becoming so rich, died of overeating.

❧

Though the depiction of brahmins in the main body of the Pali Canon is by no means so crude – and one does well to remember that several of the Buddha's chief disciples are supposed to have been of brahmin origin – the actual practice of brahminism is harshly criticized. In some texts, this criticism is direct and the main target is the same as it was for the Jains: sacrifice, particularly animal sacrifice.

A remarkable canonical poem,[4] thirty-two verses long, recounts how in days of yore brahmins led exemplary lives of poverty and marital chastity, and enjoyed long and healthy lives. They regarded cows as their greatest friends and benefactors. But then they became envious of the luxury in which kings were living, and persuaded the kings to pay them to conduct animal sacrifices. At first these did not include cows, but the brahmins got greedier. 'Then, when the knife fell on a cow, the gods and ancestors, Indra and the *asuras* and *rakkhasas*[5] shrieked "Wickedness!" Formerly there were three diseases: desire, lack of food, old age. Through the attack on cattle, ninety-eight arrived.'[6] This text has unusual features: so far as I am aware, it is the only one in which killing cows is singled out as even wickeder than other killing; and the mythologizing link between sin and the arrival of disease on earth suggests satire, as in the *Aggañña Sutta* (see below). I therefore suspect that we have lost the poem's specific context. It remains a powerful indictment.

The Buddha's fundamental criticism of brahmins is that they do not live up to their stated ideals. Brahmin terms remain as metaphors for those ideals. Thus at the end of one sermon[7] the Buddha explains who can rightly be called a renunciate (*samaṇa*), and then who can rightly be called a brahmin, a *nahātaka*, a *veda-gu*, a *sottiya*, an *ariya*, and an *arahat*. It turns out that the answer is in each case identical and concerns evil states of mind which keep one in *saṃsāra*. But in each case the first word, which says what one has done to those evil states, is different, and uses wordplay. Thus, for instance, he says that the word for brahmin means one who has expelled (*bāhita*) those bad states.[8] The next three terms are all Pali forms of Sanskrit words which can literally only refer to brahmins:

a *nahātaka* (S: *snātaka*) has recently taken a ritual bath to mark the end of his formal study of the Veda; a *veda-gu*[9] has learnt a whole Veda; a *sottiya* (S: *śrotriya*) is likewise a Vedic scholar. The word *ariya*, connected to Aryan, is also a social status; brahmins apply the term to the top three *varṇa* (see below); the Buddha frequently applies it to himself, his teaching and his followers, as in the 'Four Noble Truths'. Only the final term, *arahant*, is not a brahmin term indicating a precise status. However, it fits in nicely nevertheless, for I have argued in Chapter 4 that the Buddha borrowed it from the Jains.

❧

The *Khandhaka* section of the Pali *Vinaya* begins as follows. On gaining Enlightenment, the Buddha sits under the Bodhi tree for a week, experiencing the bliss of liberation. In the three watches of the night (presumably of each night) he contemplates the Chain of Dependent Origination, and then utters a stanza, of which the first half is the same each time. In this repeated verse he refers to himself as a brahmin. Then at the end of the week he moves to a banyan tree, where he spends another week in a similar manner. Then a brahmin happens along. He is the Buddha's first human contact since Enlightenment. This brahmin is not named, but the text characterizes him by a word found only in this passage,[10] *huhuṅka*; this seems to be onomatopoeic and to mean something like 'snooty'. The brahmin asks the Buddha[11] what features make a brahmin – a question found elsewhere in the Canon too. The Buddha answers that a man can rightly claim to be a brahmin if he has seven features: he has expelled evil characteristics (*bāhita-pāpa-dhammo*), he is not snooty (*huhuṅka*), he has no moral stains, he restrains himself, he has reached the end (that is, the perfection) of knowledge (*vedanta-gu*), he has lived the holy life (*vusita-brahma-cariyo*) and has no arrogance towards anyone in the world. Obviously, these seven features overlap. Three terms in the list – *bāhita-pāpa-dhammo, vedanta-gu* and *vusita-brahma-cariyo* – play on brahmin terminology. For the brahmin, *Vedānta* refers to the *Upaniṣads*, but the Buddha takes it more generally to refer to the culmination of true knowledge. Similarly, 'brahman conduct', which is the literal meaning of *brahma-cariyā*, has likewise been given a different referent by the Buddha (see the Appendix). The message of the list as a whole is plain. The Buddha is telling brahmins that they have no right to be proud, because all the virtues and accomplishments that they claim he has in full measure – indeed, in fuller measure, because he understands what the terms should really refer to.

The same message is graphically repeated, but in another way, only a few paragraphs later in the text. The Buddha hesitates about whether to preach. People are too full of desire (*ālaya*) and will not pay heed. Brahmā, the supreme creator god of brahminism, reads his mind and takes alarm. He appears before the Buddha, kneels before him on his right knee, and three times begs him to preach, promising that some will understand. Only when the Buddha agrees does he return to his heaven.[12] The Buddhist claim to supersede brahmin teaching could not be more blatant.

SATIRES OF BRAHMIN SACRED TEXTS

If one is quite unaware of the Buddha's historical context, it is not obvious that Brahmā's begging the Buddha to preach presents the god in a satirical light. The satirical tone is, however, hard to miss in the *Brahmajāla Sutta,* which in the Pali tradition is the first *sutta* in the *Dīgha Nikāya* and thus the first *sutta* in the entire *Sutta Piṭaka.* This *sutta* purports to set out systematically all views concerning the self and the world which present them as eternal or as coming to an end. In the section on those who hold the self and the world to be partly eternal and partly not, the first example given is the following.[13] I quote the translation of T. W. Rhys Davids,[14] because I could not improve on it, and I enjoy its Victorian style.

> Now there comes a time, brethren, when, sooner or later, after the lapse of a long, long period, this world-system passes away. And when this happens beings have mostly been reborn in the World of Radiance, and there they dwell made of mind, feeding on joy, radiating light from themselves, traversing the air, continuing in glory; and thus they remain for a long long period of time.

(This description is also found in the next *sutta* discussed below, the *Aggañña Sutta,* and is probably borrowed from there.) The text continues:

> Now there comes also a time, brethren, when, sooner or later, this world-system begins to re-evolve. When this happens the Palace of Brahmā appears, but it is empty. And some being or other, either because his span of years has passed or his merit is exhausted, falls from the world of radiance, and comes to life in the Palace of Brahmā. And there also he lives made of mind, feeding on joy, radiating light from himself, traversing the air, continuing in glory; and thus does he remain for a long long period of time.
>
> Now there arises in him, from his dwelling there so long alone, a dissatisfaction and a longing: 'O! would that other beings might come to join me in this place!' And just then, either because their span of years had passed or their merit was exhausted, other beings fall from the World of Radiance, and appear in the Palace of Brahmā as companions to him, and likewise are made of mind, etc.[15]
>
> On this, brethren, the one who was first reborn thinks thus to himself: 'I am Brahmā, the Great Brahmā, the All-seeing, the Ruler, the Lord of all, the Maker, the Creator, the Chief of all, appointing each to his place, the Ancient of days, the Father of all that are and are to be. These other beings are of my creation. And why is that so? A while ago I thought, "Would that they might come!" And on my mental aspiration, behold the beings came.'

The other beings have seen that Brahmā appeared first and they later, and accept his deluded deduction that therefore he must have created them. He is longer-lived, more good-looking and more powerful than they are. Then one day someone is reborn on earth, takes up meditation and succeeds in recollecting his former births – up to the point where he was reborn in that world of Brahmā. He concludes that he was created by Brahmā, and that Brahmā is eternal, while he and those like him are not.

As Rhys Davids remarks in a footnote to his translation: 'The story was a favourite one, and three recensions of it have been preserved (*MN* I, 326–331; *SN* I, 142–4, and *Jātaka* no. 405).'[16]

The first book of the *Bṛhad-āraṇyaka Upaniṣad* contains several creation myths. Here is the beginning of the fourth chapter, in Olivelle's translation:

> [1] In the beginning this world was just a single body (*ātman*) shaped like a man. He looked around and saw nothing but himself. The first thing he said was, 'Here I am!', and from that the name 'I' came into being. Therefore, even today when you call someone, he first says, 'It's I,' and then states whatever other name he may have. That first being received the name 'man' (*puruṣa*), because ahead (*pūrva*) of all this he burnt up (*uṣ*) all evils. When someone knows this, he burns up anyone who may try to get ahead of him. [2] That first being became afraid; therefore one becomes afraid when one is alone. Then he thought to himself: 'Of what should I be afraid, when there is no one but me?' So his fear left him, for what was he going to be afraid of? One is, after all, afraid of another. [3] He found no pleasure at all; so one finds no pleasure when one is alone. He wanted to have a companion. Now he was as large as a man and a woman in close embrace. So he split (*pat*) his body into two, giving rise to husband (*pati*) and wife (*patnī*).

He then experienced the pleasure of sexual intercourse, and first produced human beings. The couple then took other shapes and

> created every male and female pair that exists, down to the very ants. [5] It then occurred to him: 'I alone am the creation, for I created all this.' From this, 'creation' came into being. Anyone who knows this prospers[17] in this creation of his.

Surely the story from the *Brahmajāla Sutta* about how Brahmā acquired the delusion that he was the Creator is a spoof on this passage.

In the *Mahā Taṇhā-Saṇkhaya Sutta*, after talking about fire, the Buddha says, 'Monks, do you see that this [neuter] has come into being?' I wrote in Chapter 8 that it was unclear to what the pronoun 'this' referred, and suggested that he might have pointed at something in front of him. I went on:

> Patrick Olivelle has convincingly shown that this is how we have to interpret some passages in the early Upaniṣads in which deictic pronouns are used.[18] There is even a passage early in the *BĀU* (1.4.6), a cosmogonic narrative, which reads: 'Then he churned *like this* and, using his hands, produced fire ...'

In fact, this production of fire immediately follows the last words I have just quoted. Can we doubt any longer that the Buddha knew this text?

❧

In another text, the *Aggañña Sutta*,[19] the Buddha parodies Vedic creation myths on a far larger scale and with further-reaching consequences. I have devoted a lengthy article to this,[20] so here I shall only summarize my conclusions. They are quite important for our view of the Buddha and his capacity for humour and irony. The text purports to give an account of the origin of the world and of society, meaning in particular of kingship and of the caste system. It has been taken seriously as such an aetiological account by the entire Buddhist tradition, which has traced all royal lineages from the first king, Mahā Sammata, presented in this text. In so doing the tradition ignores the fact that the Buddha strongly deprecates taking any interest in such matters, as I have amply demonstrated in the previous chapter. Moreover, his teaching of causation denies that the world can have an origin; but the text gets round this by reliance on a theory, here implied rather than stated, that the world goes through periods of what one might call contraction and expansion. When it is contracted, everything below the very highest heavens, those well above where the gods lived, is destroyed; but those high heavens serve as the abode of etherial beings, described already in the *Brahmajāla Sutta* as quoted above: mind-made, in other words immaterial, but flying around feeding on joy. These beings are instances of the kind of paradoxical creatures who are immaterial and yet have such material characteristics as movement and feeding; I discussed them in Chapter 5 as part of the Indian religious heritage, just as ghosts are of ours, but cast doubt on whether the Buddha believed in such things. Be that as it may, they are the device by which the Buddha turns what Vedic literature intends as a true cosmogony into an account of why such a thing appears to us to be about the origins of the world, but is no such thing if properly understood.

In the passage quoted above from the *BĀU*, there is a good deal about the origins of language: right at the start, the text explained how the Sanskrit words for 'I' and for 'man' came into being. The word for 'man', *puruṣa*, is etymologized by means of a really poor attempt at punning. The *Aggañña Sutta* is full of this kind of etymologizing. On the other hand, the Buddha purports to explain the origin of simple little words and expressions: in the same style as the *BĀU* explains the origin of the word 'I', the Buddha explains the origins of an expression which I translate as 'We've had it' (*ahū vata no*), making up a myth about what people had had and then lost. How can this be anything but humorous? Indeed, I submit that it is a good joke. The kind of etymologizing that produced *puruṣa* he uses, for example, to produce the names of the four estates (*varṇa*) which in brahmin theory constitute society. The best joke of this kind is where he analyses the brahmin word for a teacher of the Veda, *adhyāyaka* in Sanskrit and *ajjhāyaka* in Pali, to mean a non-meditator.

I must emphasize that this is not a trivial or merely incidental point. No one who reads the *Brāhmaṇa*s and early *Upaniṣad*s can fail to notice how often they explain Sanskrit words and expressions by means of puns – often quite poor ones – and thus claim to reveal esoteric truths about the nature of reality. We have seen that the Buddha, by contrast, did not attach importance to the language in which his message was conveyed. He recognized the conventional nature of language, just as he recognized the conventional nature of the caste system. In this book we have come across several instances of how the Buddha used punning and wordplay to convey his new ideas. Perhaps one could even say that his tactic of accepting the opponents' terms, such as *karma*, and then turning them round to mean something quite different, was simply stretching such an expository method to its limits.

Awareness of how important the use of language was to the Buddha's teaching method should convince us of the benefit to be gained by studying his words in Pali. Although Pali has been shown to be somewhat different from the Buddha's own probable dialect, even so, the Pali canonical texts are the closest we can get to his actual words. However, the process of trying to record and remember those words in a variety of dialects down the centuries must inevitably have obscured many pieces of wordplay, some of which would no doubt have elucidated for us pieces of text which are now obscure. I hope that scholars will continue to try to unearth these, but of course we must accept that much has surely been lost forever. All compounded things are impermanent.

That the Buddha is setting out both to deny the brahmin view of the origin of society and to make fun of it becomes clear at the outset of the *Aggañña Sutta*. Two brahmin converts tell the Buddha that other brahmins are roundly abusing them for having left the brahmin estate and gone over to join the ascetics, whose status is that of *śūdras*. The full meaning of this passage, as of much that follows, depends on the ambiguity of the Pali word *vaṇṇa*. As explained in the 'Background Information', *vaṇṇa*, like Sanskrit *varṇa*, refers to the four estates of society (brahmin, *kṣatriya*, *vaiśya*, *śūdra*), while its primary meaning is 'colour', and by extension it means 'complexion' or 'good looks'. The four estates were assigned the symbolic colours of white, red, yellow and black respectively. (Though I know of no allusion to this in a Sanskrit text earlier than the *Mahābhārata*, I believe there is a reference to it in the Canon.[21]) It is also possible that the typical brahmin was fairer than the typical *śūdra*, or at least perceived to be so. Thus the brahmins are said to claim that their *vaṇṇa* is white and the other is black. We may assume that the brahmins considered those who had joined the Saṅgha to have *śūdra* status because the Saṅgha kept no caste rules of purity, but made people from all castes live together and accept food from anyone; we can further assume that they were blacker because they rapidly became sunburnt, like *śūdra* labourers.

At the same time the brahmins are reported as saying (para. 3): 'The brahmins are pure, non-brahmins are impure. The brahmins are Brahmā's own children, born of his mouth, born of Brahmā, created by Brahmā, heirs of Brahmā.' They describe the Saṅgha as 'shaven-headed little ascetics, menial, black, born of the feet of the kinsman'. The kinsman in question is the brahmins' kinsman, Brahmā.

The commentary on this passage[22] is very terse and does not reveal which allusions the commentator has caught, except that he does say that the feet at the end are Brahmā's feet. The author of the subcommentary, however, makes it clear that he understands the allusion to the *Puruṣa-sūkta* (*Ṛg-veda* X, 90). He says[23] that the brahmin tradition has it that the brahmins were born from Brahmā's mouth, the *kṣatriyas* from his chest, the *vaiśyas* from his thighs and the *śūdras* from his feet. He also reports, no less accurately, that the brahmins are born from Brahmā's mouth because they are born from the words of the Veda (*veda-vacanato*) and that they are Brahmā's heirs because they are worthy of the Vedas and Vedāṅgas.[24]

The first words of the Buddha's reply (para. 4) are that in making these insulting remarks the brahmins have forgotten their own traditions. As we have seen, he claims time and again that the brahmins have forgotten that the true brahmin is a virtuous person, not someone born into a particular social group. The Buddha then consoles his brahmin disciples with a joke: how can brahmins say they are born of Brahmā's mouth, when we can all see that they are born from the wombs of their womenfolk, who have periods, become pregnant, give birth and give suck? The Buddha does not have to spell out that this means that the brahmins have the same impurities from birth as other human beings.

The Buddha then points out that it is enlightened beings who enjoy the highest worldly prestige, and that they may come from any social background. People from any of the four estates may be wicked (para. 5) or virtuous (para. 6). When talking of vice and virtue the Buddha uses the words for black and white which were used to describe the *vaṇṇa* just above. He then (para. 7) refutes what the brahmins have said by remarking that all four estates have good and bad people in them, but whoever is enlightened is rightly considered top. That righteousness is held to be the best he shows by referring to King Pasenadi (para. 8); the other Sākyas have to behave deferentially to King Pasenadi, but the king shows to the Buddha the same deference that the other Sākyas show to him.

This last argument is typical of the Buddha's pragmatism. For instance, when he sets out to detail the benefits of becoming an ascetic, the very first benefit that he talks of is the change in circumstance of a slave who always had to wait on his master, but after becoming an ascetic receives deference and material help from his former master.[25]

The Buddha then goes a step further (para. 9). 'You', he says, 'are of various births, names, clans and families, and have left home for homelessness.' (Though the 'you' is literally addressed to the two brahmin disciples, the Buddha is looking beyond them to the whole Saṅgha.) 'If you are asked who you are, state that you are ascetics, sons of the Sākya.' But those who have firm faith will properly reply, '"I am the Blessed One's own child, born of his mouth, born of the Dhamma, created by the Dhamma, heir of the Dhamma." For the Buddha is designated "Dhamma-bodied, Brahma-bodied, become Dhamma, become Brahma".' This echoes word for word the brahminical formula quoted above, substituting for Brahmā first the Buddha and then the Dhamma, his Teaching. The Buddha is making a serious point, but in language which to his followers must have sounded at least playful, and to brahmins scandalous. At first he sounds as if he is equating himself with Brahmā, the creator god, but after a few words he makes clear that the real equation he is making is not of persons but of teachings: his teaching is, for his followers, the true Veda. In the final sentence of the paragraph he hammers home the point that what counts about him is not his individuality but his teaching; he makes the same point elsewhere, in the formula, 'He who sees me sees the Dhamma and he who sees the Dhamma sees me.'[26] In the formulation he gives here, the language leaves open a further implication, because in the compounds *Brahma-kāyo* and *Brahma-bhūto, brahma-* could be masculine (as suggested by the equation in the previous sentence: the Saṅgha are the Buddha's sons just as the brahmins are Brahmā's) or neuter[27] (equating the Buddha's Dhamma with *brahman* in the sense of Veda/ultimate truth).

At this point (para.10) the Buddha embarks on the aetiological myth which occupies more than half the text and gives it its name. In this myth the state of the world in general and of society in particular is ascribed to moral failings, particularly greed and laziness. Interested readers should read the text, at least in translation,[28] and my comments published in the article.

SATIRIZING THE JAINS

By no means is it only brahmins that the Buddha makes fun of. He can also be playful when criticizing Jains. While brahmins are criticized above all for their hypocrisy and pretensions, which cover a multitude of moral failings, the Jains are criticized for their pointless austerities. In a *sutta* entitled 'The Short *Sutta* on the Blazing Mass of Suffering',[29] the Buddha recounts how one evening he went for a walk on a mountain in Rājagaha and came on a lot of Jains standing perfectly immobile, trying to expunge the bad karma they had accumulated in former lives.[30] The Buddha's audience would have understood that this practice went with rigorous fasting and other extreme austerities. The Buddha cross-examines these immobile self-torturers, and establishes that they know neither what bad karma they have accumulated nor how much remains to be expunged. So the Buddha tells them that from the way that they are suffering right now, he can deduce that those who have performed acts of bloodshed and cruelty, if reborn as human beings, become Jain ascetics.[31]

Jains are thus utterly misguided. But on the whole they are not as bad as brahmins. In the *Kandaraka Sutta*[32] the Buddha talks about those who torture themselves and others. The picture of self-torturers is the usual one describing the Jains. But they torture only themselves. Who torture both themselves and others? A king or a rich brahmin. Such people institute large-scale animal sacrifices. In preparation for the sacrifice the sponsor,[33] his chief wife and his brahmin chaplain have to undergo austerities; they dress in skins, sleep on the ground and subsist on only a tiny quantity of milk. Then many, many animals are slaughtered, trees are felled, grass is cut, and a huge workforce suffers terrible conditions.[34]

EXTENDED – EVEN PLAYFUL – USE OF 'BRAHMIN' AS A METAPHOR

Not all the Buddha's many references to brahmins are negative, let alone satirical. Nor are they necessarily literal. Brahmins and their claim to hierarchical superiority were such a prominent feature of the Buddha's environment that it was natural to use the term 'brahmin' metaphorically. In our society elephants figure in everyone's imaginative repertoire, to such an extent that when a hamburger is advertised as 'jumbo' we instantly know that this is merely a claim that it is very large, not that it is made of elephant meat. Let us take as an example a *sutta*[35] in which the Buddha visits a brahmin village, and a brahmin remarks to him that he looks so radiantly fit and well that he must surely have easy access to very large and comfortable beds – of which he lists many varieties.

The Buddha says no, ascetics are not permitted to use such beds; and indeed the ninth of the ten precepts prohibits the use of what are literally called 'high and big beds' (*uccā-sayana-mahā-sayana*). The word *sayana* means either 'bed' or simply the posture 'lying down', so 'bed' in the following translation stands for what in Pali is a pun.

The Buddha then says that he has access at will to three kinds of high and big beds: the divine (*dibba*), the brahmic (*brahma*) – excuse the coinage – and the noble (*ariya*). After going on his alms round he goes into a wooded area, puts some grass and leaves together, sits down on them crosslegged, with his back straight, and enters a state of full awareness. This much is common to all three cases. In the first case, he then practises all four *jhānas*. Then, whether he walks, stands, sits or lies, his posture is divine; so, when lying, he has obtained at will a divine 'high and big bed'.

In the second case, after establishing awareness the Buddha practises the four states of 'staying with Brahmā' (the topic of Chapter 6): kindness, compassion, empathetic joy and equanimity. Then, whether he walks, stands, sits or lies, his posture is brahmic; so, when lying, he has obtained at will a brahmic 'high and big bed' – perhaps we could say, a bed worthy of Brahmā.

In the third case, the Buddha simply realizes that he has totally destroyed, so that they can never recur, passion, hatred and confusion. Then his posture, whatever it is, is noble, *ariya*. We have seen above that, like noble, *ariya* is another social metaphor.

In this *sutta*, brahmic trumps divine and is in turn trumped by noble. If we try to unpick this literally, going word by word, we shall get into a mess. But the point of the *sutta* is so simple and obvious that I need say no more about its message. What I aim to demonstrate by quoting it is simply how the Buddha did not merely use social metaphors, but used them playfully.

The Buddha's appropriation of brahmin terms must in their eyes have come very close to what Christians call sacrilege. He did it under the guise of telling them that he was a reformer, recalling them to their ancient ideals. Nevertheless, many of them must have found it irritating, to say the least, and it indicates that the Buddha had powerful protectors and supporters.

Chapter 13

IS THIS BOOK TO BE BELIEVED?

This book began as a set of lectures. Just as I was completing them, a foreign colleague posted on Indology Net, of which I am a member, the question whether anything had recently been published which showed whether the Buddha or the *Bṛhad-āraṇyaka Upaniṣad* came first. So I posted to the network a list of seven of my publications concerning passages in the Pali Canon in which the Buddha can be shown to refer to surviving passages in the *Upaniṣads*, mostly in the *BĀU*. I added:

> [U]nless we subscribe to the view that the Buddha was omniscient and could therefore respond to texts which would be composed in the future, I do not understand how his references to important passages in the *BĀU* etc. can fail to be interpreted as showing that they already existed when he preached.

This elicited the following response from a professor of Buddhism at a famous American university:[1]

> Whoa, slow down! Yes, the Buddha (qua literary character) may refer to Upanisadic passages in some suttas, but that 'the Buddha' (or variants thereof) appear in literary works composed in India up through (at least) the 15th century AD. As, presumably, the works Prof. Gombrich is referring to are from the Pali, this still puts them at no more (for sure) than pre-4th century, with the possibility that they were redacted ca. 1st cent. BC, with the further possibility that parts of them date a few centuries earlier. There is no solid (i.e. non-confessional) evidence that I know of to link them to Gotama

(the man who started the ball rolling in whatever unknown way he did).

So, as far as I can tell, to claim (comme 'les palisans'[2]) that the Upanisads in question (or the relevant passages therein) must date from a period prior to when Gotama 'preached' merely because they are alluded to in Pali sources (which do tend to be centered around the literary conceit of Gotama 'preaching') is rather to outrun the evidence at our disposal.

This is, of course, not a novel objection on my part – and one I know Prof. Gombrich is well-aware of – so I was surprised to see it so glossed over in his post ... Have we become so unskeptical, then, that we can speak so blithely about what the Buddha (as opposed to the various literary representations of 'the Buddha') knew and didn't know with such specificity? ...

❧

I have tried in the pages above to show that the Buddha's main ideas are powerful and coherent. If I had a more thorough knowledge of the Pali Canon than, alas, I can claim, I would have made a better job of it; but surely I have done enough to show that this coherence is not imposed by my fantasy, but exists in the texts. Yet, according to the fashionable view represented by my critic, Buddhism, which at least in numerical terms must be the greatest movement in the entire history of human ideas, is a ball which was set rolling by someone whose ideas are not known and – one may presume from what he writes – can never be known. So the intellectual edifice which I have described came together by a process of accumulation, rather like an avalanche. I am reminded of the blindfolded monkeys whose random efforts somehow produce a typescript of the complete works of Shakespeare.

KARMA IN HISTORICAL CONTEXT

One need not start expounding the Buddha's ideas where I have, but I think it helps to make sense of the material if one begins with his theory of karma. On the one hand, this substitutes ethics for ritual, and here the Buddha is as it were facing the Brahmins. The Jains had probably anticipated the Buddha in this respect, but their theory was philosophically crude. One of the Buddha's greatest intellectual achievements was his capacity for abstraction, and his treatment of karma, when contrasted with that of the Jains, illustrates this.

As explained in Chapter 3, the brahmin metaphysic of *Vedānta* holds that in reality every *ātman* is identical with the world *ātman* (= *brahman*) and therefore every individual *ātman* is the same. Individuality is therefore an illusion – and so, therefore, is individual responsibility. With his theory of karma, the Buddha not only established individual responsibility, but more generally argued for a principle of individuation.

The Buddha's theory of karma not only substituted ethics for ritual, but made intention, a private matter, the final criterion for judging ethical value. This was a great step forward in the history of civilization, because it meant that on the ethical plane all human beings are in a general sense equal, even if they differ in their capacity for making sound moral judgements.[3] Furthermore, the Buddha took the extremely bold step of claiming that we are the masters of our own destinies, each responsible for our fates. I have suggested that the social conditions of his time must have been quite unusual for this to carry any plausibility with his audiences. Rarely in human history, before very recent times, has this doctrine of individual responsibility caught on.

I hope to have shown that not merely the origin but also the character of these ideas can be seen more clearly if we consider them in their historical context. Among the salient features of this context, both Jainism and the socio-economic conditions have certainly exercised an important influence. However, two other influences stand head and shoulders above the rest.

The first is brahminism. I think that failure to understand the Buddha's relation to brahminism, and above all how he used its vocabulary figuratively, has resulted in massive failures of understanding by later generations – indeed, those misunderstandings may even have begun during the Buddha's lifetime. The most important failure, the subject of Chapter 6, was to grasp his teaching that love and compassion can be salvific for the person who cultivates those feelings to the highest pitch.

The second crucial influence, in my opinion, is that the Buddha was aware of other cultures. This made it possible for him to realize that the caste system, and hence the whole brahmin theory of society, was man-made and simply did not apply elsewhere. Similarly, it must have influenced the Buddha's view of language. Implicitly, but clearly enough, he rejected the brahmin view that Sanskrit had a unique relation to reality. He saw that his meaning could be conveyed in different languages and dialects, even though he may well have urged his followers to remember his precise words to help them preserve his message.

NON-RANDOM PROCESS

Philosophically, it is of crucial importance that the Buddha conceived of karma as a process. Moreover, since ethics cannot work unless agents have free will, karma is an indeterminate process. On the other hand, it can also not be a random process, otherwise there would be no guarantee of a connection between action and result.

It was not his theory of karma alone which led the Buddha to reinterpret what we normally consider to be objects as processes. He derived inspiration from Vedic speculation about fire, and saw it as a non-random process which was appetitive and yet operated without an agent, simply coming to an end when the fuel ran out. He took this as a model both for consciousness and more generally for how the life and experience of a living being (typically, of course, a human being) could be self-generating processes for which it was otiose to posit any additional, unchanging entity to act as an agent.

If what we normally take to be objects in the world around us are not really stable, but are processes, all changing (albeit not at random), whether slowly or fast, our interpretation of what our senses perceive is never perfectly accurate. The main culprit here is language, for we give names to what we perceive; it is the fixity of these names which does most to mislead us.

Thus, if we operate entirely through language, which provides our conceptual apparatus, we shall always find ourselves at some remove from the truth. The Buddha had himself succeeded in breaking through what I may thus call the veil of language – not his metaphor – and confronting the reality beyond words, and thus beyond impermanence and beyond suffering. This experience, an auto-revelation, would bring an end to rebirth and all the suffering which that inevitably involves; it was thus the one thing really worth achieving. One could only achieve it for oneself, but a teacher could point the way. At the same time, the inadequacy of denotative language strongly encouraged the use of analogy and metaphor for that purpose.

I certainly do not intend to claim that the Buddha anticipated all the main discoveries of modern psychology – discoveries which themselves, of course, are hypotheses and may in time be superseded. Obviously he could know nothing about such matters as the difference between the central nervous system and the cerebral cortex, so his accounts of perception and action, however brilliant, could not go into the kind of detail discussed nowadays. Nevertheless, the similarity between some of his ideas and the picture painted by modern cognitive psychology is certainly striking. Nowadays perception is regarded as an activity, a kind of doing. Moreover, 'Perception is inherently selective,'[4] which means that it cannot be dissociated from volition. Both of these propositions would (as explained in Chapter 10) have the Buddha's complete assent.

Modern psychology further holds that every action is an interaction with the world and affects the actor.[5] The Buddha did not perhaps say exactly this about perception or cognition, but he certainly problematized the dividing line between the actor – for him, the synergy of five sets of processes – and the environment; we recall that in the first *khandha*, the *rūpa khandha*, are included not only the senses but also their objects. While I think that Sue Hamilton is correct to say that the Buddha's theory of cognition does not settle the issue between realism and idealism, and indeed can be interpreted either way, that is only true when the theory is taken in isolation, ignoring the Buddha's soteriology – which for him was what really mattered! He would have agreed with modern psychologists in declining to accept idealism: there really is a world out there, even if we cannot know it precisely. This is as fundamental for the Buddha as it is for most of us; for were there no distinction between a person and the world, including other people, his entire soteriology would make no sense at all. We are the heirs of our own karma; my karma and yours cannot be the same. By the same token, if you achieve nirvana and I do not, it is I who continue to be reborn, not you. That these distinctions were blurred in Mahayana thought has misled many students of earlier Buddhism.

Yet in one way he made the fact that every act affects the actor the very cornerstone of his teaching. We are back to karma again. Every bad intention, we have seen, makes you worse, every good intention makes you better. As explained in Chapter 2, karma, morally relevant volition, is the dynamic that moves us through our lives (infinite in number), and is what provides the principle of continuity and coherence throughout those lives. In the context of that dynamic, karma is the same as *saṃkhārā*, a term which refers both to the process of constructing (our lives seen in prospect) and the result of that process (our lives seen in retrospect).

In Chapter 1 I wrote that the No Soul doctrine has led people to the diametrically wrong notion that the Buddha did not believe in moral responsibility or personal continuity, whereas in fact he had an even stronger theory of those things than any non-Buddhists would accept today. Analogously, when it comes to the moral sphere he gave so strong a form to the idea that actors are affected by their actions that he propounded an irrefutable form of that theory, for, if the effect of a moral act is not forthcoming within one lifetime, rather than accept refutation the theory holds that the effect will come in a future life.[6]

DEVELOPMENTS TOWARDS AND IN THE MAHAYANA

I am aware that many Buddhists, if they read this book, will find surprises in it. Perhaps I should approach this topic too from the basis of karma. I showed in my first book that the rigour of the doctrine of responsibility for one's own fate was evidently hard to sustain even within the Pali/Theravada tradition, and that it was mitigated, from very early times (probably from around the time of the Buddha's death) by the doctrine of what in English is called the Transfer of Merit.[7] This is not the place to go into that; those interested can consult my book. The further the doctrine of karma moves from centre stage in a Buddhist tradition, the more scope there is also for change in other elements, both theoretical and practical. The flame of the Buddha's teaching on karma has flickered in every Buddhist tradition and every traditionally Buddhist country, but has never been quite extinguished. The Japanese, at the furthest edge of the pre-modern Buddhist world, came up with a good pair of terms, meaning 'own power' and 'other power': by and large, Buddhists, and particularly the more sophisticated Buddhists, have known that Buddhism teaches that their salvation lies within their own power, but they have also turned to the other power, typically the benign power of Buddhas and *bodhisattvas*, to give them a helping hand.

The Sanskrit word *Mahā-yāna* means 'Great Path' (to salvation); to many of its adherents it is known as *Bodhisattva-yāna*. Thus the belief that one should aspire to salvation as, or through the aid of, a *bodhisattva* is the hallmark or defining characteristic of the Mahayana. A *bodhisattva* transfers merit to other beings; one could go so far as to say that the doctrine of the *bodhisattva*, the true hallmark of the Mahayana, is built on Transfer of Merit.[8] The word *yāna* is a pun, for besides 'path' it means 'vehicle'.[9] Thus for the *bodhisattva* it is a path, for those to whom he transfers merit it is a vehicle.

It is widely taught that the Mahayana differs from earlier Buddhism in two other respects. On the one hand, it is claimed that whereas earlier Buddhism applied the doctrine of No Self only to living beings, the Mahayana applied it to all entities. (In Sanskrit the former doctrine is called *pudgala-nairātmya*, the second *dharma-nairātmya*; in the latter case it is clearer in English to speak of a lack of essence than a lack of self.) The other alleged difference is that the Mahayana laid far more stress on altruism. Whether or not these claims were justified as criticisms of other Buddhist traditions at the time when the Mahayana arose, as criticisms of what the Buddha taught in the Pali Canon they are invalid. This conclusion should, I humbly suggest, improve relations between modern followers of the Theravada and the Mahayana.

In my view the Mahayana most strikingly differed from earlier traditions by its extraordinary glorification of the Buddha and its multiplication of Buddhas and future Buddhas (*bodhisattvas*), creating a host of what in a comparative perspective must be called divine figures, who became objects of prayer and worship; and this was the corollary of down-playing the role of karma.

BUDDHIST DEVOTION: AN UNINTENDED CONSEQUENCE?[10]

Shortly before his death, according to the Canon, the Buddha refused to appoint anyone to succeed him as leader of the Saṅgha. The monks, he said, should take refuge in themselves, not in anyone else, and take refuge in the Dhamma, nothing else.[11] As with the Kālāmas, this shows the Buddha asking people to think for themselves, but also sure that they will find his teachings to be the best.

The glorification of the Buddha, and the ascription to him of a status far above the human, surely began even during his lifetime. The history of religions and ideologies is full of ironies. Both

Christianity and Marxism can claim to spring from sympathy with the poor and powerless; both at times in history have been instruments of oppression in the hands of ruthless rulers. However noble, however intelligent, the founders of these movements may be, they cannot even foresee, let alone avoid, all the unintended consequences of their words and actions. Just as people too accustomed to obedience may parrot, 'I must think for myself,' the Buddha's followers have always chanted, 'I go to the Buddha for refuge. I go to the Dhamma for refuge. I go to the Saṅgha for refuge.' This triple formula is found in many passages in the Canon itself. It gives expression to an emotion; it need not indicate a refusal to think. And yet ...

Were I writing a history of Buddhism, I would give a culpably one-sided picture if I missed out the devotional side and the ritual and magic it has engendered. This example, Taking Refuge by saying the quoted formula three times, occurs many times in the Canon, and many other passages show evidence of the same tendency. When, as a frail old man who realizes that death is near, the Buddha tells the monks to take refuge in themselves – an unusual expression[12] – I suspect that his wording was intended as a rebuttal of the already popular formula. And yet the very same text, only a couple of pages later, has the Buddha claiming that he could if he pleased prolong his life for an eon. While I cannot believe that both passages accurately record the Buddha's sentiments, that his portrayal as godlike began and even flourished during his lifetime seems extremely probable.

The Buddha declared ritual to be useless or worse. The growth of Buddhist rites and liturgies was surely a wholly unintended consequence of the Buddha's preaching. Buddhist ritual and devotion have found no place in this book, for it has been about what the Buddha thought.

BE LIKE THE KĀLĀMAS: FIND OUT FOR YOURSELF

Coming to the end of writing this book has brought me back to the Buddha's advice to the Kālāmas. I could not imagine a better conclusion. Throughout the book so far I have kept the lid on the exasperation which, I explained at the start, has helped to motivate me. Yes, the world is full of ignorance and silliness; but what can measure up to the idiocy of what educated people are prepared not just to say but even to publish about Buddhism? Every day brings new examples. Even today, as I took a break after lunch from writing this, I read in the *Times Literary Supplement*, a justly respected journal: 'Buddhism proposes a state in which there are no pronouns, because there is no "I". Masculine and feminine are just illusions in a world that is nothing more than a dream.'[13] With such lunacy on every side, what is the poor inquirer to do?

I suggest that readers take as a provisional hypothesis, a working basis, that what I have written is more or less correct; and then test it on the touchstone of their own experience by reading the evidence, the texts of the Pali Canon. Then, if they think the evidence is against me, they should say so publicly, and we shall all be the wiser. One should not be browbeaten by perfectionists and intellectual snobs who say that translations are useless. Certainly it is incomparably better to read the texts in translation than not to read them at all.

But if one finds the texts interesting, why not try learning Pali? I have explained that the matter of the texts cannot be wholly detached from their manner, of which the most important feature is their language, which has its own culture and history. Nowadays most English speakers grow up with the disadvantage that they no longer learn any Latin at school; indeed, most of them learn nothing, or next to nothing, about grammar in any language. This makes learning an inflected language like Pali harder than it used to be. But most people in the western world do still at least speak a mother-tongue which is related to Pali, being Indo-European. And for Pali they need not learn a new script, since the Pali Text Society has published all the texts, as well as grammars and dictionaries, in the Latin script.

The study of Pali has almost died out in the western world; few universities still offer it at all. If one reader in a thousand takes it up, we could see not merely an amazing revival of Pali studies, but an informed interest in the Buddha's ideas and practices on a scale never known before. Impermanent, no doubt – but why worry about that?

APPENDIX

THE BUDDHA'S APPROPRIATION OF FOUR (OR FIVE?) BRAHMINICAL TERMS

This book shows how the Buddha both borrowed and twisted brahminical terminology. Five cases which seem to me important but not central I have here segregated in an appendix so that readers who find my discussions too technical can lighten their load by skipping them.

i. Brahma-cariyā (see Chapter 6)

This is the Pali form of the Sanskrit *brahma-caryā* , literally 'brahma-conduct'. This was the technical term for the prescribed first stage in the life of a brahmin or other high-caste boy. The boy had to be initiated into the study of the *Veda,* an initiation which turned him into a member of society. In theory, at least, he stayed in this status and followed its prescribed way of life until he married, being now qualified to perform at least the basic daily rituals by himself. While the *raison d'être* for this period in his life was to learn the sacred texts (and the rituals they accompany), a salient characteristic of the lifestyle was chastity. So, by what we could call slippage between meaning and reference, *brahma-caryā* came to mean 'chastity', normally in the sense of total sexual abstinence.

The Buddha frequently uses the term *brahma-cariyā* both in a wider and in a narrower sense. The narrower sense is the same as in brahminism: chastity. Moreover, again as in brahminism, its use in the wider sense always includes the narrower sense. But he uses it in a wide sense not to refer to a stage in the life of a high-caste male, but to the life of any member of the Saṅgha. We usually translate it 'the holy life', which is perfectly reasonable, but of course has lost the resonance which the term had in Indian society. It was on a par with his frequent claim that the true brahmin was someone who followed the Buddhist path (see Chapter 12).

Occasionally, however, the Buddha uses the word to refer not so much to a holy life as to the goal of that life. Thus, in the text quoted in Chapter 6 about his being criticized by a brahmin for allegedly helping himself alone, the Buddha replies, as I mentioned, that his disciples will dwell in the supreme state of immersion (*ogadha*) in *brahman* conduct (*brahma-cariyā*). Elsewhere he uses the same word and immersion, *ogadha*, with *nibbāna*, so it is clear that here he is using *brahma-cariyā* as a synonym for nirvana. If we return to the literal meaning of *brahma-cariyā*, it is indeed very close to the literal meaning of *brahma-vihāra*. So it is not surprising if the figurative meanings given to the terms by the Buddha are also close – though not identical.

ii. Saṃkappa (see Chapter 7)

The second step on the Noble Eightfold Path is called *sammā saṃkappa*, which is usually translated 'right resolve' or 'right intention'. That makes good sense: in order to embark on the right course of ethical behaviour, which leads into the right kinds of use of the mind, one needs to have both appropriate belief and appropriate motivation. The Sanskrit equivalent to *saṃkappa*, *saṃkalpa*, has several meanings; but I am not aware that it has been pointed out that it is a technical term in brahminical ritual.[1] When embarking on a ritual, the performer is supposed to make an explicit statement of intent, which normally includes his name, the date and the purpose of the ritual, whether worldly or spiritual. Since it is fundamental to the Buddha's message that he was substituting ethics for ritual, it is perfectly fitting that at the outset there should likewise be such a substitution, the correct mental attitude being a prerequisite for successful performance. This of course makes sense only in the original formulation of the Eightfold Path, as in the First Sermon; when that is reformulated as a sequence of three developments, in morality, concentration and understanding, and the Eightfold Path is re-jigged to suit that sequence, putting right intention last makes no sense at all.

iii. Ekodi-bhāva

In Chapter 4 I showed that the Buddha borrowed an important term, *āsava*, from the Jain tradition to formulate his teaching, even though the word carried connotations which his capacity for abstraction had rendered inapplicable. I suggest that he similarly borrowed from *Vedānta* certain words which have puzzled interpreters ever since. In the second of the ranked series of meditative states called *jhāna*, the Buddha stills all discursive thought and attains what is called the *ekodi-bhāva* of his mind.[2] The Canon contains other forms derived from this, like the verbs *ekodi-karoti*, 'to make *ekodi*' and *ekodi-bhavati*, 'to become *ekodi*'. Everyone agrees that this refers to one-pointedness of thought, elsewhere called *cittassa ekaggatā*, and yet the derivation, and hence the precise meaning, of *ekodi* remain obscure. In Buddhist Sanskrit *ekodi* is rendered *ekoti*. Quite a few Sanskritizations by the later tradition are wrong, but in this case I believe that this is the right solution. I think that in this state the Buddha (or the meditator following in his footsteps) is said to have the feeling (*bhāva*) which can be verbalized by the word 'one' in the masculine singular — *eko*; and that this refers to the same sensation of unity as is said to characterize many mystical experiences the world over, and more particularly that which is referred to in the *BĀU* as 'I am *brahman*'. I am not, of course, saying that the Buddha on his way to higher things had a Vedāntic gnosis; my claim is that, as with the word *karman*, he is borrowing that language in order to charge it with new meaning.[3]

iv. Puthujjana

I have a similar theory about this word. It is used, technically and frequently, to refer to people (*jana*) who have not even become stream-enterers on the path to Enlightenment. In other words, they are spiritually at square one. The word *puthu* is often found by itself, and the PED *s.v.* rightly says that it may correspond to Sanskrit *pṛthu*, 'many' or 'broad', or to *pṛthak*, meaning 'separated, individual'.[4] However, in the separate entry under *puthujjana*, presumably being influenced by the commentaries, it ignores the second meaning; so modern scholars favour such translations as 'one-of-the-many-folk' or '*hoi polloi*'. But the double *jj* is then a problem. In Buddhist Sanskrit the word is *pṛthag-jana*, and again I think that is right.

Phonetically the double *jj* is thus accounted for. Someone who has no sensation of oneness could surely be referred to as 'separate'.

There is in fact a verse in the Canon which contains the unusual expression *puthu attā*. I have alluded to the passage in Chapter 6 (text to n. 21), but referred readers who want a full discussion to my *How Buddhism Began* (pp. 62–4). There I translated the relevant line: 'For others too the separate self is dear.' I commented: 'It refers to the common sense view of the individual, the moral agent. But the term seems to allude, by implication, to a contrasting view of self, a "non-separate" self, the Upaniṣadic cosmic self.'

v. Papañca (see Chapter 10)

In Sanskrit and Pali, *pañca* means 'five'. So *papañca* looks as if it should mean 'quintuplication'. Could this make sense? In Sāṃkhya philosophy, and also sometimes in the *Mokṣadharma* section of *Mahābhārata* XII, the world evolves from a primal unity into sets of five, such as the five senses and the five great elements (*mahābhūta*),[5] so the multiplication of entities could fittingly be described as quintuplication. However, those texts postdate the Buddha by centuries, and in any case early Buddhism has six senses and four great elements. The word *papañca* does not seem to occur in Vedic literature early enough to be known to the Buddha. However, we have plenty of evidence that the Buddha was familiar with the first book of the *Bṛhad-āraṇyaka Upaniṣad*. In 1.5.3 this text lists the five kinds of breath (*āna*) which are said to permeate the human body; this list became canonical for the entire subsequent history of brahminism. The text says that all these are nothing but *prāṇa*. *Prāṇa* is the standard word for what we call 'breath', the breath of life. So the *Upaniṣad* is saying that we make five things out of what is really just one. Moreover, that one thing is life-breath. 'Several Upaniṣads equate breath with life and even with a person's self.'[6] (Remember that *ātman* may originally have meant 'breath'.)

The text as we have it does not use any word for quintuplication. However, the central message of the text as a whole is that we are bound to the cycle of rebirth by our ignorance of an essential unity, that of the *ātman*: we conceptualize multiplicity – in this case ideating five entities – where really there is only one.

At this point I must not be misunderstood. The Buddha was no Vedāntin, urging us to see the essential unity behind apparent but delusory multiplicity. He was, indeed, opposing that doctrine. But what I am suggesting (though in this case on rather slender evidence) is that here again, as with the words *ekodi-bhāva* and *puthujjana*, he was appropriating brahminical terminology. His argument was not that by using language we had *too many* concepts, but rather that none of them did justice to the truth.

And there is another point which risks being misunderstood. The Buddha is denying that we can distinguish, either perceptually or linguistically, between clear-cut *substances*. But he is not denying that we can distinguish between *processes*. The process of feeling, for example, is different from the process of willing. And, to take the most important example of all, your karma and my karma are by no means the same thing!

NOTES

Full details of publications appear in the Bibliography.

CHAPTER 1

1. *sabbe saṃkhārā aniccā.* The translation of *saṃkhārā* in this passage as 'compounded things', following T. W. Rhys Davids, has become usual. The term will be fully discussed in Chapter 9.
2. For more on this semantic problem, see my 'Understanding early Buddhist terminology in its context', pp. 74–101.
3. In Pali it is called the *Tipiṭaka,* which literally means 'that which consists of three baskets'.
4. In the Bhabra edict, the inscription in which he exhorts his subjects to learn certain named Buddhist texts, the emperor Asoka refers to the texts as *dhamma-paliyāya,* i.e., *pariyāya.*
5. This early terminology corresponds rather closely to the later distinction in Sanskrit between *sūtra* and *śāstra,* though the latter pair of terms refers to genres of text.
6. Perhaps I should add that in the Mahayana the term refers particularly to earlier non-Mahayana teachings, which are thus claimed to fall short of the full truth.
7. T. W. Rhys Davids, 'Introduction to the Kassapa-Sīhanāda Sutta,' *Dialogues of the Buddha, Part 1,* pp. 206–7. I quote the whole passage in *How Buddhism Began,* pp. 17–18.
8. Karma and nirvana are the two Buddhist doctrinal terms which I assume to have become naturalized in English and are therefore not italicized.
9. *AN* III, 415.
10. The term 'impermanent' does not, of course, necessarily imply that something is changing all the time, and I believe that in some contexts the Buddha did not intend the term to carry this strong sense. But expositions gloss this over; and in the *abhidharma* the doctrine was

systematized to mean constant change: it was even attempted to specify the speed of change.

11. In the Theravada/Pali tradition, these stories are conventionally said to number 550. Some of them are found in all major Buddhist traditions.
12. p. 40.
13. P: *sīla-bbata-parāmāso.*
14. Most of the last four paragraphs is taken from my *Theravada Buddhism: A Social History*, pp. 69–70.
15. *AN* I, 188–93.
16. Gombrich, *Theravada Buddhism*, pp. 83–8. This is of course not to deny that the Buddha's ideas can be, have been, and should be applied to politics and public affairs.
17. In Sanskrit the word is *kuśala.*
18. See L. S. Cousins, 'Good or skilful? – *Kusala* in Canon and commentary' (1996), especially pp. 143–8.
19. *Vin.* I, 49 para 20, 46 para 10.
20. This refers to their being written down for the first time. But our earliest physical evidence, our oldest manuscripts, of most texts is not nearly that old, and each copying brings further errors, including interpolations. For a summary account of our evidence for the Pali Canon, see my 'What is Pali?' in *A Pali Grammar.*

CHAPTER 2

1. I have thus accepted the criticism, first I believe made by Dr Sue Hamilton, of my earlier usage; I mention it in *How Buddhism Began* (2006), p. 37, n. 9.
2. The normal word is 'fruit' (*phala*). But occasionally the same thing is referred to as a 'harvest' (P: *apadāna*, literally 'reaping'). This latter word was Sanskritized as *avadāna* and its original meaning then forgotten. But like the Pali work entitled *Apadāna*, an *avadāna* was originally a story of how a deed in a former life bore fruit in the present.
3. *DN* I, 53–4.
4. *SN* IV, 230–1 = *sutta* xxxvi, 21.1. The same list at *AN* II, 87.
5. This is because the commentary (*Sārattha-ppakāsinī*, III, 81–82) instances being run over by a truck, being bitten by a snake and falling into a pit.
6. In this I am following the same entry in *PED*, *s.v. parihāra*, but choosing the first meaning given: 'attention, care'; the list of examples begins with *gabbha-parihāra*, 'care of the foetus'.
7. Thus Margaret Cone, *A Dictionary of Pāli: Part I* (2001), *s.v. opakkamika.* Peter Harvey has kindly pointed out to me (personal communication) that, at *MN* II, 218, the Buddha asks some Jains about their ascetic

practices; Ñāṇamoḷi and Bodhi translate: 'When there is intense exertion (*tippo upakkamo*), intense striving, do you then feel intense, painful, racking, piercing feelings due to intense exertion (*tippā tamhi samaye opakkamikā dukkhā tippā kaṭukā vedanā vedaniyatha*)?' This would be an act of violence perpetrated on oneself in rigorous asceticism. The commentary (see n. 5 above) says that the reference is to being beaten up on the grounds that one is a thief or adulterer; though this is ludicrously over-specific, it is plausible inasmuch as it refers to an act of violence perpetrated on one by others.

8. Richard Gombrich, *Precept and Practice* (1971), p. 150.
9. *AN* II, 80. The other three are the scope of a Buddha, the scope of a meditator and the world. The *sutta* gives no further explanation, so what is meant in these other cases is obscure.
10. *DN* I, 82–3.
11. There is a great deal of information in Greg Bailey and Ian Mabbett, *The Sociology of Early Buddhism* (2003), though I disagree with their interpretation of how it relates to the rise of Buddhism.
12. D. D. Kosambi, *The Culture and Civilisation of Ancient India in Historical Outline* (1965), pp. 100–1. Recent work on the Buddha's date – on which most other dating depends – means that for 'sixth century' we should now read 'fifth'.
13. *Ibid.*
14. Michael Willis, 'From relics to rice: early Buddhism and the Buddhist landscape of central India', lecture given at School of Oriental and African Studies, University of London, 23 January 2007.
15. Richard Seaford, *Money and the Early Greek Mind*, p. 317.
16. *Ibid.*, p. 293.
17. *Mahā Parinibbāna Sutta, DN, sutta* xvi; *DN* II, 73–9.
18. Gananath Obeyesekere, *Imagining Karma: Ethical Transformation in Amerindian, Buddhist, and Greek Rebirth* (2002), Chapter 3.
19. *Ibid.*
20. *MN* II, 149.
21. *Vin.* I, 152.
22. Steven Collins, *Selfless Persons* (1982), Chapter 4.

CHAPTER 3

1. The *Kauṣītakī Upaniṣad* (I, 2) has a slightly different version, which divides the dead into only two groups.
2. This discovery was the main reason why I found it necessary to publish a new edition of my *Theravada Buddhism: A Social History* in 2006.
3. Gananath Obeyesekere, *Imagining Karma: Ethical Transformation in Amerindian, Buddhist and Greek Rebirth.*

4. *Ibid.*, p. 15.
5. *Ibid.*, p. 74.
6. *Ibid.*, p. 75.
7. Joanna Jurewicz, 'Prajāpati, the fire and the *pañcāgni-vidyā*' (2004). She expanded her interpretation in a paper delivered at the 14th World Sanskrit Conference in Edinburgh, in July 2006, and a revised form of this may now be read on the website www.ocbs.org.
8. The word *pitṛ*, 'father', is used in the plural to refer to patrilineal ancestors.
9. Jāta-vedas is a name of Agni, fire personified [RFG].
10. Jurewicz, *op. cit.*, p. 53.
11. W. J. Johnson, *Harmless Souls* (1995), pp. 23–4.
12. E.g., *MN* III, 71–2. Here the Buddha characterizes this as the lower of two forms of right view, meritorious (*puñña-bhāgiya*) but still corrupted (*sāsava*) and thus to be transcended by supramundane (*lokuttarā*) right view. On this, Bhikkhu Bodhi, guided by the commentary, comments: 'We may understand that the conceptual comprehension of the four truths falls under mundane right view, while the direct penetration of the truths by realising Nibbāna with the path constitutes supramundane right view' (*The Middle Length Discourses*, pp. 1327–8, n. 1103). Thus the factual content of the two forms of right view is the same, but one understands it by different means. This subtlety smacks to me of the *abhidhamma*.
13. *BĀU* 4.3.7–9. The translations I give from the *Upaniṣads* are mostly those of Patrick Olivelle in *The Early Upaniṣads*, except that I have anglicized the spelling.
14. The ambiguity of this sentence will be explored below.
15. Erich Frauwallner, *History of Indian Philosophy* (1973), pp. 36–61. Alas, the translation is seriously inaccurate, so anyone who can should use the original German work, *Geschichte der indischen Philosophie* (1953).
16. *BĀU* 1.4.10. Later tradition took *tat tvam asi*, 'thou art that' (*Ch. Up.* 6.8.7–6.16.3) to mean the same thing, but modern scholarship has cast serious doubt on that interpretation. See Joel Brereton, '"*Tat Tvam Asi*" in context' (1986).
17. That God both transcends the world and is immanent in it is an idea familiar to Christian theologians.
18. See n. 16 above.
19. *BĀU* 6.2.15.
20. *Ch.Up.* 5.10.1: *śraddhā tapa ity upāsate.* This is obscure: 'who reverently understand faith to be austerity'? 'who reverently understand austerity to be faith'?
21. *BĀU* 6.2.16.
22. *Ch.Up.* 5.10.6.
23. These are the top three of the four estates (*varṇa*) of society according to the brahmin classification. See 'Background Information'.

24. *Ch.Up.* 5.10.7.
25. *BĀU* 6.2.16.
26. *Ch.Up.* 5.10.8.

CHAPTER 4

1. In his 'Observations on the sect of Jains' (1807) Henry Thomas Colebrooke was the first modern scholar clearly to distinguish Jainism from Buddhism, but he thought Buddhism to be the older.
2. Paul Dundas, *The Jains* (1992), p. 42.
3. Richard F. Gombrich, 'The significance of former Buddhas in Theravādin tradition' (1980).
4. Dundas, *op. cit.*, pp. 28–9.
5. *DN* III, 117–18; *DN* III, 209–10; *MN* II, 243–4.
6. Padmanabh S. Jaini, *The Jaina Path of Purification* (1979), p. 51.
7. Colette Caillat, *Les expiations dans le rituel ancien des religieux jaina* (1965), p. 50. In contrast to the ancient tradition of the solitary ascetic, followed by the *jinakappa*, the *therakappa* monks were not allowed to be alone, or normally even in pairs. Caillat does not relate this to the question of preserving the tradition; I owe this idea to a conversation with Will Johnson.
8. *Jina*, literally 'conqueror', is one of the titles of a 'ford-maker'.
9. *Thera* is another title shared between Jainism and Buddhism.
10. Dundas, *op. cit.*, p. 42.
11. Jains are not always clearly differentiated from other contemporary religious groups, such as the *Ājīvikas*, whose doctrines were markedly different but whose ascetic practices were probably similar. However, I believe that none of my arguments are affected by this slight lack of clarity.
12. In particular, Nalini Balbir, 'Jain–Buddhist dialogue: material from the Pali scriptures' (2000), and further references there cited.
13. W. B. Bollée, 'Buddhists and Buddhism in the early literature of the Śvetāmbara Jains' (1974).
14. Dundas, *op. cit.*, p. 81, citing the *Bhāgavatī*.
15. W. J. Johnson, *Harmless Souls* (1995), p. 6. I know Will Johnson for an excellent scholar and have relied heavily on his first chapter, on the earliest Jainism known to us.
16. *Sūyagaḍaṅga* 2.4.10, cited by Johnson, *op. cit.*, p. 17.
17. Johnson, *op. cit.*, p. 13.
18. *Ibid.*, p. 28.
19. *Dasaveyāliya* 6.5, quoted in Johnson, *op. cit.*, p. 22.
20. Johnson, *op. cit.*, p. 30.

21. *Ibid.*, p. 16.
22. *Ibid.*, p. 17.
23. For references to both sides of the controversy, see Balbir, *op. cit.*, p. 12, n. 34.
24. Johannes Bronkhorst, *The Two Traditions of Meditation in Ancient India* (1993); Richard Gombrich, 'The Buddha and the Jains: a reply to Professor Bronkhorst' (1994); Johannes Bronkhorst, 'The Buddha and the Jains reconsidered' (1995).
25. Johnson, *op. cit.*, p. 17.
26. See note 15 above.
27. *Vin.* III, 212.
28. *Vin.* III, 245.
29. I should make it clear that this general idea was quite widespread.

> As for Vedic religion, there is sufficient evidence that not only animals but also plants as well as seeds and even water and earth were ... believed to be living and even sentient, and fire and wind had at least a personalized, divine aspect ... Even in post-Vedic Hinduism, at least the view that plants and seeds capable of germination are sentient beings is still well documented, although some ... disagree. (L. Schmithausen, *The Problem of the Sentience of Plants in Earliest Buddhism* (1991), p. 3)

30. *Bījagāmā-bhūtagāmā samārambhā paṭivirato samaṇo Gotamo DN* I, 5. This question has been exhaustively treated by Schmithausen, *op. cit.*
31. *Vin.* I, 137. See also *Vin.* IV, 296.
32. This is the eleventh *pācittiya* rule (*Vin.* IV, 34).
33. Schmithausen simply translates '[people] regard trees as living beings' (*op. cit.*, p. 14) and sees no ambiguity.
34. Ute Hüsken, 'The legend of the establishment of the Buddhist order of nuns in the *Theravāda Vinaya-Piṭaka*' (2000).
35. In fact she uses the verb: *kammaṃ taṃ nijjaressāmi* (v.431).
36. *Elders' Verses* I, p. 142 (note on v.81 of the *Theragāthā*).
37. *Ehi Bhadde* (v.109). I am indebted to Bhikkhunī Juo-Hsüeh for drawing the significance of this to my attention.
38. Richard F. Gombrich, '*Pātimokkha*: purgative', in *Studies in Buddhism and Culture in Honour of Professor Dr. Egaku Mayeda on His Sixty-fifth Birthday*, The Editorial Committee of the Felicitation Volume for Professor Dr. Egaku Mayeda (eds). Tokyo: Sankibo Busshorin, 1991, pp. 33–8.
39. *Vin.* I, 104.
40. For instance, *DN* I, 84.
41. *MN, sutta* 2.
42. Peter Harvey, personal communication.
43. By Ludwig Alsdorf, cited approvingly by Johnson, *op. cit.*, p. 14.

44. *AN* II, 196–200, discussed in Gombrich, 'The Buddha and the Jains' (1994), pp. 1091–3.
45. See *PED s.v.* for many renderings and text references.
46. Umāsvāti's *Tattvārtha-sūtra*, perhaps the first Jain work to be written in Sanskrit, is dated between 150 and 350 AD.
47. Jaini, *op. cit.*, p. 97.
48. *Ibid.*, p. 162, n.11. These words are both Prakrit and a good deal of phonetic variation is thus unremarkable.
49. See *ibid.*, pp. 258–60, for an excellent account of the Jain *arhat* and a comparison with the Buddhist concept.
50. *Jitā me pāpakā dhammā, tasmāhaṃ Upaka Jino* (*Vin.* I, 8 = *MN* I, 171).
51. There are exceptions: Māra, himself a personification of death, has three daughters: thirst (*taṇhā*), lust (*rati*), disgust (*arati*).
52. Buddhaghosa gives as one of five possible *nirutti* (derivations) of *arahant* that he destroys his enemies, who are passion, etc. (*Visuddhi-magga*, p.198); and Lance Cousins has pointed out to me that this occurs several times in the Pali commentaries. We must remember that, unlike etymologies in our sense, *nirutti*s are not mutually exclusive; so this does not prove that the historical origin of the term was remembered.
53. Johnson, *op. cit.*, pp. 28–9.
54. *Ibid.*, p. 46.

CHAPTER 5

1. *BĀU* 4.3.7.
2. This is summarized in 4.3.34.
3. Richard F. Gombrich, 'Old bodies like carts' (1987).
4. *BĀU* 4.4.1–3, abbreviated.
5. 2.3.6 and 4.2.4 = 4.5.15.
6. To identify one's *ātman* with *brahman* is 'at the same time the truth to be discovered and the end to be attained' (Charles Malamoud, 'Inde védique. Religion et mythologie').
7. *Vijñānam ānandaṃ brahma* (*BĀU* 3.9.28). Another classic description of *brahman* is as reality (*satyam*), knowledge (*jñānam*) and infinite (*anantam*) (*Taittirīya Up.* 2.1).
8. 'He [*ātman*] is also breath divided into three' (*BĀU* 1.2.3).
9. *Sabbadā va sukhaṃ seti brāhmaṇo parinibbuto* (*SN* I, 212).
10. *sak-kāya-diṭṭhi.* The Sanskrit equivalent would be *sat-kāya-dṛṣṭi.* I have devoted an article to this: 'Vedānta stood on its head: *sakkāya* and *sakkāya-diṭṭhi*'.
11. *Visuddhi-magga*, p. 204.
12. *SN* I, 62. The inset lines are a verse.

13. The commonest technical terms for this in the Hindu tradition are *nirguṇa* and *saguṇa* respectively.
14. The word was originally a *karmadhāraya* compound, not a *bahuvrīhi.*
15. *DN* II, 157. The rest of the verse runs: *uppāda-vaya-dhammino// uppajjitvā nirujjhanti. tesaṃ vūpasamo sukho.*
16. Wan Doo Kim, 'The Theravādin Doctrine of Momentariness: A Survey of Its Origins and Development', D.Phil. thesis, Oxford University, 1999, pp. 62–4.
17. *AN* I, 152 = *sutta* III, 47. Kim plausibly suggests that this *sutta* derives from the *SN sutta* just cited.
18. How this happened in Theravada has been traced by Wan Doo Kim in his fine thesis, alas still unpublished.
19. *AN* V, 269.
20. Richard F. Gombrich, *Precept and Practice* (1971), p. 163.
21. Sue Hamilton, *Identity and Experience: The Constitution of the Human Being According to Early Buddhism* (1996), pp. 156–64.
22. See p.177 of my article 'The Buddhist attitude to thaumaturgy' (1997).
23. *MN* I, 265–6.

CHAPTER 6

1. Personally, I am not always on the side of the sophisticates. But that is irrelevant to my argument.
2. See below, Chapter 12. *Brahman* is named in verse 6.
3. *AN* I, 168–9.
4. *Aṣṭasāhasrikā-prajñāpāramitā* xxx, trans. E. Conze, *The Perfection of Wisdom in Eight Thousand Lines and Its Verse Summary*, Bolinas, CA (1973), p. 163.
5. I Corinthians, 13. How to translate P: *mettā* = S: *maitrī* is a dilemma, as further explained in the text below.
6. I have published this discovery twice before, in *How Buddhism Began: The Conditioned Genesis of the Early Teachings* (2006), pp. 58–64, and *Kindness and Compassion as Means to Nirvana* (1998). However, those publications seem to have had little impact, so I hope here to have improved the presentation.
7. *Visuddhi-magga* IX, §108, trans. Ñyāṇamoli (*sic*), *The Path of Purification*, 2nd edn, Colombo, 1964.
8. *appamāṇa.* However, in the *Metta Sutta* the (synonymous) word is *aparimāṇa,* perhaps because of the exigency of the metre.
9. The name of the *Chāndogya* appears in garbled form as *Chandoka* early in the *Tevijja Sutta* (*DN* I, p. 237).
10. *DN, sutta* xiii.
11. *DN* I, 81–4.

12. *Gahapati vā gahapati-putto vā aññatarasmiṃ vā kule paccājāto* (*Tevijja Sutta*, p. 250, para. 41).
13. *DN* I, p. 251, para. 80.
14. *DN* I, p. 251, para. 77.
15. There is a misconception abroad that the nirvana at death is differentiated by being called parinirvana. This is wrong. Either form of nirvana can be called parinirvana (P: *parinibbāna*; S: *parinirvāṇa*) with no change in meaning.
16. Unpublished paper delivered at a meeting in Oxford, September 2004.
17. 'I am quite deliberately inconsistent in translating many Pali words. Not only do meanings vary with context; it can simply be helpful to see that a Pali word has more than one possible rendition in English' (Gombrich, *How Buddhism Began*, p. xviii).
18. I owe this observation to Lance Cousins.
19. In the list of four the word is *muditā*; in the context of empathy with merit it is *anumodanā*.
20. *Sutta-nipāta* I, 8 = vv. 143–52. The text is quite often referred to as the *Karaṇīya Metta Sutta*; *karaṇīyaṃ* is its first word.
21. *Le Mahāvastu*, ed. É. Senart, vol. III, p. 421, lines 18–19.
22. The conversation occurs twice in the *Upaniṣad*, at II, 4, and IV, 5; the relevant passage is the same in both versions.
23. *SN* I, 75.
24. Gombrich, *How Buddhism Began*, pp. 62–4.
25. *Ibid.*, pp. 85–6.
26. *Visuddhi-magga* IX, §124, trans. Ñyāṇamoli.
27. I have studied a *sutta* in the *Majjhima Nikāya* which presents an amusing satire on Brahmā and the Brahma heavens: Richard F. Gombrich, 'A visit to Brahmā the heron' (2001).
28. For some detail see Gombrich, *Kindness and Compassion*, p. 11. The ramifications of denying that *ceto-vimutti* is true liberation became vast: see Gombrich, *How Buddhism Began*, pp. 112 ff..
29. *Dhammasaṅgani*, para. 1056.
30. *Ibid.*, para. 1054. I am grateful to Sarah Shaw for drawing my attention to these *abhidhamma* passages.

CHAPTER 7

1. Quoted in obituary of Max Perutz, *The Times*, Thursday 7 February 2002, p. 21.
2. *The Burlington Magazine*, February 2002, p. 113.
3. *Daily Telegraph*, 27 March 2002.

4. Karl R. Popper, *Conjectures and Refutations* (1963). The first chapters of this book contain detailed expositions of this position. Here let it suffice to quote from the 'Preface' (p. vii):

> The way in which knowledge progresses ... is by unjustified (and unjustifiable) assumptions, by guesses, by tentative solutions to our problems, by *conjectures.* These conjectures are controlled by criticism; that is, by attempted *refutations,* which include severely critical tests. They may survive these tests; but they can never be positively justified: they can never be established as certainly true nor even as 'probable' (in the sense of the probability calculus) ... As we learn from our mistakes our knowledge grows, even though we may never know – that is, know for certain. Since our knowledge can grow, there can be no reason here for despair of reason. And since we can never know for certain, there can be no authority here for any claim to authority ...

5. Translation is more fully discussed in section VI of my 1993 paper 'Understanding early Buddhist terminology in its context'.
6. Richard F. Gombrich, 'Dating the Buddha: a red herring revealed' (1992).
7. Ricoeur coined the term to describe such major theories as those of Marx and Freud which claimed that one had to suspect in one's sources systematic bias on the principles they explained. He was not referring to simple jejune scepticism, but to finding a meaning below the surface.
8. Przemyslaw Szczurek, '*Prajñāvādāṃś ca bhāṣase*: polemics with Buddhism in the early parts of the *Bhagavadgītā*' (2003). Moreover, Madeleine Biardeau sees many passages in the *Mahābhārata* in this light: see *Le Mahābhārata: un récit fondateur du brahmanisme et son interprétation* (2002), especially pp. 120–8.
9. For a concise survey of the Pali language and its use in texts, see my brief article 'What is Pali?' in *A Pali Grammar* (1994).
10. Oskar von Hinüber, *The Oldest Pali Manuscript* (1991).
11. This enables me to correct a misprint on p. xxvi of my article 'What is Pali?': this committal to writing is said to have occurred in the first century AD. Luckily, the next sentence makes clear that this should read 'BC'.
12. By 'canonical' I mean much the same as *Buddha-vacana,* 'the word of the Buddha'. The latter is slightly narrower than 'canonical', because in a *sutta,* for example, it does not include details such as when and where the sermon was delivered, which are supposed to have been added at the First Council (see next section).
13. P: *saṃgīti* or *saṃgāyanā.*
14. See Richard F. Gombrich, 'The history of early Buddhism: major advances since 1950' (1988), section 3, pp. 16–19.

15. *Vin.* I, 196 = *Ud.* V, 6. In the latter passage it says that the monk recited sixteen poems, in the *Vinaya* merely that he recited 'all'.
16. *Sumaṅgala-vilāsinī* I, 22–3.
17. For more on the similarities in form between the Pali Canon and Vedic literature, see Richard F. Gombrich, 'How the Mahāyāna began' (1990), pp. 23–4.
18. *Manusmṛti* III, 1.
19. Alexander Wynne, 'The oral transmission of the early Buddhist literature' (2004).
20. K. R. Norman, 'The Four Noble Truths' (1982).
21. Erich Frauwallner, *The Earliest Vinaya and the Beginnings of Buddhist Literature* (1956), p. 67.
22. *SN* V, 420–4.
23. Richard F. Gombrich, 'Three souls, one or none: the vagaries of a Pali pericope' (1987).
24. *Early History of Buddhism in Ceylon* (1953).
25. This was called *eka-vākyatā.*
26. *AN* II, 135. I discuss this issue in *How Buddhism Began* (2006), pp. 22–4.
27. This principle is known by the Latin phrase *lectio difficilior potior* (The more difficult reading is to be preferred).
28. Ernst Waldschmidt, *Die Ueberlieferung vom Lebensende des Buddha* (1944–48).
29. *DN* II, 156.
30. *DN* II, 84, for the full version.
31. This term is further discussed in the Appendix.
32. *DN* I, 124.
33. Popper, *op. cit.*

CHAPTER 8

1. Exactly the same applies when these words have the further prefix *pari-*, e.g., *parinibbāna, parinibbuta.* We have seen a use of the latter in Chapter 5, n. 9. See also Chapter 6, n. 14.
2. Printed as prose in the PTS edition, but Ludwig Alsdorf pointed out that the passage is in verse.
3. Sanskrit *tri-doṣa.* This term is also found in Vasubandhu's *Abhidharmakośabhāṣya.*
4. Sue Hamilton, *Identity and Experience: The Constitution of the Human Being According to Early Buddhism* (1996) and *Early Buddhism: A New Approach* (2000). Both this chapter and Chapter 10 owe a great deal to these two books.

5. In my book *How Buddhism Began* (2006), pp. 67–8, I further connect this to the short sermon about the burden (*SN* III, 25–6), which through pedantic literalism gave rise to the Buddhist school of *pudgala-vāda*; but this topic is not relevant here.
6. The extra *k* in *kkhandha* when it occurs as the second member of a compound is just an arbitrary spelling convention.
7. Bhikkhu Bodhi, *The Connected Discourses of the Buddha* (2002), pp. 589–90.
8. For a fine study of the complex history of these two terms, see Soon-il Hwang, *Metaphor and Literalism in Buddhism: The Doctrinal History of Nirvana* (2006).
9. This was apparently forgotten at a very early stage. Because of phonetic similarity, *upādi* in this context was changed to *upadhi*. The latter means 'basis, foundation', and in particular was used to refer to the basis for craving (*taṇhā*). As this made satisfactory sense, no one noticed that there was even a problem with the original terms.
10. G. E. R. Lloyd, *Demystifying Mentalities* (1990), pp. 20–1.
11. *Kosmogonia Rygwedy. Myśl i metafora* [*Cosmogony of the Ṛgveda. Thought and Metaphor*] (2001). My quotations in the following passage, unless indicated otherwise, are drawn from the unpublished draft English version.
12. In theory this should be done at dawn, twilight and dusk. The dawn recitation is the most important.
13. For the next seven paragraphs I am wholly indebted to my friend Professor Joanna Jurewicz of the University of Warsaw; on occasion I even use her words.
14. So, incidentally, is Soma; but to discuss that would take us too far afield.
15. This is the latter part of *Mahābhārata*, book XII.
16. Joanna Jurewicz, 'Prajāpati, the fire and the *pañcâgni-vidyā*' (2004). See also Chapter 3, n. 7.
17. This is obscured by Eggerling's translation: 'This, then, weighed in his mind'; the Sanskrit has simply *tad evâsya manasy āsa*: 'Just that was in his mind.'
18. Jurewicz, *op.cit.*, p. 67.
19. For Vessantara, see the beginning of Chapter 12 below.
20. We recall how the Buddha made an advance in the conscious use of abstractions. The mind is therefore the organ which perceives abstractions. 'Mind' is *manaṃ* and 'ideas' *dhamme*, both here being in the accusative.
21. Patrick Olivelle, *The Early Upaniṣads* (1998), pp. xxi–xxii, p.8, and note to passage cited.
22. In this sense *mahā-bhūta* is commoner than *bhūta*.
23. *SN* II, 11–12.
24. There is a large collection of *sutta*s about causal chains: the *Nidāna-saṃyutta* of the *Saṃyutta Nikāya*. Most of them are about the Chain of

Dependent Origination, but a few concern the chain of the four foods. The most substantial, with vivid similes, are *suttas* 63 and 64 (= *SN* II, 98–104).

25. *Mano* means 'mental', so adds nothing.
26. Alexander Wynne, *The Origin of Buddhist Meditation* (2007). The book is based on his Oxford D.Phil. thesis, 2003.
27. I have discussed the relationship between these two kinds of meditation in Chapter 4 of *How Buddhism Began* (2006).
28. Jurewicz has shown that this is the true meaning of the deceptively simple compound *nāma-rūpa*, literally 'name and form'. See next note.
29. Joanna Jurewicz, 'Playing with fire: the *pratītyasamutpāda* from the perspective of Vedic thought' (2000).
30. This is the *Yogācāra* or *Vijñānavāda* school.
31. The vision of the poets of the *Ṛg Veda* may have been of a less static world, for their word for the underlying system of the world, *ṛta*, is connected with a verbal root (*ṛ*) meaning 'go'.
32. Walpola Rahula pointed out the similarity to Heraclitus, but did not connect it to fire, in *What the Buddha Taught* (1959), p. 26, n. 1.

CHAPTER 9

1. *Vin.* I, 40.
2. This hypothesis, by which I explain why a *dhamma* is called a *dhamma*, is more fully explained in *How Buddhism Began* (1996), pp. 35–6.
3. In some traditions this introductory section, a very popular text, acquired a separate identity under the Sanskrit title of *Catuṣ-pariṣat-sūtra*.
4. *Vin.* I, 11.
5. Pali: *avijjā, saṃkhārā, viññāṇaṃ, nāma-rūpa, saḷ-āyatanaṃ, phasso, vedanā, taṇhā, upādānaṃ, bhavo, jāti, jarā-maraṇaṃ.*
6. *DN* II, 55.
7. I owe this observation to members of the audience when I gave this chapter as a lecture at S.O.A.S. (see Preface).
8. Joanna Jurewicz, 'Playing with fire: the *pratītyasamutpāda* from the perspective of Vedic thought' (2000).
9. *Ibid.*, p. 81.
10. *Ibid.*, p. 100.
11. Joanna Jurewicz, 'The *Ṛgveda* 10.129: an attempt of interpretation' (1995), pp. 141–50. Later publications which give a great deal more evidence for her interpretation are unfortunately still available only in Polish.
12. There is an alternative spelling: *saṅkhārā*.
13. Jurewicz (2000), p. 82.
14. *Ibid.*, pp. 89–91.

15. *Ibid.*, pp. 100–1.
16. Erich Frauwallner, *Geschichte der indischen Philosophie* (1953), vol. 1, p. 211.
17. This interpretation also explains why 'desire' appears to figure twice in the chain, once as *saṃkhārā* and once as *taṇhā*: the two come out of different contexts. See also the further discussion of *saṃkhārā* below.
18. This might also help us to interpret a famous crux in the *Bṛhad-āraṇyaka Upaniṣad* (4.4.10), but I cannot explore that here.
19. See especially Frauwallner, *op. cit.*, pp. 200–3. Also useful is Bhikkhu Bodhi, *The Connected Discourses of the Buddha* (2000), pp. 44–7.

CHAPTER 10

1. For a thorough and authoritative account of how the five *khandha* combine to create conscious experience, see Sue Hamilton, *Identity and Experience: The Constitution of the Human Being According to Early Buddhism* (1996). I must warn readers that my attempt to summarize this without lapsing into obscurity has resulted in some over-simplification.
2. An even commoner term is *saḷ-āyatana*, 'the six domains', but this term covers both the six faculties and their objects; the faculties are called 'pertaining to the self' (*ajjhattika*) and their objects 'external' (*bāhira*) *āyatana*. Sometimes there are only five *indriya*, the mind not being counted, but the system settles down to counting six.
3. '... *viññāṇa* only functions when there are other concomitant mental states which are primarily of a volitional nature.' Hamilton, *op. cit.*, p. 87, based on *SN* II, 65f.
4. Hamilton, *op. cit.*, pp. 54–5, 92.
5. Noa Ronkin, *Early Buddhist Metaphysics* (2005).
6. *DN* I, 45, trans. Ronkin, *op. cit.*, p. 245.
7. Ronkin, *ibid.*
8. Hence the common compound *nāma-rūpa*, 'name-form', as explained in Chapter 9.
9. Norman Brown, 'Theories of creation in *Rig Veda*' (1965), p. 27.
10. This kind of analysis, called S: *nirukti*, P: *nirutti*, has nothing to do with grammar.
11. See my article 'The Buddha's book of Genesis?' (1992).
12. For some of my views on the Buddha's attitude to language I am indebted to the excellent (unpublished) thesis by Isabelle Onians, 'Language, Speech and Words in Early Buddhism', M.Phil. thesis in Oriental Studies, Oxford, April 1996.
13. *Vin.* II, 139.
14. *Vin.* II, 108, where the Buddha prohibits reciting his teaching in a drawn-out musical tone. Onians shows that this must be taken together with the *chandaso* prohibition.

15. He thus moved Pali in the direction of being for Theravada Buddhists what Sanskrit was for brahmins. But the move also had advantages. See my *Theravada Buddhism* (2006), pp. 153–5.
16. Alexander Wynne, 'The oral transmission of the early Buddhist literature' (2004).
17. *MN, sutta* 139.
18. *MN* III, 234. See Onians, *op. cit.*, p. 8, and work by K. R. Norman there quoted.
19. This is the brahmin view of Indian vernacular languages.
20. *MN, sutta* 121, *Cūla-suññatā Sutta.*
21. In the *Cūla-suññatā Sutta* at *MN* II, 108, he uses the synonyms *abhisaṃkhata* and *abhisaṃcetayita.*
22. 'There is no suggestion that the world is *merely* conceptual, only that it is *saññā* that interprets it according to our level of insight.' Hamilton, *op. cit.*, p. 60.
23. Ronkin, *loc.cit.*
24. The *locus classicus* for this use of *papañca* is *MN* I, 109, in the *Madhupiṇḍika Sutta.* The wording is obscure, the commentary hopeless, and I suspect that the text is corrupt. However, I agree that the general purport is fairly clear, so that although I am unconvinced by much of the detailed discussion by other scholars, I here refrain from going into it further.
25. To my surprise, neither cataphatic nor apophatic is given in the *Oxford Shorter English Dictionary* or in *Webster's.* But they can successfully be Googled on the internet. Readers should be warned that spelling varies between cataphatic and kataphatic.
26. *BĀU* 2.3.6.
27. *Taittirīya Up.* 2.4.
28. I draw my example from Michael Coulson, *Teach Yourself Sanskrit* (1976), p. 111.
29. William James, *The Varieties of Religious Experience* (1985), pp. 380–1.
30. Walpola Rahula, *What the Buddha Taught* (1959), p. 10.
31. Richard F. Gombrich, 'Another Buddhist criticism of Yājñavalkya' (2002).
32. On the undecided questions see Ninian Smart, *Doctrine and Argument in Indian Philosophy* (1964), pp. 33–7. See also p. 167 below.
33. Rahula, *op. cit.*, p. 40.
34. See Chapter 5, n. 6.
35. These poems, the *Thera-* and *Therī-gāthā*, are illustrated and discussed in my monograph *Religious Experience in Early Buddhism* (1998), pp. 14–18. I explain that it is quite possible that the authors had not had dramatic experiences similar to the Buddha's Enlightenment, but had reached the sensation of being enlightened by a more routinized path.
36. James, *loc. cit.*

37. See Chapter 6, n. 14, above. There is useful material on the terminology in Bhikkhu Bodhi, *The Connected Discourses of the Buddha* (2000), pp. 49–52.
38. Some students find this unsatisfactory and persist in asking pointless questions, but I do not understand why they find this so different from the accepted fact that we do not know, and never shall know, just what dying feels like for anybody.
39. *Ud.* VIII, 3 = pp. 80–1.
40. I think this may be the route by which the Hua Yen school arrived at their doctrine that everything conditions everything else.
41. *SN* II, 17. It is in the *Nidāna Saṃyutta,* a title which indicates that that section of the text primarily concerns Dependent Origination.

CHAPTER 11

1. *MN* II, 260. The word for 'craving' here is *taṇhā,* literally 'thirst', so that we are confronted with a harsh mixed metaphor. It would seem that *taṇhā* had become accepted as a technical term and its metaphorical character was no longer vivid.
2. This recalls the formulation by Clifford Geertz, that religion offers at the same time a model *of* and a model *for.* (See Clifford Geertz, 'Religion as a cultural system', in *The Interpretation of Cultures,* 1976, p. 123). I have applied this to (brahminical) *dharma* in 'Is Dharma a good thing?' (1997).
3. Paul Williams, *Buddhist Thought* (2000), p. 40. I strongly recommend the whole section 'The Buddha's attitude to his teaching: the arrow and the raft', pp. 34–40.
4. *AN* IV, 203.
5. Williams, *op. cit.,* p. 245 (n. 1 to Chapter 1).
6. This applies particularly to Chapters 8 to 10 above.
7. *SN* V, 437–8.
8. *MN* I, 482.
9. Bhikkhu Ñāṇamoḷi and Bhikkhu Bodhi, *The Middle Length Discourses of the Buddha* (2001), p. 1276, n. 714.
10. *MN, sutta* 12.
11. *MN* I, 395. We can deduce that the last remark refers to flattery.
12. *Cūlamāluṅkyā Sutta, MN, sutta* 63. What I have put in direct quotations is an abbreviated version of *MN* I, 431.
13. That actions have unintended consequences is a salient feature of Karl Popper's view of history and society. See my *Theravada Buddhism* (2006), pp. 15–18.
14. Williams, *op. cit.,* p.38.
15. *MN* I, 394.

16. *MN* II, 197.
17. On this occasion he says he is not *ekaṃsa-vādo*, which one could translate 'arguing one-sidedly'.
18. Ñāṇamoḷi and Bodhi, *The Middle Length Discourse of the Buddha*, p. 1303, n. 909.
19. *AN* II, 46, quoted in Walpola Rahula, *What the Buddha Taught* (1959), p. 64.
20. Rahula, *op. cit.*, p. 63.
21. Williams, *op. cit.*, p. 39.
22. *AN* II, 135.
23. The terms are explained at *Puggala-paññatti* IV, 5 (= p. 41).
24. There are different readings and consequently different interpretations of the name of this second type.
25. For more on the Buddha's condemnation of literalism see my *How Buddhism Began*, pp. 22–4.
26. *Theravada Buddhism: A Social History*, p. 79.
27. For example, at *AN* IV, 59–63, he ranks seven motives for making gifts. The highest is 'for the decoration and equipment of the mind'.
28. *DN* II, 85–6.
29. *Theravada Buddhism: A Social History*, p. 80.
30. Why has the unusual English word 'mindfulness' come to be preferred to 'awareness' as the standard translation for *sati*? Another attempt to make the East more mysterious?
31. I feel fortunate that Sarah Shaw's admirable survey of canonical passages dealing with meditation should have appeared while I was preparing the lectures on which this book is based. Sarah Shaw, *Buddhist Meditation: An Anthology of Texts from the Pali Canon* (2006).
32. See *How Buddhism Began* (2006), Chapter IV, especially pp. 123–7.
33. *DN, sutta* 2.
34. As he writes, 'meditation' (*bhāvanā*) includes 'all our studies, reading, discussions, conversation and deliberations' on 'ethical, spiritual and intellectual subjects'. 'To read this book, and to think deeply about the subjects discussed in it, is a form of meditation' (Rahula, *op. cit.*, p. 74).
35. *Vin.* III, 21, etc.
36. See note 13 above.
37. T1428, translated by Buddhayaśas in 410 AD.
38. Richard F. Gombrich, 'Popperian Vinaya: conjecture and refutation in practice' (2007).
39. *Vin.* I, 77.
40. I. B. Horner translates this stock expression: 'This is not for pleasing those who are not (yet) pleased, nor for increasing the number of those who are pleased.' But this makes the two results mean the same. I think therefore that *bhiyyo* here means more in quality rather than in number.
41. *Vin.* IV, 128–30.

42. It is in the Dharmaguptaka version of the *Khandhaka*, so its omission here in the Pali must simply be due to textual corruption. Moreover, the Dharmaguptaka version makes it clear that the issue concerns only full ordination. Logically this must be right: the mention of *pabbajjā* is anachronistic, as this is the start of the account of how that came to be a separate institution with a lower age requirement.
43. Though the *Vinaya* is not squeamish about mentioning sexual offences, it is worth noting that no case is ever mentioned of a monk abusing a novice or being suspected of doing so.
44. The five *sīla*, the eight and the ten *sikkhāpada* (both of which sets begin with *sīla*).
45. *MN* I, 220 (*Mahāgopālaka Sutta*).
46. *DN* III, 187 (*Sigālovāda Sutta*).

CHAPTER 12

1. V. Fausbøll (ed.), *Jātaka*, vol. vi, London, 1896, pp. 479–596. Translated and illustrated by Margaret Cone and Richard F. Gombrich as *The Perfect Generosity of Prince Vessantara* (1977).
2. For a survey of the story's diffusion, see Cone and Gombrich, *op. cit.*, pp. xxxv–xliv.
3. The word has no meaning, but suggests the Sanskrit verbal root *jṝ*, 'to age, to decay'.
4. *Brāhmaṇa-dhammika Sutta, Snip.*, vv. 284–315.
5. *Asura* and *rakkhasa* are two classes of non-human beings whose moral and cosmic standing is no higher than that of humans – in fact, *rakkhasa*s are demons.
6. *Snip.*, vv. 310–11.
7. *Mahā Assapura Sutta, MN* 39; *MN* I, 280.
8. This pun is of interest to philologists, because it very strongly suggests that in the Buddha's dialect the word *brāhmaṇa* was pronounced *bāhaṇa*, which is indeed one of the several forms of the word found in the inscriptions of Asoka.
9. There is in fact no precise Sanskrit equivalent to *veda-gu*, though the meaning is obvious; the word is formed by analogy with *vedanta-gu* (see next paragraph).
10. The passage recurs at *Ud.* 3.
11. *Vin.* I, 3.
12. *Vin.* I, 5–7.
13. *DN* I, 17–18.
14. T. W. Rhys Davids (trans.), *Dialogues of the Buddha*, Part I (1899), pp. 30–2.

15. Rhys Davids translates this last phrase as 'in all respects like him', which I have changed for fear of ambiguity.
16. Rhys Davids, *op. cit.*, p. 31, n. 1.
17. The word which Olivelle translates 'prospers' is *bhavati*, so I would prefer to translate more literally 'comes into being', even though this sounds paradoxical.
18. *The Early Upaniṣads* (1998), pp. xxi–xxii, p. 8, and note to passage cited.
19. *Dīgha Nikāya, sutta* xxvii.
20. 'Aggañña Sutta: the Buddha's book of Genesis?' (1992).
21. *AN* I, 162.
22. *Sumaṅgala-vilāsinī*, P.T.S. edn, III, 861–2.
23. *Dīghanikāyaṭṭhakathāṭīkā Līnatthavaṇṇanā*, P.T.S. edn, III, 47.
24. These are Sanskrit texts, auxiliary to the Vedas, on such subjects as phonetics.
25. *Sāmaññaphala Sutta, DN* I, 60–1.
26. *SN* III, 120.
27. This ambiguity in the word *brahma-* has been explained in Chapter 3.
28. T. W. Rhys Davids and C. A. F. Rhys Davids, *Dialogues of the Buddha*, Part III (1921), pp. 77–94.
29. *Cūla Dukkha-kkhandha Sutta, MN, sutta* 14. Though *khandha* is usually translated just 'mass', I have explained in Chapter 8 that it is often short for *aggi-kkhandha*, a blazing mass of fuel.
30. This is an accurate description of the Jain practice of *nijjarā*; see Chapter 4.
31. *MN* I, 93.
32. *MN, sutta* 51.
33. At this point the text refers only to the king and his chief queen; I assume that if the sponsor (*yajamāna*) is a rich brahmin, he and his first wife take these roles.
34. *MN* I, 343–4. The same criticism of brahminical sacrifice is spelt out at greater length in the *Kūṭadanta Sutta, DN, sutta* 5; see especially *DN* I, 141–2.
35. *AN* I, 180–5.

CHAPTER 13

1. I have quoted the whole message verbatim, merely omitting two short allusions to other postings on the Indology net.
2. *Sic.* The professor presumably means 'palisants', i.e., people who study Pali.
3. This is not a fundamental inequality, in that it is due to their moral history, especially in former lives.

4. Ulric Neisser, *Cognition and Reality* (1976), p. 55.
5. 'Perception and cognition are usually not just operations in the head, but transactions with the world. These transactions do not merely *in*form the perceiver, they also *trans*form him. Each of us is created by the cognitive acts in which he engages.' Neisser, *op. cit.*, p. 11 (italics original).
6. There are exceptions: comparatively trivial acts, whether good or bad, may never come to fruition because they simply get crowded out by more significant acts. The technical term for such a superseded act in Theravada is *ahosi kamma.*
7. Richard F. Gombrich, *Precept and Practice* (1971); 2nd edn (with changed title), *Buddhist Precept and Practice* (1991), Chapter 5, especially pp. 226–40. This overlaps heavily with my article '"Merit transference" in Sinhalese Buddhism: a case of the interaction between doctrine and practice,' *History of Religions*, 11 (2), 1971: 203–19.
8. *How Buddhism Began* (1996), pp. 56–7.
9. See my article 'A momentous effect of translation: the "vehicles" of Buddhism' (1996), 1992.
10. See Chapter 11, n.13.
11. *DN* II, 100.
12. P: *atta-saraṇa.*
13. *TLS*, no. 5479, 4 April 2008, p. 18.

APPENDIX

1. *Baudhāyana Śrauta Sūtra* 2.1. I am indebted to Joel Brereton and Patrick Olivelle for this reference.
2. The *locus classicus* is *DN* I, 74.
3. The *di* derives from *ti*, the Prakritic form of Sanskrit *iti*, used to mean 'close quotes'. I interpret the *d* for *t* as a Prakritic intervocalic voicing of a stop, which was not recognized and thus remained unchanged by the early redactors.
4. The second vowel, *u*, is just a case of vowel levelling.
5. The five elements are earth, air, fire, water and space; Buddhism omits space. There is a different list of five elements very near the end of the *Aitareya Upaniṣad* (3.3), but I doubt that this is relevant.
6. Patrick Olivelle, *The Early Upaniṣads* (1998), p. 23. For a full discussion, see Erich Frauwallner, *History of Indian Philosophy* (1973), pp. 55–60.

BIBLIOGRAPHY

PRIMARY SOURCES

Buddhist sources

Texts

References to Pali texts are to the editions of the Pali Text Society.

Aṣṭasāhasrikā prajñāpāramitā, ed. P.L. Vaidya. Darbhanga: Mithilāvidyāpīṭha, 1960.

Dharmaguptaka Vinaya T1428. Tokyo: Taisho Shinshu Daizokyo Kankokai, 1962.

Senart, É. (ed.). 1882–97. *Le Mahāvastu*. 3 vols. Paris: L'Imprimérie nationale.

Translations

Bodhi, Bhikkhu. 2000. *The Connected Discourses of the Buddha* [trans. of *Saṃyutta Nikāya*]. Oxford: Pali Text Society; Somerville, MA: Wisdom.

Conze, E. 1973. *The Perfection of Wisdom in Eight Thousand Lines and Its Verse Summary*. Bolinas, CA.

Davids, T. W. Rhys. 1899. *Dialogues of the Buddha*, Part I [trans. of *Dīgha Nikāya* I]. London: Oxford University Press.

Davids, T. W. Rhys, and C. A. F. Rhys Davids. 1921. *Dialogues of the Buddha*, Part III [trans. of *Dīgha Nikāya* III]. London: Oxford University Press.

Ñāṇamoḷi, Bhikkhu. 1956. *The Path of Purification* [trans. of *Visuddhi-magga* by Buddhaghosa]. Colombo: R. Semage.

Ñāṇamoḷi, Bhikkhu, and Bhikkhu Bodhi. 2001. *The Middle Length Discourses of the Buddha* [trans. of *Majjhima Nikāya*], rev. edn. Oxford: Pali Text Society.

Norman, K. R. 2007. *Elders' Verses*, Vol. 2. [trans. of *Therīgāthā*], 2nd edn. Lancaster: Pali Text Society.

Pruden, Leo M. 1988–1990. *Abhidharmakośabhāṣyam* by Vasubandhu [English trans. from the French trans. by Louis de la Vallée Poussin]. Berkeley: Asian Humanities Press.

Brahminical sources

Doniger, Wendy O'Flaherty (trans.). 1981. *The Rig Veda: An Anthology*. Harmondsworth: Penguin.

Olivelle, Patrick (ed. and trans.). 1998. *The Early Upaniṣads*. New York: Oxford University Press.

Olivelle, Patrick (ed. and trans.). 1999. *The Dharmasūtras: The Law Codes of Āpastamba, Gautama, Baudhāyana, and Vasiṣṭha*. Oxford and New York: Oxford University Press.

Jaina sources

For *Sūyagaḍaṅga* and *Dasaveyāliya*, see W. J. Johnson below.

Jaini, J. L. (ed. and trans.). 1920. *Tattvārthādhigamasūtra* by Umāsvāti. (*Sacred Books of the Jains*, vol. II), Arrah.

SECONDARY SOURCES

Adikaram, E. W. 1953. *Early History of Buddhism in Ceylon*, 2nd edn. Colombo: Gunasena.

Bailey, Greg, and Ian Mabbett. 2003. *The Sociology of Early Buddhism*, Cambridge: Cambridge University Press.

Balbir, Nalini. 2000. 'Jain-Buddhist dialogue: material from the Pali scriptures,' *Journal of the Pali Text Society*, **26**: 1–42.

Biardeau, Madeleine. 2002. *Le* Mahābhārata*: un récit fondateur du brahmanisme et son interprétation*, 2 vols. Paris: Éditions du Seuil.

Bollée, W. B. 1974. 'Buddhists and Buddhism in the early literature of the *Śvetāmbara* Jains', in L. S. Cousins *et al.* (eds), *Buddhist Studies in Honour of, I. B. Horner*. Dordrecht: D. Reidel, pp. 27–39.

Brereton, Joel. 1986. '"*Tat Tvam Asi*" in context,' *Zeitschrift der Deutschen Morgenländischen Gesellschaft*, **136**: 98–109.

Bronkhorst, Johannes. 1993. *The Two Traditions of Meditation in Ancient India*, 2nd edn. Delhi: Motilal Banarsidass.

Bronkhorst, Johannes. 1995. 'The Buddha and the Jains reconsidered,' *Asiatische Studien/Études Asiatiques*, **49**(2): 330–50.

Brown, Norman. 1965. 'Theories of creation in *Rig Veda*', *Journal of the American Oriental Society*, **85**(1): 23–34.

Caillat, Colette. 1965. *Les expiations dans le rituel ancien des religieux jaina*. Paris: E. de Boccard.

Colebrooke, Henry Thomas. 1807. 'Observations on the Sect of Jains'. Calcutta: *Asiatic Researches IX*.

Collins, Steven. 1982. *Selfless Persons*. Cambridge: Cambridge University Press.

Cone, Margaret. 2001. *A Dictionary of Pāli: Part I*. Oxford: Pali Text Society.

Cone, Margaret, and Richard Gombrich. 1977. *The Perfect Generosity of Prince Vessantara*. Oxford: Clarendon Press.

Coulson, Michael. 1976. *Teach Yourself Sanskrit*. London: Hodder & Stoughton.

Cousins, Lance S. 1996. 'Good or skilful? – *Kusala* in Canon and commentary,' *Journal of Buddhist Ethics*, **3**: 136–64.

Davids, T. W. Rhys. 1899. 'Introduction to the *Kassapa-Sīhanāda Sutta*,' in *Dialogues of the Buddha*, Part 1. London: Pali Text Society.

Davids, T. W. Rhys, and William Stede. 1921–25. *The Pali Text Society's Pali–English Dictionary*. Chipstead, Surrey: Pali Text Society.

Dundas, Paul. 1992. *The Jains*. London and New York: Routledge.

Frauwallner, Erich. 1953. *Geschichte der indischen Philosophie*, 2 vols. Salzburg: Otto Mueller.

Frauwallner, Erich. 1956. *The Earliest Vinaya and the Beginnings of Buddhist Literature*. Serie Orientale Roma VIII. Rome: IsMEO.

Frauwallner, Erich. 1973. *History of Indian Philosophy* (trans. V. M. Bedekar), 2 vols. Delhi: Motilal Banarsidass.

Geertz, Clifford. 1976. *The Interpretation of Cultures*. London: Hutchinson.

Gombrich, Richard F. 1971. *Precept and Practice*. Oxford: Clarendon Press.

Gombrich, Richard F. 1971. '"Merit transference" in Sinhalese Buddhism: a case of the interaction between doctrine and practice', *History of Religions*, **11** (2), 203–19.

Gombrich, Richard F. 1980. 'The significance of former Buddhas in Theravādin tradition', in S. Balasooriya *et al.* (eds), *Buddhist Studies in Honour of Walpola Rahula*. London: Gordon Fraser, pp. 62–72.

Gombrich, Richard F. 1987. 'Old bodies like carts', *Journal of the Pali Text Society*, **11**: 1–4.

Gombrich, Richard F. 1987. 'Three souls, one or none: the vagaries of a Pali pericope', *Journal of the Pali Text Society*, **11**: 73–8.

Gombrich, Richard F. 1988. 'The history of early Buddhism: major advances since 1950', in A. Das (ed.), *Indological Studies and South Asia Bibliography: A Conference 1986*. Calcutta: National Library Calcutta.

Gombrich, Richard F. 1990. 'How the Mahāyāna began', in Tadeusz Skorupski (ed.), *The Buddhist Forum*, Vol. 1. London: School of Oriental and African Studies, University of London, pp. 21–30.

Gombrich, Richard F. 1991. *Buddhist Precept and Practice*, 2nd edn. Delhi: Motilal Banarsidass.

Gombrich, Richard F. 1991. '*Pātimokkha*: purgative', in The Editorial Committee of the Felicitation Volume for Professor Dr. Egaku Mayeda (eds), *Studies in Buddhism and Culture in Honour of Professor Dr. Egaku Mayeda on His Sixty-fifth Birthday*. Tokyo: Sankibo Busshorin, pp. 33–8.

Gombrich, Richard F. 1992. 'The Buddha's book of Genesis?' *Indo-Iranian Journal*, **35**: 159–78.

Gombrich, Richard F. 1992. 'Dating the Buddha: a red herring revealed,' in Heinz Bechert (ed.), *The Dating of the Historical Buddha/Die Datierung des historischen Buddha,* Part 2 (*Symposien zur Buddhismusforschung,* IV, 2). Göttingen: Vandenhoeck & Ruprecht, pp. 237–59.

Gombrich, Richard F. 1992. 'A momentous effect of translation: the "vehicles" of Buddhism', in *Apodosis: Essays Presented to Dr. W. W. Cruickshank to Mark His 80th Birthday.* London: St Paul's School, pp. 34–46.

Gombrich, Richard F. 1993. 'Understanding early Buddhist terminology in its context', in *Pali Daejangkang Urimal Olmgim Nonmon Moum II [A Korean Translation of Pali Tipitaka, Vol. II].* Seoul, pp. 74–101.

Gombrich, Richard F. 1994. 'What is Pali?' in W. Geiger, *A Pali Grammar,* trans. B. Ghosh, rev. and ed. K. R. Norman. Oxford: Pali Text Society, pp. xxiii–xxix.

Gombrich, Richard F. 1994. 'The Buddha and the Jains: a reply to Professor Bronkhorst', *Asiatische Studien/Études Asiatiques,* **48**(4): 1069–96.

Gombrich, Richard F. 1997. 'The Buddhist attitude to thaumaturgy', in Petra Kieffer-Pülz and Jens-Uwe Hartmann (eds), *Bauddhavidyāsudhākaraḥ: Studies in Honour of Heinz Bechert on the Occasion of His 65th Birthday.* Swisttal-Odendorf: Indica et Tibetica, pp. 166–84.

Gombrich, Richard F. 1997. 'Is Dharma a good thing?', *Dialogue and Universalism,* **11–12**: 147–63.

Gombrich, Richard F. 1998. *Religious Experience in Early Buddhism.* Eighth Annual BASR Lecture, 1997 (*British Association for the Study of Religions Occasional Paper* 17), printed by the University of Leeds Printing Service, Leeds.

Gombrich, Richard F. 1998. *Kindness and Compassion as Means to Nirvana* (1997 Gonda Lecture). Amsterdam: Royal Netherlands Academy of Arts and Sciences.

Gombrich, Richard F. 2001. 'A visit to Brahmā the heron', *Journal of Indian Philosophy,* **29** (April): 95–108.

Gombrich, Richard F. 2002. 'Another Buddhist criticism of Yājñavalkya', in *Buddhist and Indian Studies in Honour of Professor Sodo Mori.* Hammatsu: Kokusai Bukkyoto Kyokai, pp. 21–3.

Gombrich, Richard F. 2003. 'Vedānta stood on its head: *sakkāya* and *sakkāya-diṭṭhi*', in Renata Czekalska and Halina Marlewicz (eds), *Second International Conference on Indian Studies: Proceedings* (*Cracow Indological Series*; IV–V). Krakow: Ksiegarnia Akademicka, pp. 227–38.

Gombrich, Richard F. 2006. *How Buddhism Began: The Conditioned Genesis of the Early Teachings,* 2nd edn. London: Routledge (first published by the Athlone Press in 1996).

Gombrich, Richard F. 2006. *Theravada Buddhism: A Social History,* 2nd edn., London & New York: Routledge.

Gombrich, Richard F. 2007. 'Popperian Vinaya: conjecture and refutation in practice', in Birgit Kellner *et al.* (eds), *Pramāṇakīrtiḥ: Papers Dedicated to Ernst Steinkellner on the Occasion of His 70th Birthday.* Vienna: Arbeitskreis für Tibetische und Buddhistische Studien Universität Wien, pp. 203–11.

Hamilton, Sue. 1996. *Identity and Experience: The Constitution of the Human Being According to Early Buddhism.* London: Luzac Oriental.

Hamilton, Sue. 2000. *Early Buddhism: A New Approach.* Richmond, Surrey: Curzon.

Hinüber, Oskar von. 1991. *The Oldest Pali Manuscript.* Wiesbaden: Akademie der Wissenschaften und der Literatur, Mainz, Abhandlungen der Geistes- and Sozialwissenschaftlichen Klasse, 6.

Hüsken, Ute. 2000. 'The legend of the establishment of the Buddhist order of nuns in the *Theravāda Vinaya-Piṭaka*', *Journal of the Pali Text Society*, **26**: 43–69.

Hwang, Soon-il. 2006. *Metaphor and Literalism in Buddhism: The Doctrinal History of Nirvana.* London and New York: Routledge.

Jaini, Padmanabh S. 1979. *The Jaina Path of Purification.* Berkeley and Delhi: University of California Press and Motilal Banarsidass.

James, William. 1985. *The Varieties of Religious Experience.* London: Penguin Classics.

Johnson, W. J. 1995. *Harmless Souls: Karmic Bondage and Religious Change in Early Jainism.* Delhi: Motilal Banarsidass.

Jurewicz, Joanna. 1995. 'The *Ṛgveda* 10.129: an attempt of interpretation', in Przemyslaw Piekarski *et al.* (eds), *Proceedings of the International Conference on Sanskrit and Related Studies.* Kraków: Enigma Press, pp. 141–50.

Jurewicz, Joanna. 2000. 'Playing with fire: the *pratītyasamutpāda* from the perspective of Vedic thought'. *Journal of the Pali Text Society*, **26**: 77–103.

Jurewicz, Joanna. 2001. *Kosmogonia Rygwedy: Myśl i Metafora [Cosmogony of the Ṛgveda: Thought and Metaphor].* Warsaw: Wydawnictwo Naukowe Semper.

Jurewicz, Joanna. 2004. 'Prajāpati, the fire and the *pancāgni-vidyā*', in Piotr Balcerowicz and Marek Mejor (eds), *Essays in Indian Philosophy, Religion and Literature.* Delhi: Motilal Banarsidass, pp. 45–60.

Keown, Damien. 2000. *Buddhism: A Very Short Introduction.* Oxford and New York: Oxford University Press.

Kim, Wan Doo. 1999. 'The Theravādin Doctrine of Momentariness: A Survey of Its Origins and Development,' D.Phil. thesis, Oxford University.

Kosambi, D. D. 1965. *The Culture and Civilisation of Ancient India in Historical Outline.* London: Routledge and Kegan Paul.

Lloyd, G. E. R. 1990. *Demystifying Mentalities.* Cambridge: Cambridge University Press.

Malamoud, Charles. 1981. 'Inde védique. Religion et mythologie', in *Dictionnaire des mythologies.* Paris: Flammarion, p. 3.

Neisser, Ulric. 1976. *Cognition and Reality.* San Francisco: W. H. Freeman.

Norman, K. R. 1982. 'The Four Noble Truths,' in *Indological and Buddhist Studies (Volume in Honour of Professor J. W. de Jong).* Canberra, pp. 377–91; reprinted in *Collected Papers*, vol. II. Oxford: Pali Text Society, 1991, pp. 210–23.

Obeyesekere, Gananath. 2002. *Imagining Karma: Ethical Transformation in Amerindian, Buddhist, and Greek Rebirth.* Berkeley: University of California Press.

Onians, Isabelle. 1996. 'Language, Speech and Words in Early Buddhism,' M.Phil. thesis, Oxford University.

Popper, Karl R. 1963. *Conjectures and Refutations.* London: Routledge and Kegan Paul.

Rahula, Walpola. 1959. *What the Buddha Taught.* Bedford: Gordon Fraser.

Ronkin, Noa. 2005. *Early Buddhist Metaphysics.* London and New York: Routledge.

Schmithausen, Lambert. 1991. *The Problem of the Sentience of Plants in Earliest Buddhism. Studia Philologica Buddhica, Monograph series VI.* Tokyo: International Institute for Buddhist Studies.

Seaford, R. 2004. *Money and the Early Greek Mind.* Cambridge: Cambridge University Press.

Shaw, Sarah. 2006. *Buddhist Meditation: An Anthology of Texts from the Pali Canon.* London and New York: Routledge.

Smart, Ninian. 1964. *Doctrine and Argument in Indian Philosophy.* London: Allen & Unwin.

Szczurek, Przemyslaw. 2008. '*Prajñāvādāṃś ca bhāṣase*: polemics with Buddhism in the early parts of the *Bhagavadgītā*', in Richard F. Gombrich and Cristina Scherrer-Schaub (eds), *Buddhist Studies, Papers of the 12th World Sanskrit Conference.* Delhi: Motilal Banarsidass.

Waldschmidt, Ernst. 1944–48. *Die Ueberlieferung vom Lebensende des Buddha.* Göttingen: Vandenhoeck & Ruprecht.

Williams, Paul. 2000. *Buddhist Thought.* London: Routledge.

Willis, Michael. 2007. 'From relics to rice: early Buddhism and the Buddhist landscape of central India', unpublished paper given at School of Oriental and African Studies, University of London, 23 January.

Wynne, Alexander. 2004. 'The oral transmission of the early Buddhist literature', *Journal of the International Association of Buddhist Studies,* **27**(1): 97–127.

Wynne, Alexander. 2004. 'The Brahmavihāras reconsidered', unpublished paper given at The Richard Gombrich Celebratory Conference, St Hugh's College, Oxford, July.

Wynne, Alexander. 2007. *The Origin of Buddhist Meditation.* London and New York: Routledge.

INDEX